The **A–Z** of L~~ipreading~~

Directory of Information, Services, Organisations, Equipment and Manufacturers

Pat Saunders

The Crowood Press

First published in 1989 by
The Crowood Press
Ramsbury, Marlborough
Wiltshire SN8 2HE

British Library Cataloguing in Publication Data

Saunders, Pat
    The A–Z of Disability: Directory of Information, Services,
    Organisations, Equipment and Manufacturers
    1.   Great Britain. Services of physically handicapped persons
    I.   Title
    362.4′048′0941

    ISBN 1 85223 136 X

Line artwork by Claire Upsdale-Jones
Cartoons by Butch

Typeset by Acorn Bookwork, Salisbury, Wiltshire
Printed in Great Britain by Biddles Ltd, of Guildford and King's Lynn

'Anything to help anybody and everybody is our motto here at Stoke Mandeville, so we applaud this new 'A–Z'. Well done!'

Jimmy Savile

Dedicated to Jean, without whom neither I nor this book would exist.

Acknowledgements

There is a great deal more to writing a book like this than just putting words on paper, and when the writer is confined to a wheelchair the number of helpers multiplies. My thanks must go first to the two people most closely associated with this project – my wife, who has coped with mountains of mail, miles of typewriter ribbon and everlasting searches for missing bits of information, and my good friend Charles Priscott, who has given me an afternoon a fortnight maintaining the records and assembling the actual papers which make up this book.

For the drawings I thank Gilbert Best, and John Beaumont who drew the cartoons. Thank you to Christopher Golding, Margaret Fuller and Enid Work for reading the proofs, and to Wendy Berridge for typing the appendices. I am grateful for the use of material provided by many companies and associations – in particular, DIAL UK, the Disabled Living Foundation, the Royal Association for Disability and Rehabilitation, Hampshire Disablement Information and Advice Line, the Disability Alliance and the magazine *Caring*.

Introduction

For many disabled people, information is the key to a happy and fulfilled life. This book is a distillation of eleven years of personal contact with many thousands of disabled people, and of writing in newspapers and magazines on every aspect of disablement. Whilst every effort has been made to cover all ages and all disabilities, the writer has made deliberate selections of 'across-the-board' problems which affect many handicapped people sooner or later. This is possibly the first book a newly disabled person may acquire. It does not claim to be conclusive on every topic, but it will enable the reader to look further into those subjects which are of interest to him.

A–Z is arranged in a simple alphabetical format. If a subject is referred to elsewhere in the text, this is indicated by italic type, and you can go to that subject's initial letter and find out more about it. A manufacturer will be indicated in the text by bold type followed by (M), and the address will be found in Appendix I, whilst an organisation will be in bold followed by (O) and will be in Appendix II.

Although this is essentially an information book, it is also a miscellany of items by and about disabled people and their care-givers. So, leave it on the coffee table for a while, and from time to time open it anywhere for a few moments' amusement.

The central theme of unchanging home-spun philosophy running through the book reflects the experience of the writer in coping with disability. Some of the hard facts on subjects such as social security will change periodically and this must be taken into account. Following an ongoing policy of maximum value within the limited size of the book, the writer would therefore welcome comments from readers.

Pat Saunders

A

Access

In the world of disability 'access' means the problems of mobility and movement experienced by physically disabled people, and to some extent by those with problems of sight or hearing. These problems have two causes. The first is the disability. A paralysed person may be unable to walk; a blind person can walk but at risk of collision or falling; a deaf person may walk out into traffic. The second cause of limited mobility for the disabled person is the built environment which, broadly speaking, is designed for able-bodied people. Access is concerned with modifying the built environment to allow it to be used by some or all disabled people.

'Access' is a concept with a relatively brief history. Twenty years ago disabled people had to accept the world as it was, and for many this meant never leaving their house or even staying in just one room. Today access involves complicated technology, embracing many text books, reports, legislation, building and fire regulations, architects, local authority planners, and national and local committees. Access for a disabled person starts with movement within a room; for example, a light switch may be inaccessible to a wheelchair rider. A town may be inaccessible to a disabled person because there is no unisex public toilet. A country may be inaccessible to certain disabled people because the only air-line serving it refuses to carry them there.

Improved access may be achieved in two ways. Firstly, we can try to modify the existing environment. A flight of four concrete steps can be replaced with a ramp; a door sill can be removed; a door can be rehung so it does not take up space in a room. These are just a few of thousands of relatively simple changes which may improve the personal mobility of a disabled person. They apply equally to the domestic house or the town hall (although it must be accepted that there are many historic buildings which could not be made accessible without ruining their appearance). The second, and much better way of providing access is to incorporate it in construction in the first place, when often the cost is much less or even nothing at all. Clearly there is no extra cost involved in putting the controls in a brand-new lift lower, so that they are within the reach of a wheelchair rider.

Access in Britain has developed a clearly defined structure. At the top is the Access Committee for England which produces literature, negotiates with the government, runs an information service and promotes and co-ordinates the

activities of local access committees. This organisation has an excellent range of books and leaflets for the lay person, and you can write for a book list to the Director, **Access Committee for England** (O). They also publish a very useful quarterly magazine called *Access Action*. The second national body is the **Centre on the Environment for the Handicapped (CEH)** (O) which also publishes books and leaflets on access. They have a magazine called *Design for Special Needs* and CEH is the body to contact for information on the design of flats and houses for disabled people. The third body offering help with access, housing and mobility is the **Royal Association for Disability and Rehabilitation (RADAR)** (O); they are also an action body working with the All-Party Parliamentary Group on Disability on access legislation.

At local level, access committees seek out and identify access problems and present them to the appropriate statutory or private body. If a pavement needs dropping to enable a wheelchair to cross the road, the council will be informed. If a supermarket, church or football ground is inaccessible, the 'management' will be persuaded to change it. Where expertise is needed, the committee will provide it. Some local authorities have a full or part-time Access Officer who is normally a planner. His main role is to vet planning applications to ensure adequate provision has been made for disabled people.

From the point of view of the handicapped person living at home, problems of personal mobility come down to architectural design and the choice of the right equipment. For advice on the latter contact the **Disabled Living Foundation** (O). If there is a **DIAL** (O) in your area they will give you free information on any aspect of access.

ACROSS

The Across Trust was formed in 1972 to raise money to provide special coaches to take severely handicapped people on holidays in Europe, on tours, and on pilgrimages to Lourdes. Among the disabled would be a number who were permanently bed-borne. A whole new technology was involved in the design and construction of a jumbo-sized vehicle, which was a cross between a large coach and an ambulance. The specification included interchangeable beds and seats; air-conditioning; electric lifting and conveying hoists; flush toilets; a refrigerator for ice, drugs and plasma; hot and cold water; radio/cassette with individual earphones; electric power supplies for medical equipment; oxygen; a galley, and food provision similar to that of an airliner. These jumbo-sized ambulances became known as 'Jumbulances'. The early versions, which carried 22 passengers, were based on the Mercedes-Benz 12-metre air suspension 240hp coach chassis. The first Jumbulance made her maiden run to Lourdes in April 1973, and she was carrying a group made up largely of sick and severely disabled young people.

This was the first of six 'standard' Jumbulances, each made to carry 24 passengers, including eight lying on tubular aluminium beds. All passengers have an excellent view from the panoramic windows. These vehicles were followed by four Alligator Jumbulances each carrying 44 passengers, including up to 14 on beds. Alligator Jumbulances are 55ft (16m) long and articulated in the middle. For those disabled people who are confined to a bed or a wheelchair, those on life-support machines and those with life-threatening conditions, the ACROSS way is really the only European holiday possible.

Each Jumbulance is a miracle of engineering and a whole range of technologies – medical, catering, plumbing, TV and sound entertainment. On each coach there are lifts for boarding, hoists for the movement of passengers within the coach, ripple beds, aircraft-type reclining seats, a kitchen providing hot meals, large wheelchair-accessible toilets, and even a cabin with bunks for the off-duty drivers. Each vehicle is entirely self-supporting and no matter how severe the disability, any person accepted for travel by ACROSS could ride in one of these Jumbulances with complete confidence. Each Jumbulance costs over £200,000, making them the most

expensive vehicles in the world. There are now 12 Jumbulances in the ACROSS fleet.

Five of the standard Jumbulances take groups of disabled
pilgrims each week throughout the season to Lourdes,
taking about 19 hours from London. Each vehicle has a nine-
hour turn-round, after which they return with a group from
the previous week. ACROSS has built up a substantial base
in Lourdes, including five hotels for disabled residents.

Holidays by Jumbulance are available from April through
to October at ten venues across Europe, and are usually for a
period of seven days. Prices range from £350 to £450. There
are holidays to suit all tastes, from an energetic week in
Rheindahlen to a quiet stay in the South Tyrol. You can visit
the famous ski resort of Innsbruck, the walled city of Bruges,
Vienna, home of the Strauss waltz, Salzburg, where the
Sound of Music was made, or Rome, with the possibility of
meeting the Pope. Any one of these weeks would be the
holiday of a lifetime.

ACROSS will take physically disabled people of any age
and virtually any handicap – even those who are totally bed-
borne or terminally ill. Such is the level of medical care that
people have been known to go on holiday with pressure
sores and come home without them.

An ACROSS holiday group comprises disabled people
and volunteer helpers – in fact there are more helpers than
disabled. The group, which remains together for the whole
holiday, includes doctors, nurses, and a chaplain. The Jumbulance, with its two drivers, also remains with the group.
Volunteer helpers pay their own fares.

So popular are the ACROSS holidays that they are fairly
booked up by February each year, so it is worth while
ringing for the season's programme at the end of November.
Complete groups are collected from all parts of the country,
each choosing its own assembly point. Individual handicapped people and helpers join the Jumbulances at their
nearest motorway service station, or alternatively they can
meet at the final pick-up point which is near Waterloo
Station in London.

For more information you can write to the **ACROSS Trust**
(O).

Active

This organisation encourages the development of play, leisure and communication aids for disabled children and adults. There are many local Active groups and an information pack is available for newly-formed groups. Active is closely associated with the National Toy Library Association and local groups maintain stocks of toys and teaching aids available on loan. These range from simple wooden toys to sophisticated microchip-based equipment. Contact **Play Matters** (O).

Acupuncture

Acupuncture is an ancient Chinese therapy used as far back as 3000BC but practised in Britain only in the twentieth century. The theory is based on the concept that points on the surface of the human body connect with internal organs. Stimulating these points with fine needles gives treatment for a variety of ailments, as well as certain habits such as tobacco or alcohol abuse, or over-eating. There are over a thousand of these acupuncture points and they are divided into twelve main groups. These are joined by channels, or 'meridians', which carry the life forces of the body, which the Chinese call the 'Chi'.

The needles used are very fine and they are inserted only a few millimetres into the skin so the patient feels no pain – in fact many people speak of a feeling of extreme relaxation during and after treatment. Acupuncturists use disposable needles so there is no risk of AIDS or any other cross-infection.

In some cases only one session will produce relief, while other conditions require several treatments. Acupuncture is very effective on 40 per cent of patients and is known not to work at all on about 20 per cent. Acupuncture works well on short-term bodily disfunctions, such as headaches, menstrual and digestive problems, rheumatism, tennis elbow, hay fever and certain lung conditions. It has been found helpful for people trying to give up smoking, alcohol and over-eating. Acupuncture is an accepted treatment in some hospitals.

Contact the **Council for Acupuncture** (O) or the **British Acupuncture Association** (O).

Age Concern

Age Concern England (the National Old People's Welfare Council) is a registered charity formed in 1940. The governing body of the organisation includes representatives of 70 national organisations and six departments of state. There are about 950 local Age Concern groups in England. Age Concern England works closely with Age Concern Scotland, Wales and Northern Ireland.

The Age Concern movement provides services to elderly people, involving well over 123,000 volunteers. It also campaigns with and on behalf of elderly people, stimulates innovation and research, and works in partnership with other relevant statutory and voluntary bodies.

Age Concern groups provide a wide range of services, often including day care, visiting services, lunch clubs, over-60's clubs, and, in some areas, specialist services for physically and mentally handicapped frail elderly people. The Information, Training, and Research departments of Age Concern provide a direct service of advice and support to professionals and volunteers working with elderly people throughout the country, and grants are made to new projects and organisations.

Age Concern England campaigns on many issues affecting elderly people and aims to inform public opinion through national reports, conferences, publicity, and the promotion of research. Publications include *Your Rights* for elderly people.

For more information, contact **Age Concern England** (O).

The AID Centre

The Aid Centre (M) offers professional advice on all aspects of car purchase, vehicle hire purchase and adaptations for disability. AID will purchase the car of your choice, arrange adaptations, insurance and hire purchase, and deliver the vehicle directly to your door. Maximum repayment periods and minimum deposits are available to disabled people, irrespective of whether they are on Mobility Allowance. Any make or model is available, both British and foreign, new or used. Part exchange can be arranged.

Aids Helpline

See Telephone Services.

Alarms

Disabled or elderly people who live alone with a spouse who may be, from time to time, out of the house, can be at risk from a variety of unforeseen incidents. A fall may mean a broken limb leaving a person immobile on the floor, and many physically disabled people fall out of bed. Often the able-bodied partner alone in the house with a severely paralysed person who has fallen is unable to lift them off the floor. To the lone wheelchair rider, accidents – cuts, scalding, burns – can be dangerous if help cannot be summoned quickly. People who suffer with *angina* or other heart conditions may have life-threatening 'attacks' needing immediate attention. Any elderly or disabled person living alone may be ill with a common condition such as flu; they think they can cope but any day they may need help quickly. Even a dropped crutch can be a disaster – for a lone amputee.

Of the large number of people who die in house fires every year, many are lone elderly people. Floods from roof tanks or washing machines are harder to cope with for a disabled person who may not be able to turn off the stop-cock. Winter storms can cause actual damage to a house – again, much worse for the lone immobile occupant. Disabled and elderly people are often chosen as soft targets by intruders. People who are blind, sight-impaired or deaf have special problems with the maintenance of safety and security.

The most simple alarm is a small hand-held noise-maker which can be used indoors or out. These are often described as 'anti-mugging' devices and the smallest is the size of a lipstick (**Homecraft** (M) or **QED** (M)). Personal alarms may be battery- or gas-operated. Gas alarms are louder, more shrill and less likely to stop if dropped on concrete, and their value depends on someone being within earshot. Personal alarms can be combined with other items such as walking sticks (**Enterprise Engineering** (M)) or torches (**Homecraft** (M)). The Tumble-Alarm, which clips on to clothes, crutch or stick, sounds when it is turned from the vertical (**Trunkgate** (M)).

Simple household alarms designed to attract the attention of a passer-by have been around for years and some social services departments supply them. They are cheap, reliable and easy to use. They comprise a bell or buzzer on the outside of the house and a fixed or flashing light which may be in a front window. Activation is with a push button or pull cord. Some have an illuminated 'HELP' sign (**MAR Design Services** (M), **Gladstone Law (Electric) Ltd** (M)).

There are also sound/vision alarms operated by radio from body-worn switches (**Llewellyn Health Care** (M) or **Ridley**

Electronics Ltd (M)). The great advantage with these is that they can be operated from any room in the house.

Habit alarms are tuned to the normal activities of the user and will operate automatically if a person leaves a bed (**Aremco** (M)), if a mat is not stepped on (**Cass Electronics Ltd** (M)) or a tap is not turned on within a set period of hours (**Senflow (UK) Ltd** (M)). Some passive alarms operate automatically if the temperature rises above or falls below a fixed point.

The Possum AID system which is provided free (subject to assessment) by some health authorities consists of a speaker/ microphone and a bank of six lever switches fixed to the wall. Outside the front door is a unit comprising a microphone, speaker, red light and a loud buzzer. When the doorbell rings the user can speak to the caller and unlock the front door. In an emergency his alarm switch gives a flashing light and a buzzer sounds. The other three switches control three power points.

One of the most simple and reliable alarm devices is a cordless telephone which consists of a base unit, which has to be plugged into the telephone socket and into a power socket, and a handset, which may be carried around the house, in the garden or even next door. With some types there is an intercom facility between the handset and the base unit. There is an aerial on both the handset and the base unit, and the handset has batteries which recharge every time it is put back in the cradle. Normally up to five commonly-used numbers can be stored in the single button store. For emergency purposes these could be, for example, a family doctor, '999' and three nearby neighbours. There is also a holster provided to carry the handset attached to a belt or to hang it on the side of a wheelchair (**British Telecom** (M)). CB radio can be used as an emergency call system and in some areas local CB radio clubs have set up their own care-watch schemes for disabled and elderly people. Write for information sheets to the **Department of Trade and Industry** (O).

Where there is an able-bodied carer in the house intercoms can be useful and these may be wired in pairs or they may be cableless. Baby alarms are battery-operated and inexpensive

(Boots) – they are more practical for disabled people as, like cordless intercom, they give 'hands-free' operation. Cable-less intercoms comprise two units which plug into three-pin power sockets (Tandy).

There are a large number of emergency alarm systems which use a body-worn transmitter to activate an automatic dialling system which will alert a neighbour or a control centre, national or local. The UK 500 Carephone is a very popular system costing around £200. It is a pendant switch on a neckcord which activates a special telephone – this then dials four pre-entered numbers sequentially until somebody answers, when it delivers an emergency recorded message. You can change the numbers at will but normally you would choose neighbours or relatives who are close at hand, who are willing to help and who are usually at home. The main disadvantage is that it dials all four numbers until it is switched off. The base unit is a conventional telephone with a 31-number memory store.

All these emergency alarm systems have in common a switch worn on the body, as a pendant or on the wrist. Some switches require pressing two buttons simultaneously, whilst some provide a cancel button. Normally a large pro-truding button is best, although you are more likely to set the alarm off by accident.

You have to decide whether you want your calls to go to friends or to a control centre. Friends may mean well but could they lift you off the floor back into your wheelchair? On the other hand, friends may be willing to stay with you after the problem is solved, wait for a doctor to come, or cook a meal. Control centres are open 24 hours a day. Some systems provide two-way speech communication with the control centre and this enables you to explain the nature of the emergency and is also reassuring for you. Some centres keep a detailed information sheet on you, so they can solve your problem by the quickest and best method. However you do have to pay monitoring fees (which may be up to £3 a week), so it pays to shop around or seek advice from your nearest **DIAL** (O).

Next you have to decide whether to rent or buy. Unless you are covering yourself for a relatively short period, buying is the cheaper option. Here again it pays to see what is available and choose the one with the lowest monitoring fees. Most alarms incorporate a direct two-way speech link, but you can have this with or without a built-in telephone. This can be a 'hands-free' loud-speaker telephone for people unable to pick up a handset.

Permanently-manned control centres may be operated on a national or regional basis by the equipment makers or by local authorities. Monitoring fees by the latter are usually cheaper.

One of the largest manufacturers of emergency communications equipment is **Tunstall Telecom Ltd** (M). Over 550 local authorities and housing associations throughout the country use Tunstall equipment, covering one in twenty of the pensioners in Britain. Tunstall equipment is available with or without a built-in telephone. **Homelink** (M) 2015 is good value for those who already have a telephone. Visual and sound signals inform the user that the alarm has been pressed and that the signal has been received. This signal continues for a pre-set time, during which the alarm may be cancelled by the user. The control centre operator is able to talk to the user and initiate action. If no contact is made with the centre a local alarm is sounded.

The Vitalcall 2 gives the best of both worlds in sending alarm calls to three friends first before ringing a control centre. Separate optional units are available so that friends can deal with alarms direct. There is also a built-in timer for optional passive alarms (**Aerospace Communications Systems Ltd** (M)).

Local authority monitoring services can be as low as 40p a week and some are available for people who have acquired their own equipment. If you are about to install an alarm system for the first time, try the council first. There are over a score of major manufacturers of emergency communication equipment so it does pay to get all the information you can before making a choice. **DLF** (O) publish a leaflet *Communication – B*; **Mary Marlborough Lodge** (O) publish a book called *Communication; Which* July 1986 published comparative tests on equipments; and *Age Concern England* publish *Calling for Help*, priced £2.95.

All Party Disablement Group

When Parliament is in session, the All Party Disablement Group, chaired by Jack Ashley MP, meets fortnightly. The Group is made up of 150 members from both Houses, and the secretary is John Hannam MP. Meetings of the Group may be addressed by representatives of associations representing the views of disabled people or they may discuss major issues affecting disabled people – employment, education, community care or future legislation – in which case they invite people with specialised knowledge.

Inevitably, with the pressures of parliamentary business, attendance at some meetings may be quite low, but detailed minutes and reports are circulated so all members are able to keep up to date. Measures affecting disabled people can cut right across party boundaries and in these cases the Group speaks with a powerful voice.

Contact with the Group can be made through the Research Assistant, All Party Disablement Group, **RADAR** (O).

Alternative Medicine

In the 1970s and 1980s alternative or complementary therapy has achieved respectability, and many people now recognise the value of the non-medical approach to the treatment of certain ailments. Nowadays one in ten of all consultations is made with an alternative practitioner, and it is not unusual for a GP to refer a patient to an alternative practitioner. A *Which* survey indicated that one person in seven had used alternative therapy and of these 82 per cent claimed a total cure, or alleviation of symptoms where the ailment was incurable. Practitioners of conventional medicine also train in the alternative therapies. Doctors become skilled in *acupuncture* or hypnotherapy; physiotherapists in *osteopathy* or aromatherapy; nurses in reflexology; and dieticians in homeopathy. Five UK hospitals offer homeopathic treatment.

Conventional medicine deals with specific problems which assail particular parts of the body. It is, in effect, a form of medical crisis management. *Alternative therapy* looks at the body as a whole and the practitioner treats the person rather than the illness. Alternative therapies could never replace conventional medicine, but they can be used alongside it. A GP should feel free to refer a patient with back problems to an osteopath, or a person with anxiety problems to a hypnotherapist.

Treatment costs vary, and they are higher in London. Over the country as a whole, first treatments average from £10–£20, with subsequent sessions rather less. The costs of acupuncture, homeopathy, osteopathy and chiropractice can be covered under an insurance plan available from **Complementary Health Insurance Plan** (M).

Most GPs will recommend a good alternative therapist and local practitioners will be found in the Yellow Pages. The addresses of the national bodies are to be found in Appendix II or you can contact the **Institute for Complementary Medicine** (O). You can also ring Webster's Complementary Medicine Line on 0898 600 440.

Amnesia

People who lose their memories live lost and bewildered lives in a sort of stationary time capsule. Although it is distressing for both the sufferer and his family, there are no long-term care facilities for these unhappy individuals and a great deal of research is needed. The best help is from the **Amnesia Association (AMNASS)** (O), which is now forming regional branches throughout Britain.

Amputees

An excellent little booklet *Better Health for the Amputee* is available from the **British Limbless Ex-Servicemen's Association (BLESMA)** (O).

Angina

There are many possible reasons for a pain in the chest. Angina is one, and the pain is caused by an over-worked heart muscle which may be the result of excessive exercise increasing the heart rate. Stress which arises from too long a working day, public speaking, excessive exercise, or anger, can also bring on an angina attack. Physically disabled people are as likely to get angina as anyone else. It is very rare for angina to come on when a person is completely at rest but it is a fact that the likelihood of angina increases with age.

Angina is a frightening, crushing chest pain. Breathing increases the pain and there will be a tendency to try to hold the breath. If the person is in bed, sitting them up will ease the pain. Ceasing physical activity and relaxing will let the heart slow down to its normal rate.

A first attack of chest pain should always be reported to your doctor immediately – in a few cases the underlying cause can be serious. However, angina is a warning, probably that the blood vessels feeding the heart are filling up with fat. A sensible diet, a quieter way of life, no smoking and simple medication can control angina for many years. You can also be given emergency medication (pills or an aerosol) which will reduce the pain of an attack very quickly. It may also be interesting to learn that a natural yoghurt a day is said to help to arrest the accumulation of fatty deposits in the blood stream.

For more information about angina write to the **British Heart Foundation** (O).

Angling

Angling is a sport which, in any of its many forms, is eminently suitable for people with a variety of handicaps. It takes you out of doors, it is relaxing and time-consuming, it can be enjoyed at any level of expertise and, since it can be 'played' on even terms with ablebods, it brings an easy social interchange which is true integration. The **Handicapped Anglers' Trust** (O) is a powerful force in encouraging mentally and physically handicapped people to participate in angling.

To further this objective they have designed the Allenard Wheelyboat which is 12ft (4.5m approx) overall with a beam of 5.3ft (about 2m) and it draws about 4in (about 10cm). The hull is made of double-skinned aluminium, filled with close-celled expanded foam; load-bearing parts such as the transom are filled with solid timber. It is a bit like a miniature version of an assault craft, in that it has a hinged ramp set in the bow, enabling a wheelchair rider to enter the boat in his chair. The ramp is controlled by a hand-operated winch and it is fully buoyant, so it can be lowered on to the water in calm conditions. The boat can be propelled with a small electric or petrol outboard motor, or it can be rowed or sculled.

Although this craft has been designed for the disabled angler, it has a wide range of uses for disabled sailors in general. For example, as a tender for wheelchair riders to be taken out to a moored craft, as a river ferry or even as a sailing club rescue boat. For details write to the **Handicapped Anglers' Trust** (O).

Ankylosing Spondylitis

This is a rheumatic disease which affects the spine and, more rarely, the limb joints and tissues in other parts of the body. It is a stiffening of the joints of the lower part of the spine due to inflammation. There is no known cause but it has been shown to be about 300 times more likely to occur in people who inherit a particular white cell blood group called HLA B27. Normally this disease is found in young men between the ages of 20 and 25. It starts very gradually with early morning stiffness and pain, and sometimes it may be incorrectly confused with other back ailments. Early diagnosis is important as this disease can result in a fixation of the spine in a bent or stooping position, which would make it difficult to look straight ahead. In the early stages there is considerable pain but good treatment usually alleviates this. The condition responds to exercise and should not prevent most forms of employment.

It is now realised that ankylosing spondylitis is more common in females than was previously thought, and that some women may have a mild form without realising it – often they think it is 'just a bad back'.

There is no cure for ankylosing spondylitis, but normally the doctor can deal with the pain and it is up to the patient to look after his posture, his weight and to take exercise daily. Jobs which involve sitting in one position – at a bench or a desk, or in a motor car – should be avoided. Use a firm bed, a high chair with a firm seat and try to lie face downwards for 20 minutes each day. See a physiotherapist, get a schedule of exercise to do at home, and find out which non-contact sports you can play. Swimming is very beneficial. Maintain good health overall and take advice about your diet. *Ankylosing Spondylitis – a Guidebook for Patients* is an excellent little booklet available free from the **National Ankylosing Spondylitis Society (NASS)** (O).

Appeal Tribunals

If you have applied for and been refused a social security benefit you can ask for your case to be put to an Appeal Tribunal. Appeal Tribunals are completely independent of the DHSS and they can, subject to the law, change decisions made by Adjudicating Officers or Adjudicating Medical Officers.

Adjudicating Officers make decisions about whether the law says you are entitled to a benefit or not. Adjudicating Medical Authorities include one or more doctors, and they rule on medical aspects of applications on such benefits as Industrial Injuries Disablement Benefit, *Mobility Allowance* or *Severe Disablement Allowance*.

Appeals against refusal of *Attendance Allowance* are put by letter to the Attendance Allowance Board. There is no formal hearing but they may arrange for a further medical examination in your own home. They then send you a provisional opinion on which you can comment. Once the Board has made a final decision they will not reconsider the case for a year.

Although Appeal Tribunals are informal, claimants tend to become flustered, and often they are their own worst advocate. It is wise therefore to take a friend, or better still, an adviser from a *DIAL* or a Welfare Rights Office. Disabled people often present themselves as being much more able than they really are, but a companion can help to present a true picture. Every case needs careful preparation. Obtain letters of support from as many caring professionals as possible – tribunals give credence to care-givers able to report a long period of regular personal help to you. You should both have clearly written lists of the points you wish to make.

The leaflet you want is NI 246 from your local Social Security Office. If you are asked to attend a tribunal and, because of the disability they are considering (or because of another disability), the journey is difficult or impossible, tell the tribunal clerk. There is no point in struggling up the stairs to an appeal office on the first floor if by so doing you undermine your own case for Mobility Allowance. Expenses are paid for you and anyone who comes with you to help present your case.

If you are turned down by an Appeal Tribunal, you can ask for leave to appeal to a Social Security Commissioner, but only on a point of law.

Armchairs

Sitting is commonly accepted as a resting state, but as far as the base of the spine is concerned, it is very much like bending. The lower spine loses its natural hollow and ligaments across the back tighten. Pressure inside the disc is higher when sitting than standing and people who get backache during or after sitting may eventually rupture a lower spinal disc, unless they take care to adjust their posture.

Physically disabled and elderly people who remain seated for long periods also have to be careful to avoid *pressure sores*, so careful attention must be paid to the cushion and support surfaces. Slumping in an armchair must be avoided as this causes sheer stresses on the skin which can also result in pressure sores.

People who sit for long periods are prone to circulation problems in their legs, leading to swollen ankles, varicose veins, or ulcers and cramp pains. Preventive measures include sitting with the feet up on a stool at least as high as the seat of the chair, prescribed elastic stockings, and exercising the legs with a manual peddling machine (**Carters** (M)), or for anyone who is totally paralysed an electric pedalling machine from **Powex** (M).

Strange as it may seem, without care, sitting can be positively dangerous, so the choice of an armchair requires considerable thought. First there is the problem of sitting down and standing up. The higher the seat the easier it is to stand, since the strength needed to rise from a high seat is 20 per cent less than that used in rising from a low one. Seat heights vary within makes and from make to make but average between 16 and 20in (41 and 51cm) – try **Parker Knoll** (M) or **Renray** (M). However, remember that the seat must not be so high that the legs dangle – some people use foot stools. The arm-rests are used when standing, and these need to be the correct height. They should project from the front of the chair to enable the user to get his weight over his feet. There should be no front rail between the legs of the chair; this would prevent the user getting his feet back far enough.

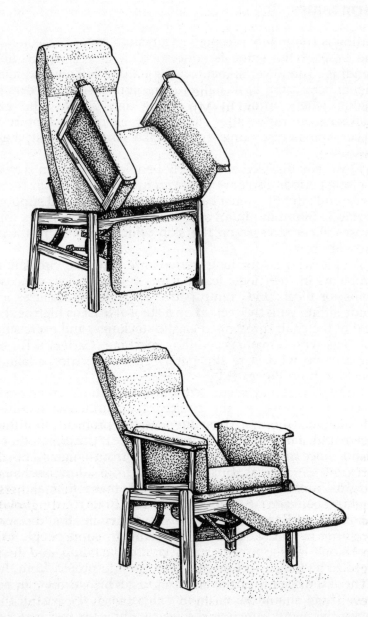

Stand-up and recline armchair.

Some severely disabled people need mechanical assistance to stand. There are spring-loaded cushions which help the act of standing and armchairs with built-in spring-loaded seats (**Powell Seat Co. Ltd** (M)). There are two kinds of electrically-powered armchair. In one the whole chair rises and tilts forward, putting the user into a standing position (**Ortho-Kinetics (UK) Ltd** (M)), while in the other type only the seat rises (**Powell Seat Co. Ltd** (M)).

The seat should slope back at an angle of about 6°. A horizontal seat is uncomfortable, but too great an angle will make rising difficult.

Looked at from the side, the spine is S-shaped, and the back of the chair should be shaped to maintain this, otherwise lower back pains will develop. The amount of spinal curvature varies from person to person, and some armchairs provide built-in adjustable lumbar support whilst others supply separate lumbar cushions (**Shackletons (Carlinghow) Ltd** (M) or **PEL Ltd** (M)). The back of the chair should slope gently backwards and be high enough to support the full length of the torso. The head should be supported just slightly to the rear of upright.

The construction of the chair should be good enough to prevent sagging of the cushion – this causes sheer stresses on the buttocks which can lead to hip pain and maybe pressures sores. Foam cushions soon lose their resilience;

open-cell foam rubber is better. The aim is to produce maximum weight distribution without touching the bottom. Hot, sweaty conditions are conducive to pressure sores, so cushion fillings and covers should allow a flow of air through the seat. A good solution is to put a piece of Mullipel on the cushion and, for real luxury, on the back too. Obtainable from **Medipost** (M), Mullipel is a machine-washable artificial fleece with many anti-pressure sore qualities.

Many armchair makers offer a variety of options. For example, fabrics are warmer than leather or vinyls; filled-in sides keep out draughts and wings are good for dozing, but a bit anti-social. Other accessories include tables, ash-trays, crutch and stick holders and foot-rests. Castors or small wheels, if fitted, should be on the front legs only.

An armchair is an expensive item to buy and it is wise to seek professional advice from a **DIAL** (O), disabled living centre or community OT, or there are useful leaflets available from the DLF, or the **Arthritis and Rheumatism Council (ARC)** (O). Some social services departments supply 'high' armchairs and others can buy them at cost price on behalf of a client. The best advice is 'Try before you buy'.

ARMS

See under Multiple Sclerosis.

Arthritis

Rheumatism and arthritis may well be the most common disabling diseases in Britain, affecting some 20 million people, and the cause of about 15 per cent of total absence from work due to sickness. This represents 44 million working days every year at a cost to the country of over £200 million in lost production.

Only one person in fifty will escape some form of rheumatism before reaching the age of 70 and women are much more likely to get it than men. Rheumatism is a word that almost defies definition, covering 'aches and pains and possible stiffness in muscles, bones, ligaments and joints anywhere in the body'. Originally 'rheum' meant a watery discharge, as in 'rheumy eyes', but, in fact, within the body liquid flow has little to do with rheumatism. Arthritis, on the other hand, has a more precise meaning as it is limited to pain resulting from a diseased joint, 'itis' meaning 'inflammation' – this results in heat, pain, swelling and redness of the skin. There are many possible causes but in all cases the thin membrane between the bones of the joint is affected and the joint becomes swollen. This may be due to infection, rheumatic fever, gout, rheumatoid arthritis, osteo-arthritis, or ankylosing spondylitis. Infective joint diseases and rheumatic fever have both become comparatively rare, but cases of the latter can occasionally cause damage to the valves of the heart.

Rheumatoid arthritis is the result of chronic inflammation of the synovial membrane which becomes thickened and folded. The disease spreads to the cartilage, wearing it away, and may eventually lead to the bones of the joint wearing, through direct contact with each other. This results in pain, swelling, stiffness and limited movement, and eventually in total immobility of the joint. There may also be general illness with anaemia and sometimes a fever. There are a million victims of rheumatoid arthritis in Britain and these include children and young adults. It is a serious illness which not only affects the joints but the whole body, and when it strikes a young husband or wife it can be a major disaster for the family.

Of the 187 true joints in the body, rheumatoid arthritis may affect almost any, and often joints will tend to be affected symmetrically down both sides of the body. The disease may start and stop in a completely unpredictable manner – it is an extremely variable disorder which can affect one or two, or many, joints in the body for a few days, a few weeks, or for years. It is the uncertain nature of the disease which produces so much anxiety and depression in those who suffer from it. However, the outlook for 50 per cent of patients is good and 20 per cent recover completely. Severe physical disability, with the need for a wheelchair, may come to about 10 per cent, but the spine is rarely affected.

Much research has been undertaken into the cause of rheumatoid arthritis. It seems to be initiated by some unknown factor, and this is followed by a disturbance in the immune system which would normally react defensively. It is, therefore, a sort of self-perpetuating vicious circle. There is no absolute cure and, even if the disease can be arrested, little can be done to repair the joint. No treatment should be attempted other than under the direct supervision of a doctor, who can offer a wide range of anti-inflammatory drugs and pain-killers which may keep the pain and stiffness at bay. These drugs help the arthritic person to soldier on as usual, maybe even carrying on a full-time job. Aspirin is often used to relieve pain and joint inflammation but for some people it may result in stomach trouble – it should not be taken by pregnant women, people with gastric ulcers, or anyone with asthma. Paracetamol is an effective pain-killer but will do nothing for joint inflammation.

Some surgical treatments are available, such as synovectomy, which is the removal of the thickened, inflamed lining of the joint. This may relieve the pain but the membrane grows back and may produce the same problems again. In some cases it may prevent further damage to the joint. Debridement is a kind of spring-cleaning of the joint to reduce pain by the removal of loose bits of bone and cartilage. Sometimes a joint can be exised leaving a gap with tough scar tissue forming between the bone ends. With some joints it is possible to interpose a layer of artificial material such as metal or plastic.

Partial replacement is the replacement of one half of a joint. Techniques of total joint replacement have made great advances in the 1970s and 1980s – often the original joint is reproduced in artificial materials. This method has been used for hip, knee and finger joints and progress is being made with ankles, elbows and shoulders. When a joint is made permanently stiff this is called 'arthrodesis' and the method is often applied to wrists and knees. The joint then becomes pain-free and is stable and strong. Probably the most spectacularly successful development is total hip replacement which is now 95 per cent successful. This has become such a routinely successful operation that there are long waiting lists.

Ankylosing spondylitis is a form of arthritis which affects thousands of people, including many formerly athletic young men. This usually affects the spine and in severe cases the joints become fused, leading to a very restricting deformity called 'poker back'. Contact the **National Ankylosing Spondylitis Society** (O).

Osteo-arthritis is often thought of as a 'wear and tear' joint condition but young people can get it and it can be inherited. The cartilage wears and flakes, and in severe cases it is completely lost, leaving bare and polished bones rubbing against each other. There is a considerable loss of function and a great deal of pain. When this condition is found in the knees or hips it can cause substantial physical disability. The spine can be affected at the base of the neck or in the lumbar region, usually as a result of heavy manual work. Fortunately with this very common form of arthritis there is no overall loss of general health. Some sportsmen (for example, wicket-keepers) tend to get osteo-arthritis later in life.

There are a number of less serious versions of arthritis. Gout is the result of too much uric acid in the body – either too much is made or the kidneys fail to remove enough. Gout is one of the most painful types of arthritis and it mainly affects men who are past middle age – it tends to run in families. It comes and goes in a random fashion but it can lead to permanent joint damage. Treatment, aimed at lowering the level of uric acid, is usually successful, and gout is now regarded as a curable disease.

On average, back pain is the reason for time off work for 60 per cent of all miners, dockers and foundry workers – these people are all involved with heavy manual work, often on uneven floors. The damage is usually to the spine where the discs, cartilages and ligaments are subjected to undue wear. Much help is available for back pain sufferers from the

Back Pain Association (O). Lumbago is just a descriptive word for low back pain, while sciatica is the term often used to indicate a pain running down the leg from the buttock. A common cause of the latter is pressure on the sciatic nerve root, maybe by a displaced spinal disc. Most backaches respond to rest, supportive clothing and avoiding strain, and many people benefit from sleeping on a firm mattress, often with a board underneath. It also pays to look at office chairs, armchairs and car seats. Tennis elbow, golfer's elbow and frozen shoulder are examples of passing forms of arthritis which afflict the more highly mobile joints; further exercise tends to aggravate these conditions.

There is a large range of equipment and aids to help arthritic people manage everyday tasks. There are gadgets to take the tops off bottles and jars in the kitchen, to pull on socks or tights in the bedroom, and to help move an unwilling body in the bathroom or toilet. Clarify the problem in your own mind then seek advice from your nearest **DIAL** (O) or **Disabled Living Centre** (O); or write to **DLF** (O).

Exercise can be helpful but you have to be careful to find your own best level. Aim for the maintenance of some degree of mobility of all joints. Walking or standing for prolonged periods should be avoided, and any exercise which afterwards causes increased pain or joint swelling lasting for two hours or more is excessive.

Rheumatism and arthritis have been with us for so long that there is a whole folklore of so-called cures and palliatives. If you sit in any doctor's waiting room you can always pick out the rheumatism sufferers – they are the ones wearing copper bracelets. The alleged curative power of copper goes all the way back to the ancient Egyptians who also used green copper-based substances as eye make-up. Records show they had their fair share of arthritis.

A fairly new book worth reading is *Relief from Arthritis* by John E. Croft (Thorsons) which describes a remarkable new product from the ocean – an extract derived from the New Zealand green-lipped mussel.

There are two national associations concerned with arthritis and both have local groups throughout Britain. **Arthritis Care** (O) provides information, mutual support, advice and practical help. They work for improved welfare and medical facilities for their members and they provide specially-adapted holiday centres and residential homes. There is a strong regional organisation and most local groups hold monthly meetings. They publish a wide range of information leaflets as well as an excellent quarterly magazine. Contact **Arthritis Care** (O). The **Arthritis and Rheumatism Council (ARC)** (O) is the only national voluntary organisation which has as its main aim the funding of research into rheumatic diseases – currently over £1½ million a year. Over the last twenty years, this research has resulted in the virtual elimination of some forms of arthritis, and has produced new treatments which have improved the prospects of over half of all sufferers. For information write to **ARC** (O).

Nearly all of us will suffer from one of the many kinds of rheumatism sooner or later. With good advice from these two excellent organisations much can be done at least to limit the effects and make it possible to live with this disability.

ASBAH

The **Association for Spina Bifida and Hydrocephalus** (O) is a welfare and research organisation which provides advisory and welfare services, practical assistance and information. There are almost 80 local associations in England, Wales and Northern Ireland. There is a separate association for Scotland. ASBAH has a team of trained field workers who support parents, families, and individuals with spina bifida and/or *hydrocephalus*, giving advice and practical help.

Support includes financial help, welfare grants and advice on a variety of topics covering aspects of disabled living, provision of aids and equipment, accommodation, social development, education, independence and vocational training, leisure and employment, and adaptations to property.

The Association has a residential centre, 'Five Oaks' in Yorkshire, which is totally accessible to disabled people. It houses a specially-designed activities centre and it is a base for a wide variety of courses including independent living, fashion, photography, fishing and arts and crafts. Interesting Study Days are organised for parents and caring professionals.

ASBAH publishes a wide range of books and leaflets as well as a bi-monthly magazine called *Link*. Video and slide sets are available for purchase.

For more information, contact **ASBAH** (O).

Association of Disabled Professionals

In 1971, when ADP was founded, a certain amount was being done to train, rehabilitate and employ disabled blue collar and clerical workers, but there were few facilities for assessing, training or employing disabled people with professional qualifications. ADP is an association of disabled people, run by disabled people. The main aim of ADP is to improve the education, rehabilitation, training and employment prospects for all disabled people. The Association has an excellent quarterly House Bulletin and it maintains close contact with Parliament. Members, 95 per cent of whom are disabled, are drawn from a wide range of professions and there is a growing Register of Professional Advisers. These are qualified and currently practising in their professions, and they have volunteered to give advice on employment in their particular fields.

Disabled people who seek training for and *employment* in the professions have to rely to a great extent on their own initiative. ADP can provide the advice, information and encouragement needed by such disabled aspirants. There are few, if any, professions that cannot be followed by disabled people. Requests for further information should be sent to Peggy M Marchant, General Secretary, **Association of Disabled Professionals** (O).

Asthma

This is a fairly common condition which affects the lungs, causing attacks of wheezing, difficulty with breathing, and coughing. It is often mistakenly called bronchitis. Asthma is caused by a narrowing of the air passages and lungs.

These attacks can have any one of many causes – allergy, exertion, infection, pollution, or sometimes even emotional pressures. Attacks can happen at any time and can last for just a few minutes or go on all night. Fairly close but random attacks can last for days. The severity of the attacks varies from a slight wheezing to an almost total inability to breathe. Severe attacks are extremely distressing both for the sufferer and those around him. Although very rare, death can result from asthma.

The past twenty years have seen vast improvements in the management of this condition. Asthmatics who formerly were significantly handicapped by this ailment now have a reasonable chance of a normal life, provided they and their families are given the necessary information. Many treatments for asthma involve breathing medicines directly into the narrowed air passages. These medicines are called bronchodilators and they give quick relief from asthma wheezing. The device used to deliver the medicine is called a nebuliser and it makes a mist out of the liquid medicine by blowing air or oxygen through it. Nebulisers are used routinely in hospitals and they are also found in GPs' surgeries and ambulances. Normally, home treatment of asthma is by prescribed pressurised inhalers, but chronic cases may need the use of a nebuliser daily. Treatment must be monitored by a doctor and the use of the nebuliser should be tapered off as soon as possible.

The **Asthma Society and Friends of the Asthma Research Council** (O), formed in 1980, has as its main objectives the provision of mutual aid and practical assistance to those with asthma and their families, informing the public about asthma and the treatments available, and raising funds for research into the causes and treatment of asthma. There is a network of local branches which hold regular meetings with talks, films, and discussions on the medical and social problems of asthma. They also make the public aware that asthmatics can live normal lives, if they are given the correct medication.

The society publishes a wide range of books and helpful leaflets as well as a regular newsletter.

Attendance Allowance

Attendance Allowance is available to mentally or physically disabled people who need a lot of help from another person. Over half a million people in Britain draw this non-contributory allowance, which is untaxed and does not normally affect other social security benefits. The low rate is for people who require help by day only and the higher rate is reserved for those who need help during the night as well as by day.

Full details are to be found in leaflet NI 205 which also contains the application form. You will be assessed by a DHSS doctor in your own home. It is a good idea to have an advocate with you – say, an advisor from your local *DIAL* – as many applicants lose Attendance Allowance through presenting themselves as being more capable than they really are. For example, many are ashamed to admit to being incontinent. Before the assessment keep a careful diary for 24 hours noting every occasion when you need help from another person. If you are turned down you can appeal within 28 days. A disabled person who is employed or in full-time higher education or living alone may still draw Attendance Allowance. The allowance may be awarded to any person from the age of two upwards; there is no upper age limit.

Audio Books

Unabridged readings of books on standard cassettes are now available from a number of commercial publishers. Prices range from £20 to £30. Write to:

Chivers Press
Windsor Bridge Road
Bath BA2 3AX

Cover to Cover cassettes
Freepost
Marlborough
Wiltshire

ISIS Audio Books
55 St Thomas' Street
Oxford OX1 1JG

Ullverscroft Soundings
The Green
Bradgate Road
Anstey
Leicester LE7 7FU

A good postal lending library of audio books is Travellers' Tales. They have an annual membership fee of £11.50 (with a standing order) or £13.80 (cash), as well as a life membership for £29.50. The average hire charge is 85p per cassette per week. Write to Travellers' Tales, Great Weddington, Ash, Canterbury, Kent CT3 2AR, or ring on 0304 812531. Most public libraries also lend out audio books.

Autism

Autism is a devastating handicap which affects the parts of the brain that control understanding, the emotions, verbal and gestured communication, and the ability to relate to others socially. There is no known cause and the condition, which is incurable, affects over 75,000 people in the UK.

The **National Autistic Society** (O), which is the only organisation working specifically for autistic people, provides day and residential centres for the care, education and training of autistic children and adults. There is an information service for parents and caring professionals, and the society owns seven schools, an adult community, a hostel and workshop and a family centre.

B

Back Pain

Back pain is as common in Britain as wet weekends and income tax – and, like these two, it is often the subject of our rather odd sense of humour. However, it is no joke for the millions of unlucky people who suffer from it. Back pain is so common that 1,500,000 people go to the doctor with it every year, and maybe a further million try fringe medicine – *osteopaths*, *acupuncture*, massage and so on.

On every weekday 90,000 men and women are away from work because of back pain. Some of them face a lifetime of agony, which will affect their earning capacity and their family life. It is reliably estimated that the cost to the country in sickness benefit, medical care and lost production tops a staggering £500 million a year. Research has shown that people who suffer with back pain are usually dissatisfied with the treatment they get. The simple fact is that back pain is very widespread, so, undeserved as it may be, there is a tendency for a busy family doctor to say 'You'll have to live with it', or even 'I've got it too'.

Whilst some cases of back pain arise from rheumatism or *arthritis*, the majority are the results of misuse of the body. Some risks are related to heavy industry – mining, steel production, dock labour – while sedentary work, such as typing, computer operating, watch repair, or long hours using a microscope, encourage bad posture resulting in back problems. Hospital staff who are much involved with lifting patients attend regular lifting courses – nurses, therapists and porters are taught how to lift patients without damaging their own backs, and they are encouraged to give tuition to patients who have back problems.

Most people seem to regard back pain as some sort of bad luck, when in fact an hour's instruction could prevent the damage which causes the pain. Of all the disabling conditions back pain is the one in which the greatest level of prevention can be achieved by proper training and education. We all use our backs throughout life so instruction should start in

'*For someone with a bad back, you got up here ruddy soon!!*'

school and 'reminder' training should be given at places of work, particularly in those jobs where the incidence of back pain is high.

The **National Back Pain Association** (O) is a registered charity whose main objectives include the promotion of research into the causes and treatment of back pain, the prevention of back pain by educating people in the correct use of their bodies, and the formation of local branches to help sufferers by providing them with useful advice and information and an opportunity to meet and learn from each other.

Much time and effort is put into raising funds to further these objectives. The Association publishes an excellent quarterly magazine, *TalkBack*, and a great many helpful publications, leaflets, posters and books on back pain and its prevention. New leaflets include *Oh, my Back!* for the general public, *Back Pain – a National Problem* for the institutional donors, and *Back to Mobility*, a cassette and booklet giving 32 simple exercises to music which can be done in the privacy of your home.

There is a wide range of products for the prevention of back pain or to help back pain sufferers. The best place to find these is the **Back Shop** (M) or the **Back Store** (M) which has the largest stock in Europe. The shop is open daily, 6 days a week, from 10am to 6pm for personal shoppers. All of their products have been tried and tested thoroughly and the vast range includes everything from ice packs to special seats for taxi drivers and office furniture. It is well worth writing for their excellent catalogue.

BACUP

See under Cancer.

Banstead Place Mobility Centre

This well-known centre has been in existence since 1982, during which time well over two thousand people have been assessed for driving a modified car or for driving an electric wheelchair or other 4mph pavement vehicle.

Support from the Ford Motor Company has enabled staff to man a mobile unit which has visited all parts of the country assessing and advising people on how their car should be modified to enable them to drive. In addition, also with the help of Ford, the centre is able to offer a free follow-up check to clients, enabling them to return to Banstead when they have their car to see the Driving Instructor and Therapist.

The Information Service handles an average of 80 enquiries each week. The centre enjoys very good co-operation from motor manufacturers and disabled people are able to have driving lessons on various adapted cars which are held on loan.

The centre also organises various courses, including three-day Driving Instructors' Courses for instructors interested in knowing more about the problems of disabled would-be drivers; one-day seminars for therapists interested in driving ability assessments for disabled people with neurological damage; and workshops for therapists to learn more about the wide range of 4mph vehicles now available.

A research programme is evaluating the long-term effect of assessment and increased mobility on former disabled clients.

For further information contact the Mobility Officer, **Banstead Place Mobility Centre** (O).

Bathroom

Pride in personal appearance as well as cleanliness in personal habits is more important for the physically disabled person than for the able-bodied person. Life in a wheelchair is not as nature intended, and hair, eyes, complexion, teeth, ears and nails all require extra care . . . and that goes for the chaps too. Because of their relative immobility, affection from personal touch is very necessary to disabled people, whether it is a handshake or a kiss and cuddle. It breaks down the barriers of foolish convention, but you cannot expect it if you are smelly and unkempt.

Looking good adds up to a lot of hard work. A mildly physically disabled person – say, a hemiplegic with one good arm – could take over an hour to wash and dress unaided. A severely handicapped tetraplegic might need two hours for his wife to lift him out of bed, put him on the loo, wash, shave and dress him and put him into his wheelchair. For disabled people an attractive appearance does not come easily and so it is well worth while putting considerable thought into the design of your bathroom and toilet.

Consider first what would be an ideal arrangement for the severely disabled person and then work back to what is feasible in your particular house, bearing in mind the capability of your particular disabled person, the cost and the available space. Although the thought may be distressing, allow for the deterioration of the handicapped person. Always take into account the needs of the other members of the family too. A good arrangement is for the wheelchair rider to have a bedroom, sitting room, 'eating' room, bathroom and toilet all on the ground floor, with good access to the front and rear and adequate floor space to move around. These parts of the house are shared with the rest of the family but they are modified for the needs of the handicapped member. It is likely the family would use bedrooms upstairs.

For the severely physically disabled person who can only be moved with great difficulty, an electric hoist on an overhead rail may be necessary (**Wessex** (M)). This should be carefully routed so the disabled person can be moved from bed to bath, to toilet, bidet or wash basin. Doorways have to be extended to the ceiling and this system is often used in a purpose-built ground-floor 'disabled' extension. Grants for part or all of the cost of major building projects like this are available from local authorities, although in some areas they are discretionary. Normally the domiciliary OT makes the initial assessment and sees the work through, in collaboration with the Housing Officer.

Disabled people who are able to walk on crutches tend to prefer separate toilets or small bathrooms where they can readily lean on the walls or the fitments in the room. However, it must be recognised that wash basins, cupboards and toilet roll holders often do not have fixings strong enough to take the full weight of a disabled person, and this is a common cause of accidents. Wheelchair users, on the other hand, need room to manoeuvre, so the minimum clear floor space should be at least 6ft × 6ft (2m × 2m) – this may need to be increased when account is taken of fixed objects such as washbasins. Additional space may also have to be allowed for if a helper is always needed in the bathroom. A bathroom door should always open against a wall, open outwards, or slide; this avoids taking up space in the bathroom. It also avoids blocking the door on the inside if the disabled person has a fall. The floor covering should be slip-resistant, and there are many floor tiles and vinyl coverings which give a good surface. Carpet is warm and attractive but difficult to dry, and may be *too* slip-resistant for the disabled walker. Loose bath mats are dangerous.

Domestic *toilet* compartments tend to be small and good for the disabled walker who can attend to his own toilet needs, but for the wheelchair user who has to be lifted on to the toilet, they can be back-breakers for the caring relative. It is better to have the toilet, washbasin and bath all in one room, where the disabled person can move the short distance from one to another, and where there is enough floor space for the care-giver to assist with transfers. Disabled people often take a long time over their toilet functions and a second toilet and washbasin may be necessary for the rest of the family.

Disabled people need a temperature of about 70°F (22°C) and while a chilly bathroom may be all right for a quick visit by the able-bodied, it could be dangerous for a handicapped person. If the house has central heating there should be a radiator in the bathroom, preferably close to the loo. A ceiling light fitment which incorporates a radiant heat element helps with drying after a bath. The Luxaire Body dryer (**Clos-o-Mat** (M)) dries the whole body with an oscillating jet of warm air.

Some form of alarm is essential and for most people it is enough to keep a small hand bell on the floor beside the toilet.

The location of the large main items in the bathroom should take account of the special needs of the disabled person. Space will be needed on one side or the other of the toilet for the person who make a sideways sliding transfer from his wheelchair. It may be necessary to have a high cistern for the person who needs a helper to stand behind the toilet to lift him out of the wheelchair backwards. Support rails (**Llewellyn** (M)) may be fixed to the wall, floor, or toilet pedestal.

The range of specialised baths for disabled and elderly people is very wide, and expert advice is necessary before making a choice. The introduction of reinforced acrylic has meant that baths can be made in any shape, and, since bathing seems to have become a social activity, any size too. The smallest conventional baths are about 1500mm long and heights vary from 16in (40cm) to 22in (56cm), which may be preferred by an ambulant disabled person. The average height of a wheelchair is 18in (45cm) and many disabled people use sideways transfers to get into the bath. The bottom of the bath should be flat and slip-resistant. It would be natural to choose a bath with built-in handles but often these are too low for disabled people. Lever taps should be within reach of the bather and a pop-up waste plug helps those with poor grip. At the head of the bath there should be a smooth-tiled or cork-covered shelf about 16in (40cm) wide to facilitate lateral transfer from the wheelchair to the bath.

The bath may also incorporate a shower with curtains or sliding screens. **Shires** (M) make a bath with a circular end for the shower. A handset-type shower incorporated with the taps is very useful for the person who needs help with bathing. The connection should be long enough to be used at the wash basin for shampooing hair. Chrome or plastic support rails may be fixed to the wall to suit the disabled person for entering the bath.

44

The level and type of disability will determine the best method of getting in and out of the bath. Certainly the newly-disabled person and their care-giver should be trained by an *occupational therapist, physiotherapist* or care attendant until they can manage alone with safety. Most paraplegics can manage lateral transfers from the wheelchair to the shelf at the head of the bath and then forward into the bath. If no shelf is possible there is a wide range of bath boards available from **Homecraft** (M). Bath seats enable the body to be lowered into the water in stages. It is possible to use a portable hoist to put a disabled person in the bath but this needs 5in (12.5cm) clearance under the bath for the base of the hoist.

A better system is a P & L Bath Lifter (**Llewellyn** (M)) or an Autolift (**Mecanaids** (M)). These are essentially the same but since each has distinctive features, both should be considered. Each consists of a plastic seat with a back, attached by a sturdy curved metal arm to a vertical pole. Winding a handle causes the seat to rise vertically until the disabled person is high enough to be rotated over the bath; he can then be lowered into the water. A loo-type seat enables the bottom to be washed before entering the water. This type of hoist may be clamped to the side of most baths, or, if the floor is suitable, fitted in a socket on a large metal base plate.

Another method is the Mangar Bath Lift (**Mangar Aids Ltd** (M)) which is a sort of concertina with a seat on the top. Placed in the bath, it is raised and lowered with air pressure from a low-pressure electric compressor outside the bathroom. In the raised position this permits a sideways sliding transfer from the wheelchair. An alternative is the Messerli Dip Seat (**Llewellyn** (M)) which clamps to the sides of the bath. The seat is controlled by counter-balanced springs, so no external power is needed.

There are a number of baths with built-in corner transfer ledges and seats (**Nicholls & Clarke** (M)) and baths with removable sides, enabling a direct sliding transfer to the floor of the bath (**Aremco** (M)). The well-tried Parker Bath has a built-in seat giving easy entry through a lift-up side. The bath can be reclined giving full immersion. This is found in many hospitals but it is also available in a domestic version (**Parker Bath Developments Ltd** (M)). The Appollo Bath has a moulded seat which can be elevated, giving easy transfer from the wheelchair. When the seat is at its lowest point it is recessed into the bath, permitting full-length immersion (**Hampshire Medical Developments Ltd** (M)).

The water temperature needs to be checked, particularly by those without sensory nerves who could be scalded without feeling pain. For these a small round floating thermometer is available. For those who regularly lose the soap, shower soap has a cord to hang it around your neck. Nail brushes are available with suction discs enabling one-handed use. Back scrubbers can be made from coat hangers and there are soap dispensers, special brushes, combs and electric tooth-brushes. All of these aids are in a large catalogue available free from Boots the Chemist.

Washbasins should be positioned at a height to suit the needs of the disabled person – normally 24–32in (60–80cm) from the floor. Some ambulant and all wheelchair riders wash seated so they need to get as close to the basin as possible. The ideal shape is rectangular with the front rim narrow and the trap underneath set as far back as possible to give knee room (**Nicholls & Clarke** (M)). There are a number of washbasins and vanitory units with flexible plumbing permitting height adjustment (**Pressalit Ltd** (M)). Both basin and bath should be fitted with lever taps (**Belco** (M)).

Bathing should be enjoyable and there are few greater pleasures than relaxing in a hot bath. However, for some disabled people a shower is more suitable, and some local authority 'disabled' houses provide showers only. A shower should have a smooth entrance to take the front wheels of the wheelchair or the feet of the disabled walker, a non-slip floor and suitable support rails, thermostatically-controlled water supply, and lever controls for water supply and tem-perature. Some people shower in a 'wet' wheelchair or sani-trolley. Often recommended is the Chiltern 100 shower unit (**Nicholls & Clarke** (M)). For those who have to shower sitting down a strong folding seat is essential (**Pressalit** (M)). There should be alternative positions for the shower-head. There are a number of 'total hygiene' free-standing units which can be put in the corner of a bedroom. These provide a toilet, washbasin, mirror, shaving point, light and shower. The earliest of these was the 'Triad' from **Stannah Lifts Ltd** (M).

If there is enough floor space, a bidet may be useful and for disabled women the Pentland (**Nicholls & Clarke** (M)) is about 18in (457mm) high for easy transfer from a wheelchair. It has a polished wooden seat and you sit upon it in the same way as a toilet – that is, the opposite way to a normal bidet. In the bathroom, mirrors, shelves and cupboards should be at heights suitable for the disabled user.

Advice is available from your local *DIAL*, community OT, or Health Visitor and if you have a *Disabled Living Centre*, pay them a visit; they will have a demonstration 'disabled' bathroom. The **DLF** (O) Information Service has an excellent leaflet (No 7B) entitled *Personal Care*, and very useful too is *With a Little Help* (Volume III) by Philippa Harpin.

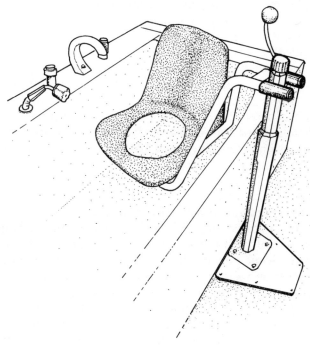

Bath lifter.

Batteries

Wheelchairs, scooters and 'golf-buggy' type electric personal vehicles have traditionally been powered by 12 or 24 volt motors using standard car batteries. As there can be a danger from acid spillage, the batteries are always in acid-proof boxes and there is a move towards 'sealed-for-life' or gel batteries. Car batteries are designed to give a burst of power which is immediately followed by recharging, and any other drain on the battery normally only occurs when the engine is turning and the battery is being recharged. Many wheelchair manufacturers now use deep cycle batteries which are designed to give a constant power output over the whole discharge cycle. Information on these can be obtained from Crompton Batteries Ltd, Stephenson Street, Newport, Gwent NP1 0XJ.

The batteries of an electric wheelchair used indoors for twelve hours or more need recharging every night. Outdoor wheelchairs are normally put on charge after every outing of two or three hours. Modern battery chargers switch off automatically as soon as the battery is charged, and some have coloured lights to indicate the state of the charging process. It is essential to top up batteries regularly with battery fluid, and the terminals should be covered with Vaseline. In winter the batteries of an unused electric wheelchair should be regularly charged, and in exceptionally cold (sub-zero) temperatures batteries should be brought indoors. As a pair of batteries for an outdoor electric wheelchair could cost upwards of £200 it does pay to care for them.

With an outdoor wheelchair it is difficult to estimate how much power is left in the battery and this tends to limit the use. The 'Curtis' Battery Meter is a sort of 'petrol gauge' for electric wheelchairs. It is a small box about the size of a cigarette packet which has an adhesive patch allowing it to be attached to the control box. On the top of the gauge is an LED presentation giving ten divisions, from 'Full' to 'Empty'. The gauge is wired directly to the battery. A tiny plug and socket in the wire provides for its disconnection when not in use. With this device, when you are a mile or so away from your house in the wheelchair it is easy to check that you have

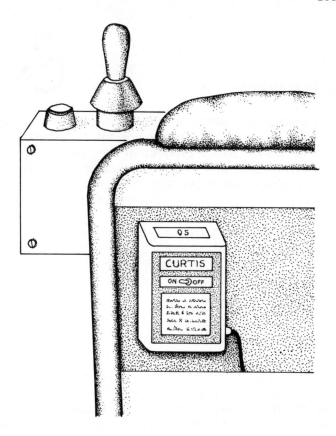

Curtis gauge.

sufficient battery power left to get you home. Write to Curtis Instruments (UK) Ltd, 51 Grafton Street, Northampton NN1 2NT.

BAWD

See under Wheelchairs.

Bird Watching

Bird watching is a pleasant occupation for wheelchair riders which can be enjoyed from a window overlooking the garden, or in local parks. Enjoyment is enhanced if you can recognise the birds and you know something about their habits, and this is where the Royal Society for the Protection of Birds comes in. They publish a range of books and leaflets, as well as catalogues of field glasses and equipment, to help handicapped people enjoy this absorbing hobby. For more information, write to Anthony Chapman, **RSPB** (O).

Blindness

Some forms of blindness are hereditary and every year some babies are born completely blind. Many more people are blinded through accidents, and diabetes can also be a cause. People who are blind should register with their local Social Services Department – this will bring them entitlement to social security, equipment and services. A registered blind person is entitled to increased personal income tax allowance, and a deaf-blind person is likely to be entitled to Attendance Allowance. Most Social Services Departments employ trained social workers to deal with the problems of the blind, and they also provide a wide range of aids, including radios, working closely with the local voluntary associations. A useful first step is to contact your local *DIAL* for a list of national and local blind organisations and equipment manufacturers, concessions for TV licences, travel on BR, dog licences, and parking. Some county social services run rehabilitation schools for the blind, day centres, and homes for the elderly blind.

Of the many voluntary associations for the blind the largest is the **Royal National Institute for the Blind** (O). The RNIB sells many specialised aids – often at as little as one third of the real cost – and also publishes a comprehensive catalogue. The RNIB has a number of residential homes, holiday hostels and hotels, and runs courses for blind students in physiotherapy, audio typing, telephone operating, piano tuning and computer programming. They can provide an escort service for cross-country journeys too.

Friends and relatives in daily contact with blind people can get a useful book of advice from the RNIB. For example, whenever you meet a blind person you should always introduce yourself by name and shake hands. If you lead them to a chair, put their hand on the back and let them seat themselves. At home never tidy a blind person's belongings and avoid leaving things about the place which they could trip over. Always say if you are leaving the room.

Personal mobility is important for blind people and thousands have benefited from the canine navigators supplied by the **Guide Dogs for the Blind** (O). There are training centres at Bolton, Exeter, Forfar and Leamington Spa. Most of the dogs are Labradors and the training takes about five months. The blind owner then has a month's residential course. For a blind person the harness handle is the vital new connection with freedom and independence.

Other organisations providing equipment or services for blind people include the **National Federation for the Blind** (O), who have branches all over the country. They publish an excellent guide to the rights of blind people who are looking for jobs. Also well worth a letter are the **National Library for the Blind** (O), **Electronic Aids for the Blind** (M), the Moon Branch of the **RNIB** (O), and **National Music for the Blind** (O), which is the only charity authorised by the Post Office to send complete programmes of music via the Freepost system for the blind. This service sends three cassettes weekly to each person – a newspaper called *Guiding Star*, music and a talking book.

Given training, blind people can 'read' Braille or Moon, interpreting raised dots or symbols with the tips of the fingers. Most public libraries stock books in these formats and there are a number of national lending libraries. Optacon is a portable reading device comprising a tiny camera which is moved over the print associated with a tactile device for fingertip reading. It will also read a VDU and it is sold by **Sensory Information Systems** (M). This firm also make the Vincent Work Station, which is essentially a talking typewriter. The Kurzweil Reading Machine from John Bradburn (Microsystems) Ltd is a controllable electronic device which will read print verbally aloud.

In Touch is a weekly radio programme for blind listeners on BBC Radio 4. For summaries in Braille, or on a C60 cassette, write to **In Touch** (O). Taped books are available for temporarily blind patients in hospital from the **British Library of Tape Recordings for Hospital Patients** (O). National and local newspapers and certain magazines are available from the **National Newspaper and Magazine Tape Service** (O). Calibre is a free lending library of books for children and adults recorded on standard tapes.

Many sports are played by blind people. Cricket and football are both played by blind teams, using sonic balls, and there is even an annual blind cricket festival. Archery and darts are popular, and blind athletes compete in track and field events as well as in swimming. Many blind people ride and a few, using a cap with built-in radar, go in for show jumping. The cap has earphones which bleep; the volume gives the range from the jump and the frequency the direction. Blind yachtsmen steer boats using tactile compasses and a number have crewed on deep-sea trips on the square-rigged *Lord Nelson*.

The Manpower Services Commission offers many services and aids to enable a blind person to work in an office or shop-floor environment, and where training is required the MSC will defray the cost of a sighted 'reader'. A number of home-based jobs involving computers are also within the reach of blind people. Would-be writers can get much help from the **Blind Authors Association** (O) of which membership is free.

It is possible to modify many items of domestic equipment to make them safer or easier for blind people to use and it is well worth getting the appropriate leaflets from the Gas and

Electricity Boards. There are control knobs with Braille markings and tactile switches, and lights can be replaced by sound warnings. **Candy Domestic Appliances** (M) make a 'Braille' washing machine (model 611). Most banks offer special services including Braille statements and a template for signing cheques. The **Brunel University Research Unit for the Blind** (O) will provide information on request from their Directory of Agencies for the Visually Disabled.

Story

Tale of the Dog

In America small internal airlines are much like buses in this country. A single journey may involve several stops at small airfields where some people board and leave the aircraft and the rest stay in their seats. It is not unusual on such brief stops for the pilot to get out and walk around the aeroplane to stretch his legs.

A famous blind pianist was travelling to his next engagement accompanied by his Labrador guide dog. At the next stop-over the pilot climbed out of his seat, came back down to the blind man and offered to walk the dog. Holding the dog harness as he walked away from the aircraft towards the small terminal building, he wondered what it must be like to be blind. He decided to walk a little with his eyes shut. Inside the building a very nervous lady passenger said to the receptionist 'Am I too late for the next departure?' 'No Ma'am,' she replied, 'there's the pilot.' The lady turned and watched with horror the uniformed pilot, coming towards her, eyes shut, led by the guide dog.

Blind Writers

Aspiring blind authors can get advice and the opportunity to air their problems by contacting Mr John May, The Blind Authors' Association, Brierdene, Croit e Quill Road, Lonan, Isle of Man (0624 781349). Mr May will supply full details in return for a blank C90 cassette.

Story

Worth a Try

A blind man entered a public house with a tiny chihuahua on a lead. The landlord started to escort him back to the entrance saying 'I'm sorry Sir, dogs are not allowed in here; we only allow guide dogs.' The blind man said 'But this is my guide dog.' The landlord replied 'But how can that little thing be a guide dog?' The blind man bent down and felt around vaguely, saying 'Blimey, have they given me the wrong one again?'

BOLD

This organisation promotes and encourages blind and partially-sighted people to take part in outdoor recreational and leisure pursuits. Blind Outdoor Leisure Development is run by Mr Peter Lobley, BOLD, 26 High Street, Cherry Willingham, Lincoln, Lincolnshire (Lincoln 751950).

Books

There are many books for disabled readers, and the following titles include some of the standard works which have run into several editions. Most of these books should be available in any public library, and many will also be available from large bookshops.

General Reference

The Directory for the Disabled, Ann Darnbrough and Derek Kinrade (**Woodhead-Faulkner** (M))
Children with Mental Handicaps, Fred Heddell (Crowood Press)
Children with Physical Handicaps, Renee Myers (Crowood Press)

Social Security

Disability Rights Handbook (**Disability Alliance** (O))
Rights Guide to Non-Means-Tested Social Security Benefits (**CPAG** (O))
National Welfare Benefits Handbook (**CPAG** (O))

Holidays

Holidays for the Physically Handicapped (**RADAR** (O)) (available from WH Smith & Son Ltd)
Access at Channel Ports, Gordon Couch and David Barrett (**RADAR** (O))
A Guide to Countryside Recreation for Disabled People (**Country Landowners Association** (O))

Equipment

Equipment for the Disabled (a series of 13 books, regularly updated) (**Mary Marlborough Lodge** (O))

Health

Health Help (**Harper & Row** (M))

Retirement

'Letts Retirement Guides', *House and Garden, Leisure and Travel, Good Health, Finance* (**CLIO Distribution Services** (M)) *Good Retirement Guide*, Rosemary Brown (**Gerald Duckworth & Co. Ltd** (M))

Alarms

Calling for Help (**Age Concern** (O))

Care

Caring at Home (**King's Fund Centre** (O))

Housing

House Adaptations for People with Physical Disabilities (HMSO)

Sport

Outdoor Pursuits for Disabled People, Norman Croucher (**Woodhead-Faulkner** (M)) *Textbook of Sport for the Disabled*, Sir Ludwig Guttman (**John Wiley & Sons Ltd** (M))

Braille Chess Association

See under Chess.

Breast Cancer

Many women over the age of forty are haunted by the fear that they will one day find a lump under or near the breast and this will mean they have to have a mastectomy – major surgery involving total breast amputation – to remove a cancerous growth.

The decisions needed before the operation, if any, and the management afterwards require counselling independent of both the hospital and the family. Contact the **Jeanne Campbell Breast Cancer Radiotherapy Appeal** (O) or the **Breast Care Mastectomy Association** (O).

Breast Care and Mastectomy Association

This association was formed in 1973 to advise women who had had, or were about to have, breast surgery. BCMA provides emotional support together with a practical information service which is available during office hours. There is also a telephone answering service.

When support is requested, a volunteer, who herself has had similar surgery, will visit the patient, helping her to come to terms with the operation and offering advice on prostheses and clothing. It is usually easier for a patient to air her worries freely about breast surgery to someone who has had the same fears and doubts rather than to her family who, however much they may sympathise, cannot know exactly how she feels.

The BCMA produces a wide range of literature describing the prostheses available on the NHS and listing stockists of suitable lingerie and swimwear. Literature on services is free of charge but postage should be paid by the recipient. No subscriptions are requested by the Association which has a paid staff.

The BCMA welcomes women who would like to become volunteer visitors. They are selected at least two years after surgery as they are then able to offer a reassuring example of someone leading a normal life.

For more information contact the **Breast Care and Mastectomy Association** (O).

The British Council of Organisations of Disabled People

The **BCODP** (O) was formed in 1981 by groups of disabled people who were unhappy that the representative voice of disabled people was not being heard. Until 1986 the Council was funded only from members' subscriptions, but in 1988 it received an annual grant of £10,000 from the DHSS. This provides for a London-based Development Worker and there is another Development Worker based in Derbyshire.

There are 40 member organisations, including national and local associations. Membership of the BCODP is limited to organisations which are of, rather than for, disabled people. Members' constitutions must state clearly that control of the organisation is in the hands of disabled people, and that more than 51 per cent of the governing body must be made up of disabled people.

It is the view of the BCODP that they are the democratically-elected representatives of disabled people in this country, and therefore the proper body to be consulted on any of the following:

Housing and personal support
Environmental access
Employment
Education and training
Transport
Technical aids
Finance and information
International affairs on disability
Women's issues

Through the member organisations the BCODP claims access to a large body of knowledge on these issues.

The BCODP is preparing a regional structure to improve liaison with member organisations. This will provide support for local organisations of disabled people and assist in the development of new groups. The Council is a member of the Disabled Peoples' International which was also established in 1981, and which has largely the same aims as the BCODP.

British Database on Research into Aids for the Disabled

This is a database known as BARD, which contains information on British design and development work, prototypes and research into equipment for disabled people. They have over 1,000 records divided into 31 fields. General searches can be carried out on any of the fields and more detailed searches based on the 200-word BARD thesaurus. They have a second database – BARDSOFT – on computer software for special disabled needs. Write to the **Handicapped Persons Research Unit** (O).

British Diabetic Association

See under Diabetic.

British Telecom's Protected Service Scheme

For many disabled and elderly people, particularly those living alone, their telephone is a lifeline in emergency situations. Furthermore, many people at risk use warning systems for which the telephone is an integral part. Clearly it is vital for these people that their telephone should not be disconnected for non-payment of the phone bill owing to circumstances beyond their control.

To avoid this happening, British Telecom have introduced the Protected Service Scheme under which the person at risk finds someone to act as a 'nominee' for them. This second person may be a relative, friend, professional carer or welfare worker, or it could even be a disabled association. The details of the nominee are given to British Telecom. The nominee does not have to pay the bill unless they wish to.

If a phone bill remains unpaid, British Telecom will advise the nominee, by phone if possible, and defer disconnecting the line for two weeks to enable the problem to be resolved.

To apply, simply complete the three parts of the application form and send it to the address on the back – normally your local British Telecom office. Copies of the form are available from your local British Telecom office or you can telephone them free of charge using the method detailed on the top of your phone bill.

Brittle Bones

About 2,500 people in Britain have brittle bones. In some of the milder cases, the disorder passes from one generation to another. In all the severe cases it appears without warning with no history of the disorder in either parent. Some brittle bone children are actually born with fractures, while others have their first fracture soon after birth or when they start walking. For these people bones break with frightening ease; a simple act like closing a door or switching on a television can cause a fracture, and some children have as many as fifty fractures before they reach their teens. Some never stand and have to remain in a special wheelchair and many are of short stature. A few have fingers with bones so weak that their hands are virtually useless. A nineteen-year-old may be the same size as a normal seven-year-old girl.

There is no known cure for the brittle bone condition. It is thought to be a combination of at least seven distinct disorders, all caused by abnormalities in the basic structure of the protein part of the bone. Brittle bones are not caused by lack of calcium. It may be that in the future drugs will be developed to treat some types of this disorder.

Most brittle bone children can be helped with special braces, 'space suits', custom-built wheelchairs – everything is designed to preserve their bones from fractures. These children are often quite bright and can take their education right up to university level. They can, given good support and understanding, be educated in mainstream primary and secondary schools.

The Brittle Bone Society was founded in 1972 and this registered charity now has over 1,000 members all over Britain. The two main aims of the society are the promotion of research and the provision of practical support and advice to patients and their families. Through the society affected families can get in touch with each other and share ideas on how to cope with the disorder. A regular newsletter is issued and also a range of helpful leaflets is published. Sometimes the society is able to help families with the cost of essential expensive equipment not available from statutory sources. For holidays the society has two specially-adapted caravans in the Isle of Wight and one in Scotland.

Contact the **Brittle Bone Society** (O).

C

Cancer Relief

The **Cancer Relief Macmillan Fund** (O) was founded in 1911 by Douglas Macmillan and to this day it has remained a major support for cancer sufferers and their families. The Fund is best known for its Macmillan nurses, but it also provides in-patient and day care, and financial help.

Macmillan nurses visit patients in their own homes to provide pain relief and practical support for caring relatives. Often the help they can give enables a patient to remain in his own home rather than having to enter hospital. This gives peace of mind to the patient who is able to be in familiar surroundings with his or her family.

The Fund also provides specialised care in their Continuing Care Homes where patients can learn to come to terms with their condition and what is involved with their treatment. Training is given to families to prepare for the patient returning home.

The onset of cancer in the breadwinner of a family can result in sudden financial hardship from loss of earnings and increased costs. The financial help which Cancer Relief may provide in such situations alleviates much stress and worry.

British Association of Cancer United Patients

BACUP was formed in 1985 by a very brave lady, the late Dr Vicky Clement-Jones, who was herself a cancer victim. The association has a full-time staff of eight, who provide answers to written and telephone enquiries with the help of a panel of experts, and a large computer database. Information is available on screening, treatment, research centres, transport services, patient support groups, financial help and home nursing services. BACUP's wide range of published leaflets and booklets includes *Coping with Cancer*, *Hair Care* and *Holiday Insurance*, and there is also an excellent quarterly newspaper. BACUP is complementary to, and actively working with, all the other cancer organisations. The main thrust of the association is the provision of emotional support and practical advice to those living with cancer, as well as information essential for family members and caring professionals. For details contact **BACUP** (O).

Special Care Agency

This is an agency which trains nursing and care staff to look after handicapped children and the children of disabled mothers. The agency recruits NNEB qualified staff, some of whom have, in addition, qualifications or experience in physiotherapy, Portage training or Makaton signing. The services also include nannies, maternity nurses and mothers' helps for non-handicapped children.

The aim of the **Special Care Agency** (O) is to provide staff who are trained to develop their charges physically and mentally, guiding them towards an independent life.

Carematch

This computer-based service for disabled Londoners has a database register of *residential* homes for disabled people in the London region, together with details of over 60 Cheshire homes throughout the country. The aim of **Carematch** is to cut through the frustration and confusion experienced by

disabled people and their carers, both family and professional, in seeking suitable residential establishments.

Contacting Hilary Kates, Carematch, 286 Camden Road,
London N7 0BJ, will produce a form asking for details of the
client's needs. The client will then receive a list of possible
homes to which they can make direct applications. Although
matching is confined to personal and geographical prefer-
ences, Carematch does have a telephone counsellor, Miss
Lin Barwick, who may be telephoned from 2 to 5pm Monday
to Friday on Hornchurch (040 24) 58325.

Caring Relatives

There are more women acting as caring relatives than there
are men – probably in the ratio of three to one. The carer may
be, for example, the spouse of a disabled person, a daughter
caring for an elderly parent, or the mother of a spastic child.
The level of dependency varies with the nature of the handicap, the character of the individual, housing, family finance,
and the provision of aids and services. The loading upon the
care-giver will vary from the healthy 40-year-old lady with
two helpful teenage children coping with a wheelchair-
riding grown-up son, to the lady who is over sixty caring
single-handed for a tetraplegic husband. Of all carers 43 per
cent are over sixty.

About one person in forty is severely disabled and in need
of a high level of constant care. The public at large has no
idea of the demands which this places upon caring relatives.
There are well over a million of these care-givers and if they
were paid wages it would cost the country £4–5 billion a
year. Some 68 per cent of all carers are in poor health and
over half never have even a weekend break. Improvements
in medicine have meant many disabled people have a life
expectancy as good as that of anyone else, and an increasing
number of caring relatives are dying before their handicapped charges – really from sheer hard work.

The disabled person living in his own house pays his own overheads – food, rent, rates, heating, and upkeep of the house. If he leaves home to go into a residential institution, the overheads remain the same for the wife or other member of the family. Society is now required to foot the bill for the disabled person – £100 a day for a hospital bed or £2–300 a week for nursing home care. On the grounds of humanity every effort should be made to keep disabled people in their own homes with their family; on purely economic grounds too, it is far cheaper to keep a disabled person at home. There they are cared for by a relative who receives little financial recompense although he or she is saving considerable public expenditure.

The lady who is the sole carer of a severely physically disabled husband is doing, every day, the work of three people. First, she is doing the household chores – just one pair of hands to peel every potato, to wash every dish; secondly she has to do all that her husband probably used to do, from income tax to painting the ceiling; and thirdly she has to do the equivalent of two shifts of a nurse's day caring for her husband – treatment, medicines, washing, dressing, shaving, toiletting, maybe feeding. Add to this level of sheer hard work the unavoidable worry and emotional stress and you have an unknown twentieth-century saint.

A severely disabled person can never fare better than his carer, and if, for example, she breaks an ankle, then he will suffer; he may have to enter hospital simply because there is nowhere else where his immediate personal needs can be seen to. It is therefore more important to look after the carer than the disabled person since the one is entirely dependent upon the other. Caring relatives have limited reserves of emotional and physical energy, and these, used intensively, without replenishment, will soon run out. The carer may suffer a damaged back, have a nervous breakdown, run away or ask for a divorce.

This sort of crisis can be avoided with careful planning and constant reappraisal which will give everyone enough time to stop an incipient problem becoming a disaster. First the carer must have some time of their own away from the disabled person, every day, every week and every year.

Someone coming in to play chess with a disabled person releases the carer, allowing her to pop next door for a chat, for example. A weekly visit to a day centre or a visit from a care attendant gives time for a day's shopping, WI, or sport. Two or three times a year the disabled person should spend a fortnight in a nursing home. On these occasions the carer can take a holiday, attend hospital as an in or out-patient or get house decorating and maintenance done. As far as possible, all of the carer's previous social contacts and hobbies should be maintained.

Every element of community care, from both the voluntary and statutory sectors, should be considered. *A care attendant* should call every week to attend to bathing, shampoos, nail cutting and simple exercises. Care attendants may come from the *Crossroads Care Attendant Scheme* or the Leonard Cheshire Family Support Scheme. Social workers can provide services, such as meals on wheels or *home helps*, domiciliary *physiotherapists* will monitor failing muscles, and occupational therapists can assess problems and supply equipment. Under the 1986 Disabled Persons Act local authorities have a statutory duty to assess the ability of a caring relative to continue to give care. The relevant association may provide transport, sitting services, respite care, equipment or holidays. A visit to the nearest *DIAL* will provide information and advice on specific problems, particularly social security, and an overall counselling session may be useful. The family doctor should identify the carer's health needs and provide periodical check-ups, and if the disabled person is very dependant 'what if' plans should be made to cover possible crises. What if the carer went shopping and finished up in hospital? What if she had a bad bout of flu? What if she had to go to her father's funeral 300 miles away?

The load on the caring relative can be reduced by the use of equipment which enables the disabled person to do things for himself and which helps the carer. Environmental controls, *alarm systems*, electric beds, special *armchairs*, and *toilets*, and aids to mobility all contribute to reducing the carer's worry. With over 10,000 aids on the market, random searches are pointless. The best method is to crystallise the problem in your own mind then go to an expert with a prepared

question: 'Is there a gadget which will enable me to . . .?'
Experts are to be found at *Social Services* Departments, *DIALS*
and *Disabled Living Centres*. A very useful new book is *Caring
Together* by Judy Wilson, priced at £3.95 from the **King's
Fund Centre** (O).

Considerable advice, information and practical help is
available from the **Carers' National Association** (O) which
has some 7,000 members, 61 branches and nearly 200 affili-
ated groups. They publish an excellent quarterly magazine.

If just 1 per cent of the carers of elderly people gave up,
the DHSS would have to increase spending by 20 per cent.

Caught Short

The best answer, as the Irishman said, is 'don't'! Some
disabled and elderly people may suffer with urinary *incontinence*. However, this is not the same as the disabled person
who needs a toilet when, for unforeseen reasons, it is not
possible to get to one. This often happens on long car
journeys when the disabled passenger has an urgent need to
pass urine and the car is stuck in a long traffic jam.

Very useful on such ocasions is the 'Convenient' portable
loo sold by **CC Products** (M). This complete, portable,
odourless and reusable urinal comes complete with applicators for use by male or female; the 2-litre reservoir is
vacuum-packed so it will draw liquid into itself and the
system has a non-return valve. For re-use the reservoir may
be sterilised with Milton 2.

CEH

See under Environment.

Centres for Independent Living

See under Independent Living.

Cerebral Palsy

In Britain there are over 100,000 spastic people. Cerebral palsy can occur in any family and in every 500 births one child has this disability. This condition (otherwise known as spasticity), produces uncoordinated movements and severe postural problems, and it results in many forms and levels of handicap. People who are seriously affected may have difficulty with walking, seated posture, with speech or hearing. There may be perceptual difficulties, for example in the analysis of shapes and forms and their reconstruction through drawing or assembly.

There are three types of cerebral palsy – spasticity, athetosis and ataxia. The person with spasticity has a disordered control of movement, muscle weakness and often reduced growth and development. Athetosis produces frequent involuntary movements which mask and interfere with normal movements of the whole body. Ataxia gives an unsteady walking gait and difficulty with balance.

Cerebral palsy is due to damage of that part of the brain which controls movement. Damage or growth failure of adjacent parts of the brain may also produce deafness or special learning problems. Many people with cerebral palsy are of above-average intelligence, although they may appear to be mentally retarded because of their communication difficulties.

Early recognition of the condition in very young children is most important, as it enables assessment by specialists who can define the best form of treatment and training. Good management of the condition at an early age can often bring great benefit, and it seems that some training that can be absorbed by a young child may be of little value later.

However, no way has yet been found to repair the damaged brain cells, although the damage cannot spread. Cerebral palsy is not a disease nor is it catching, and it is not generally considered to be an inherited defect.

The Spastics Society is a very large, broadly-based organisation that was founded in 1952. The society provides information, care, education, employment, holidays, welfare and residential care. It also finances a £3,000,000 research programme at Guy's Hospital in London. There are over 200 branches, centres and workshops, as well as seven schools catering for all levels of learning ability. A wide range of living accommodation is also provided, some in association with sheltered employment. The society publishes books and leaflets as well as an excellent newspaper called *Disability Now*.

For more information contact the **Spastics Society** (O).

Braille Chess Association

This is the national organisation of blind chess players. You do not need to be able to read Braille to join, nor do you need to be a strong player. Correspondence games are played in Braille or on cassette, and there are also 'over the board' tournaments and matches against foreign opponents, at home and abroad, for players of all strengths.

There is a library of chess literature in Braille and on cassette, and regular magazines in both forms, including the *BCA Gazette*. Advice is given on all aspects of chess, including the use by blind people of chess computers.

Membership is open to all blind and partially-sighted people and associate membership to sighted friends. Anyone under the age of 18 will be offered one year of free membership.

For full details write to the **Braille Chess Association** (O).

Children with Artificial Arms

The parents of children with artificial arms can obtain a considerable amount of information and practical help from **REACH**, the **Association for Children with Artificial Arms** (O). REACH was formed in 1978 by a group of parents of children who had part of an arm or hand missing. The immediate aim was to press for research and development into the technology of artificial arms. This has had some success – we have seen the arrival of the Swedish hand which is 'switched' by the user's brain, and the Southampton University hand which has, in addition, limited sensory feed-back.

REACH is now a mutual support and advice organisation, and caters for all children with any type of hand or arm deficiency. Research is strongly supported and there is a major project to discover the reasons why some children are born missing one or both arms. Parents are kept informed of new developments in prosthetics through a quarterly news-letter. There are a number of local branches.

Chiropractic

This is a form of manipulative treatment for mechanical disorders of the joints, particularly the spine. Many muscular and joint problems result from everyday activities such as carrying heavy shopping, gardening, lifting children or physically disabled relatives, or even sitting for long periods in an unsuitable chair. These are problems which cause aches and pains and they are closely related to today's style of living – bad bending and lifting habits are also risky.

The treatment by a skilled chiropractor is gentle and painless, and much safer than pain-suppressing drugs. All chiropractors undergo lengthy training before qualification and some work within the NHS. On a first visit a detailed case history will be taken and a full physical examination given, with blood pressure being measured and perhaps specimens of blood or urine taken. Treatment using manual pressure is directed towards reducing the strain on specific joints. A special treatment couch may be used to place the patient in the best position for each manipulation. Advice will be given on follow-up exercises to be done at home.

For more information write to the **British Chiropractic Association** (O).

Clothing

The following workshops make special garments for people with a wide range of disabilities; it is well worth writing for a catalogue.

Fashion Services for the Disabled
Units D10–D30
Saltaire Workshops
Ashley Lane
Shipley
West Yorkshire BD17 7SR
(0274 595966)

Merseyside Fashion for the Disabled
Tudor House
Wood Lane
Liverpool
Merseyside L27 4YA
(051 488 0444)

WDCT Fashion for the Disabled
Unit 2
Leechmore Industrial Estate
Sunderland
Tyne and Wear
(0783 674955)

Direct Community Action Group
Southall Baptist Church
Western Road
Southall
Middlesex
(01 574 4456)

Redbridge Community Care Managing Agency Ltd
The Methodist Church
Ilford Lane
Ilford
IG1 2JZ
(01 514 5143)

Colitis

See under Crohn's Disease.

College of Health

People are increasingly taking on the responsibility for their own personal health. This is evidenced by a new-found interest in jogging and aerobics, a proliferation of health food shops and advice on slimming, curiosity about food additives, a sharp downturn in the consumption of tobacco, and a slight reduction in alcohol abuse. Not so very long ago many people regarded illness as something entirely beyond their control – maybe the random act of an unfeeling God. Others thought the NHS would rectify ('free') whatever went wrong with their bodies anyway, so why bother to preserve health? Now there is a growing realisation that the NHS resources are finite, doctors are fallible humans, and preventive measures, expensive as they may be in terms of time, self-denial and money, are much cheaper than a long spell in hospital.

This was the climate of opinion that launched the College of Health in 1984. The College was so named to give it equal standing with bodies such as the Royal College of Physicians, but in practice it is really an organisation of health-care consumers. 'The purpose is to improve the education of lay people so that they can be more effective in protecting their own health and also the health of the nation. The best way to put professionals and patients on more level terms' said founder Michael Young, 'is therefore to endow patients with more information.'

'Primary care' is the accepted jargon for what you get when you go to your GP, or when the community nurse or health visitor calls on you. In fact, real primary health care is what people provide for themselves. It is not just a matter of treating our own coughs, colds, bruises and burns, but a positive way of life aimed towards preservation of good health. It involves the mother in the supermarket who opts for wholemeal bread rather than white sliced in a packet and encourages her children to eat fresh fruit and vegetables; the middle-aged jogger puffing around the park; the adolescent eagerly reading a magazine about slimming or how to get rid of spots; the young mum-to-be who refuses a cigarette; the people who play sport just for pleasure – these are the real providers of primary health care, which has more to do with prevention than cure. Quite rightly they do not think of themselves as potential patients any more than they think of themselves as fitness freaks. They are just ordinary people who do not become patients.

In association with the Consumers' Association the College of Health publishes an excellent quarterly magazine called *Which? Way to Health* which is very readable (and there are no advertisements). Typical articles would be on the crisis in the NHS, VDUs and health, exercise, vitamins, hearing aids and convenience foods.

The College of Health has set itself four objectives:

1. Prevention, both collective and individual. Collective

prevention is about housing, sensible diet, hypothermia, a food industry really interested in nutrition, air and water pollution, and conditions of work.

2. Self-care, which covers how to deal with the common injuries and ailments that affect everybody.

3. Treatment and how to make the best use of the NHS.

4. Alternative medicine, including permanent monitoring of the alternatives to orthodox medicine.

The College runs courses from time to time in conjunction with the National Extension College at Cambridge. Their database includes details of over 1,500 self-help associations dealing with topics from anorexia to scoliosis. With the help of the Patients' Association, advice can be given on members' individual problems, but not where medical diagnosis or treatment is involved.

The College of Health is a non-profit-making registered charity. The subscription is £10.00 a year and this includes the quarterly magazine. Membership is primarily for lay people, but it does include many doctors, nurses, health visitors and members of the para-medical professions. For more information contact Marianne Rigge, Director, **College of Health** (O).

Communication

A factor common to many disabled and elderly people is some level of impairment of communication, both verbal and written. Good communication involves the simultaneous ability of one person to produce an intelligible message, and one or more others to receive and understand it. Breakdowns in this everyday, but quite complicated, process may occur for many reasons. Some people are born without speech, hearing or sight, or a combination of these; others lose these senses partially or completely as a result of illness or traumatic accident. Physical disability may prevent a disabled person moving to within hearing distance; poor hand muscles may prevent writing or the ability to turn the pages of a book.

Advances in technology in recent times have produced a very large range of devices to solve communication difficulties. Electric typewriters and *computers* with a wide range of inputs are available for people who are unable to hold a pen. It is even possible to type a page using only a slight movement of one eye. Some devices produce a synthetic voice from words put in through a 'QWERTY' keyboard, or by pressing squares on a board. Deaf people can 'type' a message into a telephone which comes out the other end as speech, while people without hands can use a typewriter which turns spoken words into print.

Many devices are available from **British Telecom** (O) – to enable disabled people to communicate by telephone. For people who are unable to pick up a handset there are loud-speaking telephones, some of which will store up to 50 numbers on a single button operation. 'Claudius' is a push-button device which will speak up to 64 pre-set phrases which can be used on the telephone or for 'conversation'.

There are, in Britain, a number of Communication Aids Centres (CACs) which offer a full assessment, advice and training in the use of communication aids. Each has a comprehensive display of the latest aids. Referral is not necessary but assessment is only by appointment with the relevant CAC. The following CACs are available:

Communication Aids Centre
Charing Cross Hospital
Fulham Palace Road
London W6 8RF
(01 748 2040)

Sandwell Health Authority
  Communication Aids Centre
Boulton Road
West Bromwich
West Midlands B70 6NN
(021 553 0908)

Communication

Communications Aids Centre
Musgrave Park Hospital
Stockmans Lane
Belfast 9
Northern Ireland
(0232 669501)

Communications Aids Centre
(for children)
The Wolfson Centre
Mecklenburgh Square
London WC1N 2AP
(01 837 7618)

Communication Aids Centre
Rookwood Hospital
Fairwater Road
Llandaff
Cardiff CF5 2YN
(0222 566281)

Communication Aids Centre
Castle Farm Road
Newcastle upon Tyne NE3 1PH
(091 2840480)

Speech Therapy Department
Frenchay Hospital
Bristol
Avon BS16 1LE
(0272 565656)

The main sources of information are *Communication* from
Mary Marlborough Lodge (O); *Communication A or B* from
the **Disabled Living Foundation** (O); *Communication Aids for
the Deaf, Communication Aids for the Blind* and *Communication
Aids for Physically Handicapped People* are leaflets from **GLAD**
(O); *Low Vision Aids* from the **Library Association** (O); *Communication Aids – a guide for people who have difficulty speaking*
from **RICA** (O); and there is a useful chapter in the *Directory
of Aids for Disabled and Elderly People* published by **Woodhead-
Faulkner** (M).

Community Care Grant

See under Social Security.

Community Health Council

Wherever you live in the United Kingdom there will be a Community Health Council representing the consumer's interest in their dealings with family doctors, dentists, or hospitals. Human nature being what it is, for most of us accidents and illness are things that happen to someone else – we do not really think much about the National Health Service until we fall into its clutches, and then we passively accept gratefully whatever we are given. The average person knows little about his CHC.

There are three layers of administration in the National Health Service. At local level there are District Health Authorities (DHAs), composed of appointed lay members. A DHA may cover an area with a population of 200,000–500,000. The next layer is the Regional Health Authority (RHA), covering two or three counties. It also has appointed lay members. The RHA is responsible to the third layer, the DHSS.

The management of the NHS is therefore hardly democratic, and the main role of the CHC is to provide an avenue of accountability to the general public. The DHA and the CHC therefore have a close working relationship and normally both groups cover the same geographical area. Management is the job of the DHA; monitoring the success or otherwise of the DHA is the job of the CHC.

Most CHCs have 24 members and all give their service voluntarily (they are paid expenses). Half the members are nominated by the local authorities, a third are elected by voluntary associations and a few are nominated by the RHA. There is, therefore, a wide range of interests and the members should be evenly spread throughout the district. The

Chairman and Vice-Chairman are elected annually. CHC members serve a term of four years; they may serve a second term if they are re-nominated, but no one can serve for more than eight years. Each CHC has a full-time paid secretary supported by one or more part-time staff. CHC funding is provided by the health region and it is fairly limited – this is one reason why so little is spent on publicity. Service on a CHC demands a great deal of time and dedication.

Accessibility to the general public is very important and most CHCs have an office with something approaching a High Street location. Their main function is to ensure that the views of the public reach the District Health Authority. CHCs also have an important role in giving guidance to members of the public who wish to complain about the service they have received from some element of the NHS, and the procedure for obtaining redress. Regrettably, some CHC offices remain completely inaccessible to their most likely customers – wheelchair riders, the ambulant disabled and elderly people.

Most CHCs maintain close ties with local voluntary and statutory bodies. Public meetings, seminars and conferences are held from which shortcomings in the local health service provision soon become apparent. Waiting lists for treatment and surgery are subject to continuous scrutiny. Surveys are carried out on subjects such as hospital catering, conditions in out-patients or maternity clinics. The aim is always to monitor the quality of the service at the point of delivery.

Planning of health services is always difficult, because there is never enough money to meet what is, in effect, an open-ended demand. There will always be a conflict between hospital and community services, between one part of the health district and another, between prevention and cure, between one treatment and another – for example, how many hip replacements equal one heart transplant? Although Health Authority budgets have so many noughts they are beyond the comprehension of ordinary mortals, in fact, after you have provided for the immovable items such as wages and salaries (75 per cent), food and fuel, drugs and building maintenance, there is very little money left to make decisions about. Even so, an important role of the CHC is to decide on priorities for future developments, and to present those views to the DHA which has to take the final decisions.

A Community Health Council is an entirely independent public body with statutory rights clearly laid down by law. It is entitled to all the information it needs from official sources, and this would rarely be refused provided it concerned only the running of the service. Most CHC members are inundated with reports and papers from all levels in the Health Service – many of the local papers are of a routine periodic nature, such as consultants' waiting lists. Members may enter Health Service premises, subject to the usual courtesies. The CHC must be consulted before any hospital or other health service facility is closed; this is a powerful weapon that is frequently used with great effect. Every DHA produces a draft annual plan and the CHC is invited to comment on this before it becomes firm.

Most CHCs meet as a council once a month. A recognised number of these meetings is held in public – maybe six a year. At these, when the agenda business is over the public audience is invited to take part. This is an opportunity to make suggestions or voice complaints on any subject, large or small. Public CHC meetings are held in different parts of the district, so everybody can, at some time in the year, attend a meeting without travelling too far.

Such is the widespread and diverse nature of a CHC's business that it would be impossible to consider everything in detail at council meetings and a tiered business structure is essential. Often members are divided into small special interest groups dealing with such subjects as maternity and child care, mental handicap, hospitals, community facilities, the physically handicapped and the elderly. These groups consider specific problems in detail and submit reports to the full council. Members are usually on a regular schedule for visiting NHS premises, either to study the running of the facility as a whole, or to look at a particular problem, such as out-patient waiting time. Members may also visit individual patients.

The CHC also has to look outwards beyond its own boundaries. There are meetings with the DHA, neighbouring CHCs, Family Practitioner Committees, local authorities, and regional bodies. There are a number of health facilities of which the health region would have only one – for example, a spinal injuries unit, a renal unit, or a sterilising unit. These may be outside the district but they still have to be visited.

Public meetings are held to consider subjects of common interest – the location of a new health centre, the threatened closure of a maternity home, or the problems arising from AIDS or substance abuse. Speakers are invited and the public joins in; it is democracy in action, clumsy and time-consuming, but fair. CHCs also have certain statutory obligations, such as the need to produce an annual report.

The national co-ordinating body is the Association of Community Health Councils of England and Wales, known as **ACHCEW** (O), which, appropriately enough, can only be pronounced with a handkerchief. This body has valuable co-ordinating functions as well as acting as a clearing house for ideas coming up from member councils. As a national body representing NHS consumers they are able to make direct approaches to the DHSS.

Most disabled people have had a fairly long spell in hospital. Many, together with elderly people, continue to be semi-permanent customers of the Health Service, and it is therefore important for them to know where the CHC office is, what the CHC can do and what information it can offer. Most of the offices have a 24-hour answering service and you will find their number in the phone book.

Community Resources

All disabled and elderly people should be aware of the local resources available and it is worth making a list of the addresses and telephone numbers appropriate to your needs. This list may be compiled from the telephone book, Yellow Pages, Thompsons Directory or from local directories put together by a Council for Voluntary Service or a **DIAL** (O). Community resources may be classified broadly as statutory or voluntary.

There are two types of voluntary agency. For all the major disabilities there are national associations which have local branches offering a wide range of services. Normally it is necessary to become a member. Lists of these branches are available in public libraries, *DIAL*s or Citizens' Advice Bureaux, where you will also find listed the other main groups in the voluntary sector – the 'across-the-board' organisations, providing services available to any disabled or elderly person, either free or with a fee. In many areas *care attendant* schemes – sometimes called 'Family Support' or *Crossroads* – are available to help the caring relatives of disabled people and the service is usually free. There are also local branches of the **Carers' National Association** (O). A 'SAD', or Sports Association for the Disabled, is to be found in most towns. **PHAB** (O) – Physically Handicapped and Able-Bodied – clubs are widespread and, like the Scouts and Guides, organise activity holidays for disabled young people.

In some places many of the voluntary organisations are grouped under the umbrella of Councils of Voluntary (or Community) Service, and these are good information points. There are a few Centres on Independent Living (*CILs*), whose main function is to assist young disabled people to move out into the community from residential accommodation. Dial-a-Ride organisations provide local transport on demand for seated wheelchair riders on an individual basis, while local branches of *Age Concern* (often with their own premises) and Help the Aged cater for elderly people. Many associations for disabled people interested in the arts, hobbies or home-based employment have regular meetings staged by local branches.

Statutory services are funded from rates and taxes and they are therefore not 'free'. Health and Social Services are the two largest statutory resource services. *Social Services* is a local authority function with main offices at county level, and social workers based at local offices deal with social problems in the community overall – disabled and elderly people are only a part of their work.

Community occupational therapists, based at the Social Services Department, assess for and provide equipment, make provision for modification to private dwellings, and give advice on coping with disability. Social services provide 'Meals-on-Wheels', *home helps*, transport, day centres, *Orange Badges* and *residential care*. Good social services departments provide comprehensive leaflets on their services. Depending on the level of severity of disability, a person may become 'registered disabled' with the department.

'Health' may be divided into community health and health (mainly hospital) services. Community health involves GPs, clinics, health visitors, district nurses, health education, re-habilitation, *physiotherapy*, chiropody, *nursing homes*, psychiatric nursing, day centres and respite care. Health services, mainly hospital-based, deal mainly with the health crises in our lives – illness and injury. For each health district there is a Community Health Council and this is the best point of contact for information about any local aspect of the NHS. GPs are governed by a local Family Practitioners' Committee and you should contact the FPC if you wish to change your GP.

Disablement Service Centres are to be found roughly on the basis of one to two or three counties, often located in the grounds of a hospital. DSCs provide artificial limbs and eyes and aids to mobility – wheelchairs, walking frames, crutches and sticks.

The local council may provide grants or loans for disabled and elderly people to make alterations or extensions to their dwelling. Without a means test the council also gives 'disability discount' on rates, although this will change with the introduction of poll tax. Tokens for public transport may be available, and certain people will get rent and/or rate rebates.

Problems over social security, income tax or *VAT* (Customs and Excise) may be resolved by contacting a local office, and a disabled person with employment problems should make an appointment with the Disablement Resettlement Officer (DRO) at the local ofice of the Training Commission.

Public library reference sections are valuable sources of information on both statutory and voluntary sector resource agencies.

Computers

Some households have one or more computers. In the popular sense, a computer is a device comprising a keyboard like a typewriter, a box with slots into which you can put floppy discs and a screen which may be monochrome or colour. Many people also have a printer. These items are known as 'hardware'. Cassettes or floppy discs are the 'software' and these contain the programmes which make the computer do what you want. There are three types of programmes. Probably the largest group is the entertainment software, which represents a vast industry in itself. Next, there are literally hundreds of functional programmes from accountancy to data storage. Lastly, there are many training programmes to teach you anything from working the computer to playing bridge. You can also buy blank discs and make up your own programmes.

There are many uses for a home computer but top of the list is leisure. There are hundreds of 'Star Wars' type games suitable for all ages and intellects, while games like whist, bridge, backgammon or chess in which the machine plays against you at different levels are very good for people with poor hand control. Some point out your mistakes and one even apologises when it beats you!

The home computer, especially one with coloured graphics, is a valuable educational tool which will teach spelling, English grammar, numeracy, mathematics and technical drawing. It leads the student along a path in which he has to learn each skill before the computer takes him up the next step. Foreign languages can be learned using computers which will 'say' the words, and some computers have music so that the sounds are heard as the notes are displayed on the screen. Computers are excellent for training (sometimes from a very early age) children with impaired hearing, sight, speech or mental ability. For disabled people there are many alternative inputs to the conventional typewriter keyboard; these include expanded keyboards, simple on/off switches, suck/blow switches and even an eye switch built into a spectacle frame. Contact **Possum Controls Ltd** (M). For blind people there are computers which 'speak' the words on the screen. Computers can even control the environment – heating, lighting, drawing curtains. Write to **Voice Input** (M).

There are many people who use a computer for *home-based employment*. As a stand-alone device it can be used for secretarial services, word processing, book-keeping, tax consultancy or database management. The worker may be self-employed or he may process work brought to him by an employer at regular intervals. With a device called a 'modem' the computer may be linked through the ordinary telephone line with an employer many miles away. This enables the home-based worker to do jobs like stock control, personnel management, wages control or journalism. Home-based employment is attractive to people whose ability varies from day to day, because they can only work when they feel well. Through the Remote Work Units Scheme it may be possible to get free equipment. For information write to John McCann, Department of Trade and Industry, Information Technology Division, 29 Bressendon Place, London SW1E 5DT.

Once it is loaded, a home computer can be a great time-saver in the house. It can hold birthday dates and addresses; Christmas card addresses; household accounts; what you said last year on your income tax return; personal information – national health number, bank account number; telephone numbers; and recipes. Updating information is very easy.

Two very useful books are *Computer Help for Disabled People* by Lorna Ridgeway and Stuart McKears (published in the Human Horizons series), and *Word Processing and Publishing* by Peter Denley (published by the British Academy). Advice on computers for disabled people can be obtained from Roger Jefcoate MA, Willowbrook, Swanbourne Road, Mursley, Bucks MK17 0JA.

Conductive Education

Over 40 years ago Dr Andras Peto established a centre in Budapest for the rehabilitation of children with cerebral palsy, spina bifida and motor nerve problems. The Peto Method, later known as 'Conductive Education', became world-famous and the present director of the centre, Dr Maria Hari, claims a 70 per cent success rate with Hungarian children in restoring mobility and the ability to attend normal schools.

The Peto Centre has attracted international interest and in recent years over 200 British parents have taken their handicapped children to Budapest. The results have varied widely and some children have returned with little benefit. The Peto Method is basically a one-to-one form of physiotherapy and many British physiotherapists contend that it is little more than they have been doing for years anyway. There seems to be general agreement that an essential feature is the intensity of the training, and the overall amount over a period of months. Children may be at the Peto Centre for six months or more and this makes it a very expensive exercise because the parents are also required to remain in Budapest for the whole time. In some cases parents have sold their homes to raise the money.

In September 1987 the Foundation for Conductive Education was set up in Birmingham to evaluate the system. Eight trained conductors are working with disabled children and the foundation has acquired substantial funds. There is also a new action group called **RACE** (O) – Rapid Action for Conductive Education – with the general aim of bringing Conductive Education to Britain.

The Spastics Society says that it has been practising Conductive Education since 1960. It uses a form of team training based on the Peto Method but does not train conductors. However, it has invested considerable resources in extending its version of the method. It is estimated that there may be 16,000 children in Britain who could benefit from the method.

Contact

This organisation, now over 20 years old, takes more than 2,500 elderly people out to tea every month in private homes all over the country. Contact aims to provide a link between lonely elderly people, who are housebound and without family support, with volunteers in the same area. Each local group is made up of twelve elderly people and the volunteers commit themselves to provide an afternoon of companionship on one Sunday in each month. At a time when it is estimated that the number of people over 85 will increase by 47 per cent over the next ten years, this seems to be a very sensible idea. Write to Contact, 15 Henrietta Street, Covent Garden, London WC2E 8HQ (01 240 0630).

Contact a Family

Contact a Family is a national charity for families with children who have different disabilities or special needs.

The charity was set up in 1974 and since then has established eleven self-help projects in London, and the southwest of England. The main aim of the organisation is to link up families whose children have any disability, physical or mental, mild or severe. The theme of the organisation is 'a problem shared is a problem halved.'

Contact a Family also helps and supports over 500 independent self-help groups and contacts across the country and through them is in contact with 17,000 families of children with special needs.

In May 1987 Contact a Family set up Contact Line, a new telephone service, with the aim of putting more families in touch with each other, either locally with self-help groups or other organisations, or nationwide, linking up parents whose children have similar rare disabilities. This service became available on a national basis from May 1988. It is open between 10.30 am and 2.30 pm every weekday on

01 222 2211. The telephone lines are manned by fully-trained volunteers, many of whom are themselves the parents of children with special needs, and they are backed by the Contact a Family staff. The volunteers use comprehensive directories to pass on information to callers.

Contact Line is available for any caller – parent or professional – and can put families in touch with each other, help professionals find local and national self-help groups and other voluntary organisations, or simply offer advice and information.

Contact Line was set up with help from over 20 organisations, including the Spastics Society, *ASBAH*, Sense and MENCAP.

For more information write to **Contact a Family** (O).

Continence

Continence is a word which indicates a refreshing, new and positive approach to an embarrassing problem which afflicts many disabled and elderly people, and many ablebods, through temporary conditions such as illness or pregnancy. About 3,000,000 people in Britain put up with some level of urinary incontinence; faecal incontinence accompanies some acute illnesses and severe disabilities but it is relatively rare. In a typical town of 250,000 people there will be about 11,000 with incontinence problems, and of these around 10,000 will be receiving no help at all.

Incontinence is no longer a socially unacceptable subject. It afflicts more women than men; over the age of thirty it affects one woman in three. It can be a major handicap for many physically disabled and elderly people, and the social consequences can be devastating. It can make a person confine themselves to the house, cause them to give up sport, recreation, holidays or even employment, and it can inhibit a healthy sex life.

Incontinence exists whenever a person knowingly or unconsciously passes urine in a place and in a way that undermines their dignity. Continence involves an awareness of the need to empty the bladder and the ability to retain the urine until you get to the toilet. Incontinence is not a disease nor is it an automatic result of disability or ageing. However, it may be caused by an underlying medical disorder and even those with mild incontinence should see a doctor.

Some of the causes of incontinence are simple enough to be determined by a nurse asking routine questions. Other causes can be complicated and would involve attendance at a hospital urodynamic clinic – now sometimes called a 'continence clinic'. Incontinence may be caused by illness, childbirth, conditions affecting the bladder or womb, stress, multiple sclerosis, cerebral palsy, Down's syndrome, spinal injury, unpredictable spasm or lack of motivation arising from mental inadequacy. Stress incontinence – from laughing, physical strain, coughing or sneezing – can cause a little leak. Urge incontinence may result from an over-active muscle in the wall of the bladder. There are paraplegics and tetraplegics with neither sensation nor functioning muscles below the waist, and they will be incontinent. People with physical disabilities which prevent or limit access to a toilet may be functionally continent – there is nothing wrong with their 'water-works', but sometimes they cannot get to a toilet, maybe because it is too small for a wheelchair.

It is tempting to think you can help incontinence by reducing the amount you drink, but this may be dangerous; it is essential for health to pass an adequate amount of urine daily. If the nerves controlling the bladder are damaged, the only solution may be the use of a collection aid to give a form of social continence. There is a vast range of such aids and skilled advice is essential.

A number of treatments are possible. There are drugs which will calm an over-active bladder. For others, catheterisation – the insertion of a tube into the bladder – may be the answer. A disabled person or their carer may be taught to insert the catheter themselves, but great care must be taken with cleanliness; special catheters for self-catheterisation are obtainable from **Downs Surgical Plc** (M). There are also a number of surgical techniques. Urinary diversion, called *urostomy*, brings the urine out through the wall of the stomach to be collected in a disposable bag. This method is rarely used now. In a new and exciting technique the sacral nerves are joined to a radio-controlled, implanted bladder stimulator. Operation of a small hand-held transmitter causes the bladder to empty completely. Very new, but for first-hand accounts from satisfied users, write to the **Spinal Injuries Association** (O).

Training can help in many cases, but the exercises require considerable motivation, charts must be accurately maintained and the programme may take several months. Helpful instructions and charts are available from **Coloplast** (M). Try to lengthen the time between visits to the toilet. Pelvic floor exercises, which can be done on the toilet or in the bath, will strengthen the muscles supporting the bladder, giving improved control. One side-effect from such exercises, appreciated by both males and females, is increased pleasure from sex. Information on pelvic floor exercises is available from the **Disabled Living Foundation** (O).

For persistent urinary incontinence there are many products for the collection of urine. Padded disposable pants will absorb urine whilst leaving the skin dry. Marsupial pants have a front pouch for an absorbant disposable pad, and the newer pads contain a powder which turns urine into gel. Write to **Henleys** (M), **Nicholas Laboratories** (M), **Molylncke** (M), or **Caducee Healthcare** (M). Boots also carry a large range of incontinence products.

Males are rather better equipped by nature to cope with incontinence. A condom is fitted over the penis and to this is attached a flexible tube running to a leg bag, which can be emptied from time to time. At night a further tube joins the leg bag to a larger night bag on a stand beside the bed. The condom is attached to the penis with adhesive or double-backed adhesive tape. For disabled males without hands there are condoms with applicators permitting fitting by a carer without finger contact. Write to **Seton** (M), **Coloplast**

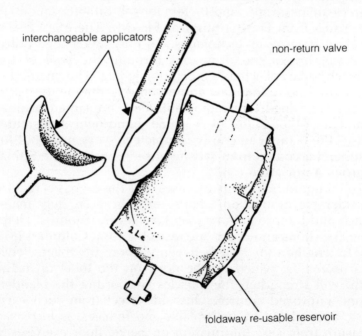

'Convenient' portable urine device (C.C. Products).

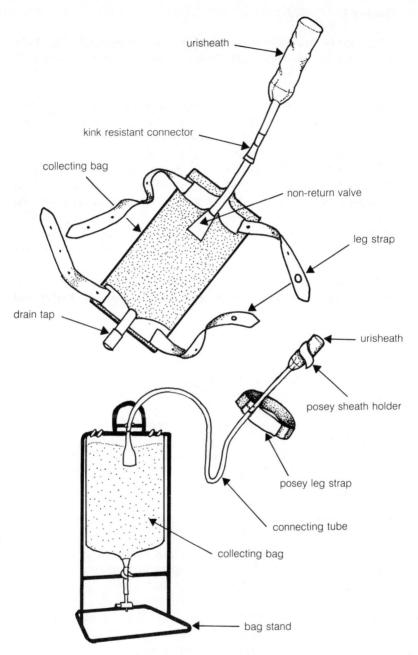

Urine collection systems – day (above) and night (below).

(M), **Home Nursing Supplies** (M), or **Medimail Ltd** (M). From **Incare Medical Products** (M) there is a range of self-adhesive condoms. Most incontinence equipment is available on prescription.

There are many sources of information and advice on this highly complicated subject. You can contact your local Continence Adviser, *DIAL*, health visitor, district nurse or community occupational therapist. You can write to the Continence Adviser, **DLF** (O); the **Coloplast** (M) Service (Also available on FREEPHONE dial 100); the **Association of Continence Advisers** (O); or **Epsom Care Centre** (M). An excellent book is *Overcoming Urinary Incontinence* by Richard Millard (Thorsons).

Regular use of a commode should not be necessary, but for the severely physically handicapped person who may have a week or so in bed with the flu, one should be held in reserve. There is also a wide range of waterproof sheets and mattress covers available. The toilet may need a raised seat or support rails. Great care is necessary to avoid odour problems and a useful product is Nilodour from **Loxley Medical Supplies** (M). Skin contact with urine causes soreness and this can be avoided by using Dermalux cream.

Full continence or good management of incontinence is well within the reach of the majority of disabled or elderly people, but it is essential to seek advice.

Conquest

This is a well-established organisation which promotes all forms of creative arts for handicapped people, with a large number of local branches providing teaching. They are experts at solving the physical problems so disabled people with a wide range of handicaps are able to discover new talents and the pleasure of creation. They publish, three times a year, an excellent magazine called *Spectrum* as well as a series of useful booklets. For disabled people, the current subscription is only £1 a year. Conquest, now ten years old, has awakened many disabled people to the pleasures of artistic hobbies. Write to **Conquest** (O).

Coping with Disability

It is quite possible to live a happy and fulfilled life confined to a wheelchair . . . Consider first your own attitude to your disability. You are only handicapped – not sick. If you become sick – and everybody does from time to time – then go to your family doctor; if you are very immobile, he will come to see you.

So you are a fit disabled person. Staying fit is harder work for disabled people than for ablebods and you must be aware of the peripheral medical problems likely to emerge as a result of your 'disabled' way of life. First you need to offset lack of movement by taking some exercise every day, together with a longer session, which may be some form of *sport*, once a week. Daily exercise could involve using a manual or electric pedalling machine while remaining seated in your wheelchair, and arms can be exercised using slings fixed over a doorway. You may not be a sporting type but it will pay you to join the local Sports Association for the Disabled and put in two or three hours a week at table tennis, archery, snooker, or whatever takes your fancy. Swimming is the best exercise of all and many people who are normally unable to stand or walk can do so in water. Swimming on a regular basis will improve your vital capacity – you will be less breathless; it will help with the action of bowels and bladder; reduce your weight and girth (think of the person who has to help you!); your circulation, particularly in your legs, will be better; and so will your appearance and feeling of well-being.

Any exercise will help to avoid *pressure sores*. A bench or table-top hobby will give sufficient movement to release the pressure points on your bottom. Given the right wheelchair cushion and bed mattress it is possible to prevent pressure sores, which are the biggest menace for wheelchair riders.

Your own mental attitude to your disability is important. First, forget the past which contains many things you can no longer do – look forwards and upwards. Disability is a door shut behind you but facing you is a corridor with doors on either side stretching away into the distance. Waiting for you to open it, every door is a new experience, a new skill to be mastered, a new friend to be made – there is so much to be done. We are all handicapped in many ways – unable to reach a high shelf, unable to do the Times crossword, unable to sing or speak in public – for every disabled person with a handicap I will show you an ablebod with a host of handicaps.

It is very easy to worry and become self-centred if you are disabled. This can be avoided by making yourself permanently busy – follow a full and carefully planned day, and you really will not have time to think about yourself. Also, the moment your head touches the pillow at bed-time you will fall fast asleep—without pills. Your day's activity should be such that you can do it alone and you should be able to start and stop each part unaided. Any social contact you have with your family or friends is a bonus which you may regard with mild irritation as it takes you away from your planned 'work'. Try to avoid sleep during the day and avoid boredom by having only small amounts of each activity.

In looking at the 'disabled' family the spot-light should be turned away from the disabled person and on to the caring relative – often the wife or daughter. It is more important to look after the health, welfare and happiness of the family care-giver than that of the disabled person. If the caring relative breaks down from physical or mental strain, over-work or stress, then the disabled person is as nothing, so always ensure that the caring relative has some 'own time' each day, each week, and a couple of times each year. It is also important to organise as much care as possible from outside the house; use the local *care attendant* or Family Support Scheme for as many hours as you can get. All this is a part of the careful planning needed to keep the carer within tolerable stress and work levels.

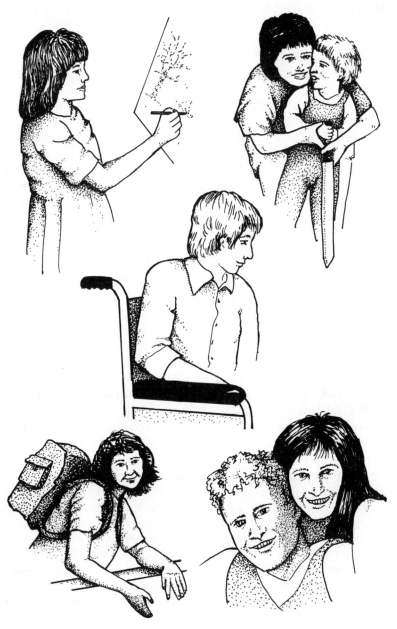

Doors open on every side for a disabled person.

Story

I See no Handicap

The level of handicap arising from a given disability varies from one person to another.

In the Napoleonic Wars, the British fleet, commanded by Admiral Lord Nelson, chased the French ships all over the eastern Mediterranean, eventually destroying them at the Battle of Aboukir Bay. Whilst on passage back to his base at Naples, Lord Nelson received a signal from England:

From: The Lords of the Admiralty
To: Admiral Horatio Nelson
It has come to the notice of their Lordships that in recent years you have become severely disabled by reason of the loss of an eye and an arm. In view of your handicaps it is strongly recommended that you immediately apply for retirement.

Nelson, who had never thought of his disabilities as handicaps, sent a very impolite refusal to their Lordships. Then he went on to win the Battle of Trafalgar . . . two years later.

The disabled person is no better and no worse than your average ablebod. You will meet discrimination every day of your life, and you just have to learn to live with it and be aware that most of it is unintentional. Remembering that most discrimination is the result of lack of knowledge or fear, always let the offending ablebod down gently. Talk to them for several minutes before you mention your university degree, Olympic gold, or that you make more in a day than they make in a week. Just think what a great time the Duke of Buccleuch must have in his wheelchair . . .

Countrywide Workshops

For many handicapped people arts or crafts provide lucrative and satisfying home-based employment. Thousands of disabled people have discovered talents they never knew they had, and some are earning more money than before they were disabled. Apart from the mundane business of earning a living the craftsman needs the motivation which can come only from selling the fruits of his labours, but achieving this has always been a problem. The disabled worker is often relatively immobile, his production rate may fluctuate with his health, and he has little spare cash to put into selling.

Countrywide Workshops, now five years old, is effectively a mail-order showcase for products made by handicapped people. They produce a very comprehensive and attractive catalogue offering clothing for both sexes, leather goods, engraved glassware, jewellery, clocks and children's toys. Some items are made to the requirements of the individual customer, or personalised with initials and in every case the goods are ordered direct from the disabled maker. If you are a prospective customer you can order a catalogue or if you wish to have your products advertised in the catalogue then write to **Countrywide Workshops** (M).

Crisis Loan

See under Social Security.

Crohn's Disease

Ulcerative colitis and Crohn's disease are types of inflammatory diseases of the bowel. These diseases affect some

50,000 people. The symptoms include diarrhoea, pain, weight loss, swollen joints and intestinal blockages. The diseases are chronic conditions which may return from time to time over the years. They tend not to occur in the young or the very old.

Ulcerative colitis is not curable but there are treatments with tablets or enemas; a severe attack may necessitate the removal of part or all of the colon. The cut end is brought out through the wall of the stomach as a small opening, over which a bag is fitted to collect waste matter which previously would have been discharged through the anus. This operation is called an ileostomy.

In Crohn's disease a part of the wall of the continuous tube (the gastrointestinal tract) which runs from the mouth to the anus becomes thickened and inflamed. Common symptoms include vomiting, constipation, loss of weight and lethargy. There is no overall cure but there are a number of drug treatments. Surgery includes resection, in which the diseased part of the tube is removed and the two healthy ends rejoined, and ileostomy or colostomy.

The **National Association for Colitis and Crohn's Disease** (O) provides a wide range of services to its 8,000 members, including information booklets, bi-annual newsletters, counselling and social events. There is a printed 'Can't Wait' card which helps gain rapid access to a toilet. Large amounts of money are raised for research.

Crossroads Care Attendant Scheme

About a million people look after their disabled or elderly relatives at home and most of them want to go on caring, but the care-givers do need support and practical help. In recent years successive governments have emphasised the benefits of disabled people staying at home. This is fine in theory, but in practice it means that the main responsibility for caring falls, not on the community as a whole, but on one person – a wife or a husband, a son or daughter. Most carers are women. Many people have to give up their jobs and their freedom in order to look after their dependent relatives at home.

The Association of Crossroads Care Attendant Schemes has pioneered the concept of giving caring relatives practical support. Their simple idea of giving such help in small quantities, at the right time, on a regular, reliable basis, really does prevent the disabled or elderly person being admitted to hospital by preserving the health of the carer. These carers and the Crossroads schemes save the country billions of pounds each year, but the cost to the carer in emotional, physical and financial terms is only just beginning to be recognised and understood.

In the space of ten years, the association has grown from a small pilot project in Rugby, Warwickshire, helping twenty-eight families with a small band of five care attendants, to a national network of caring which now helps over 9,000 families and employs 1,100 care attendants.

Crossroads care attendants are specially trained in the domiciliary care of severely disabled people, work alongside them and their carers, and liaise very closely with the statutory services. A care attendant becomes a trusted member of the family, ensuring great peace of mind because of their commonsense approach. Somebody else is sharing the load and somebody else cares.

The cutbacks in health and social services do not make the association's work any easier, but Crossroads schemes are very cost-effective and very care-effective, because they enable families to stay together. During the next decade the growing problem of elderly people living longer and increasing numbers of children born with a handicap surviving to live fuller and more meaningful lives will mean more and more strain on caring relatives. This issue needs to be properly addressed and thought through, and Crossroads have contributed to the growing awareness that caring at home places an intolerable strain on human resources.

Further details of the work of the Crossroads movement,

and where its 134 schemes are currently operating, can be obtained from the **Association of Crossroads Care Attendant Schemes Ltd** (O).

CRUSE

Cruse was founded in 1959 and it offers help to all bereaved people of any age. There are 140 local branches whose members offer counselling, advice and information, as well as contact with other people who have suffered bereavement. Branch counsellors are available to visit people, either at home or elsewhere, and regular meetings are held for widowed people providing opportunities to make new friends.

Fact sheets and other literature are available through local branches and the *Cruse Chronicle* is published ten times a year. A contact list is also maintained for members who would welcome letters from other members.

Cruse runs training courses for bereavement counsellors and monitors the statutory provision of services, and pensions and benefits.

For further information and details of your nearest branch contact **Cruse** (O).

Cystic Fibrosis

This is an inherited condition which, from birth, affects the lungs and digestive system of about one child in 1,600. It is the most common genetically-based disability in Britain. CF is incurable and it used to be a major cause of early death – now 75 per cent of children reach young adulthood.

The child with cystic fibrosis will have malfunctions in

either or both of the lungs, and the pancreas. His lungs will lack the means of defence against common bacteria such as bronchitis and pneumonia, and the sputum is very sticky and difficult to get up with coughing. The function of the pancreas fails in CF, so that the absorption of protein and fat does not take place properly, and this causes a build-up of sticky secretions. These block the pancreatic duct preventing enzymes reaching the stomach, so digestion of food is incomplete.

The CF baby may have a cough, abnormal foul-smelling stools, and fail to gain weight in spite of a large appetite. CF children lose excessive amounts of salt in their sweat, a fact which is used in very refined techniques to give a fast, accurate diagnosis. It also means the child may suffer with heat exhaustion in hot weather.

Treatment involves great attention to diet, control of lung infection and physiotherapy to keep the breathing passages clear. Certain antibiotics can prevent lung infection but chronic bronchitis will always be likely. Parents have to learn, in the baby's first few months, how to give *physiotherapy* exercises to rid the child of the sticky sputum.

The **Cystic Fibrosis Research Trust** (O), formed in 1964, now has a national network of over 300 local branches. The main aims include the provision of help and advice to affected families; the sponsorship of extensive research; to educate the general public; and to publish a range of leaflets as well as a regular newspaper. They have recently founded the **Association of Cystic Fibrosis Adults (UK)** (O) to help the CF adult live as full a life as possible.

D

Deafness

There are several levels of hearing impairment. These are sometimes defined as 'Hard of Hearing', 'Deaf with Speech', 'Deaf without Speech' and 'Acquired Deafness'. Deafness may be congenital, the result of an accident or illness or, over a period of time, caused by living in an intolerable sound environment. A child who is born totally deaf, or who becomes totally deaf before the age of seven, will have a very limited (or nil) language capability – the rest of us learn to talk simply by hearing others. Totally deaf people are unable to conceptualise the common sounds of nature (birds, weather), of civilisation (traffic, factories), or of social experience (music, conversation, church). Total deafness strikes at the need to communicate which is the very basis of all social relationships. Information and advice can be obtained from the **Royal National Institute for the Deaf** (O) or the **British Deaf Association** (O).

There are twice as many people in the 'hard of hearing' group as there are in all the other groups put together. The two most common causes of being 'hard of hearing' are ageing and living in excessive noise. Most people who are hard of hearing are able to use a hearing aid and usually they have no communication problems. The main organisation is the British Association of the Hard of Hearing.

Those people who are 'deaf with speech' – the partially deaf – have great difficulty with hearing a full range of speech, and the greater the hearing loss the lower their verbal ability. Partially deaf people may use manual sign language and many rely heavily on lip reading.

'Acquired deafness' often follows a virus attack, illness or an accident. The sudden and total loss of hearing is a traumatic experience, demanding much advice and skilled counselling over a prolonged period.

In the field of *employment* the impact of deafness can be

minimised, partly through good instruction of colleagues, and partly by the use of special equipment. If the sound of an implement requires a reaction (as in answering a telephone), then the method of attracting the worker's attention must be changed from sound only into something visual, like a flashing light, or something sensual, like a current of air. Although deafness can be a communication handicap, the impact on work is not all bad in some cases. Tasks which require a high level of concentration may be done well by a deaf person not distracted by noise or conversation. Indeed, in some very noisy work environments deafness may be a positive advantage.

Equipment for deaf people may be divided into aids which help people to hear, and aids which help people to overcome the handicaps arising from deafness. Most hospitals have an ENT (Ear, Nose and Throat) Department and they will give hearing tests and prescribe the appropriate aid. There are two main types of free NHS hearing aids – the small 'behind-the-ear' type, and the body-worn type, consisting of a small box worn on the belt or in a breast pocket with a wire leading up to the ear. The second type is the more powerful and the controls are easier to manage for anyone with poor manual control. Hearing aids require regular care and cleaning. The NHS provides servicing, replacement batteries, ear-moulds and flexible tubes. All users of NHS hearing aids are provided with a very useful booklet called *General Guidance for Hearing Aid Users*.

Hearing aids get smaller and smaller, and nowadays the smallest instruments can be concealed within the ear completely – in fact, some are put *in* the auditory canal. This miniaturisation can lead to problems with controlling the device, particularly when the user is disabled or elderly. To be effective in varying circumstances a hearing aid must be adjusted from time to time.

TELOS is a remote control transmitter for the COSMEA in-the-ear miniature hearing aid. There are no wires joining it to the piece in the ear. The small hand-held device resembles a calculator and it provides remote control on/off, volume, and noise suppression. This hearing aid is available in six different versions, for left or right ears, and it is as easy to fit as a conventional hearing aid. This is the first in-the-ear hearing aid with automatic suppression of disturbing noise in the low frequency range. The position of the instrument in the concha enables the natural function of the outer ear to be used to the maximum advantage. Sound from the front is picked up in preference to signals from the side and behind. For details write to **Seimens Ltd** (M).

A hearing aid may take months of patient effort to achieve maximum results. The human hearing system has the capacity to filter out unwanted sounds; a hearing aid magnifies all sounds, and to some extent changes them, so the brain has to relearn the identity of some of them. Maintenance – particularly keeping the ear-mould clean – is essential.

There may be problems with listening to the television or radio, and for this there are two common solutions. Some televisions are fitted with an earphone socket but this usually disconnects the speaker. Alternatively, the set may be fitted with an earphone socket in parallel with the speaker. In either case, the user wears a headset instead of a hearing aid. Alternatively, the set can be joined to a loop system – a length of wire fitted around the skirting board. This will only work with the behind-the-ear aid, with the switch turned to the 'T' position. For either system write to **A & M Hearing Aids** (M). Televisions, radios and music centres all use mains electricity and modifications should be carried out only by a skilled engineer.

The main handicap arising from hearing impairment is partial or almost total loss of communication, and there are a number of aids on the market which help with this problem. Where there is also a total absence of speech there are a number of electronic communicators which give a visual presentation of words. Among these are the Brainbank, the Canon Communicator or the Lightwriter. Write to **QED** (M), **Canon Business Machines** (M) or **Toby Churchill Ltd** (M). SPLINK is a large electronic wordboard on which there are 950 words, letters, numbers and phrases. Through a small microprocessor plugged into the aerial socket the words are displayed on the television screen, and with this two people can conduct a conversation. Write to **Medelect Ltd** (M).

Some equipment really designed for those without speech

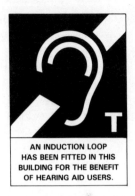

AN INDUCTION LOOP
HAS BEEN FITTED IN THIS
BUILDING FOR THE BENEFIT
OF HEARING AID USERS.

can be used in the opposite sense to communicate with deaf people. The common feature is the use of a typewriter-type keyboard to input words which appear on a display and can then be read by the deaf person. The Frank Audiodata is a microcomputer which displays on its own screen words which have been spoken to it. Write to **Sensory Information Systems** (M). For the person who is both deaf and speechless there is a computer terminal which speaks the words played on a keyboard. This is made by **Braid Systems Ltd** (M).

A hearing-impaired person will have problems with front door bells, alarm clocks, kitchen timers and telephones. The answer is to add to the sound signal a visual or sensory signal. Equipment is available from the **RNID** (O) or **New-tech Electronics** (M) which will cause every light in the house to flicker if the telephone or door bell rings. Flashing light door bells are available from **M & G Electric (Hayes) Ltd** (M). Vibralarm, a battery-operated alarm clock with an attached vibrating pad to go under the pillow is supplied by **Niagra Therapy** (M).

Some of the above aids to daily living (including the radio, television and telephone aids) are obtainable from social services departments, and most of these have trained social workers for the deaf who will be familiar with all the latest equipment, sign language and local services. The usual re-quirement before any provision can be made is for the hearing-impaired person to be registered with the Social Services Department.

There are many aids to overcome problems with the telephone. 'Phonetype' is a teleprinter used with an ordinary telephone – you type your message and it is reproduced on a similar teleprinter at the house of the person you are calling. Where two participants both have computers there is a device called a 'modem' which does the same thing. 'Vistel 2' plugs directly into the telephone socket and can communicate directly with any other Vistel user – write to the **Breakthrough Trust** (O). A newer device (supplied by British Telecom) is 'Tonto', a combined telephone and computer giving direct screen to screen communication between any two of these devices. For the hard of hearing there are 6in (15cm) diameter loud bells (Models 50C and 80C), tone ringers and the very loud 'Bedlam Loud Tonecaller'. Some telephones have a neon light in the handset which flashes when the bell rings, and others have an inductive coupler, a small coil which goes into the telephone earpiece. This can be used by turning your hearing aid switch to 'T'; this facility can be used in public buildings where an induction loop is fitted. Portable inductive couplers which can be used with any handset are available from **EPC Ltd** (M). For the hard of hearing there is an amplifying handset with a volume control and a watch earpiece enabling you to use both ears. The **RNID** (O) runs 'TED', a telephone exchange for the deaf.

It is very difficult to keep up with the flood of new 'disabled' equipment from British Telecom and I would strongly recommend their new free 1988 *Guide to Equipment and Services for Disabled Customers*. These are available from all British Telecom sales offices or you can contact BTADC – **BT Action for Disabled Customers** (M).

It is important that hearing impairment in a child should be identified as early as possible. At the pre-school stage care is available through the NHS up to the age of three, and after that there are groups within nursery classes. Above school entry age there are deaf schools at all levels, and most education authorities provide further education classes in lip reading and sign language. For the deaf parent of a young baby there is a voice-operated baby call with a flashing light. For advice write to the **National Deaf Children's Society** (O) or the **British Association of the Hard of Hearing** (O).

Story

Universal Sign Language

American author Nora Groce tells a fascinating story about Martha's Vineyard, an island off the New England seaboard, now well known as a posh American summer holiday resort for the political aristocracy.

Back in the 1700s the persecution of the Puritans and the decline in the wool trade caused whole communities in Kent to emigrate to America. Forty-eight families settled on the island later to be known as Martha's Vineyard. One of these families carried the gene of deafness. In those early days the island was economically self-sufficient, but very isolated, so there was a high level of inter-marriage until eventually over 95 per cent were married to someone to whom they were already related. Over a period of 200 years one child in four was born completely deaf.

The interesting thing was the way the islanders reacted to having a very large part of the population deaf. For them it was something unremarkable like having blue eyes or red hair. Certainly, deafness carried no stigma and it was little handicap in the island's two main occupations – farming and fishing.

Anybody on the island was likely to be deaf, so from birth the entire population learned sign language – everybody was 'bi-lingual'. The island did not have the communication barrier which isolates deaf people in our society. One elderly islander said 'People would start a sentence in speaking and finish it in sign language – especially if they were saying something dirty.'

Of course, in our society it would not be feasible for everybody to know sign language just in case they met a deaf person. However, this little story does point to the moral that it is not the disability which handicaps, it is the inability of society to cope with it.

Link (O), the British Centre for Deafened People, makes provision for people with sudden severe or total deafness. They run two-week residential courses for deaf people and their families. A relatively new development is Pro-Dogs, which is a national charity providing hearing dogs for deaf people. The dog is trained to recognise the sounds of daily living – a crying baby, a knock at the door, a telephone ringing or a boiling kettle – and he will then lead the deaf person to the source of the sound. For more information on Pro-Dogs write to the **RNID** (O).

Death of a Disabled Person

Coping with a severely disabled person over many years often brings the carer and spouse much closer than most couples. When the disabled person dies the surviving partner is likely to feel the loss more keenly than is the case with the death of an able-bodied person. There will be the normal pattern of bereavement – anger, bitterness, despair, depression and perhaps even a refusal to accept the death – all can be a part of the grieving process. The surviving partner of a deceased disabled person has all these emotional problems plus a feeling of guilt (Did I do enough for him? What can I do with all this spare time?), plus a house full of reminders (wheelchair, hoists, toilet, bath-aid), plus a sudden freedom from responsibility. It is like swimming against the tide for years – you then land on the beach but you cannot stop your limbs moving.

This unreal situation is a natural stage in grieving for a disabled partner, but if the bereaved person is gently encouraged to think and talk openly about their grief their pent-up emotions will be released. There is a need for someone outside the family – a church member, a nurse, a DIAL adviser, preferably a person who knew one or both of the couple – to act as a listening counsellor. They will need several meetings over a couple of months. At an early stage all the 'disabled' equipment should be removed from the house, even if it has to be stored in a friend's garage pending sale or donation to disabled people.

National organisations with local branches which would help include **Age Concern** (O), the **National Association of Widows** (O), the **Compassionate Friends** (M) (for bereaved parents) and **CRUSE** (O), which is for widows and their children.

If a person is dying in hospital, relatives may stay with them as long as they wish. After the death relatives may see the person in the ward or in the viewing room of the mortuary. If a person dies in a nursing or residential home, they are normally removed by the undertaker as soon as possible.

The death certificate will be issued by the GP or hospital in a sealed envelope and this should be taken to the registry office as soon as possible, together with the deceased's birth certificate and medical card. If the deceased is to be cremated the death certificate may require the signature of a second doctor. Sometimes a doctor will order a post-mortem examination in which case the coroner will be notified and it will be his responsibility to inform the registrar. Either way the registrar will issue two file copies of the death certificate and the funeral arrangements can be made.

The cost of funerals can vary considerably, so relatives should check the cost of a burial or cremation with at least two undertakers. Normally the undertakers will remove the deceased to their own chapel of rest until the funeral. Viewing days immediately before the funeral enable relatives to see the dead person.

If there are financial difficulties with paying for the funeral contact *Social Security* for help under the Social Fund. To get this you must be the person responsible for the funeral, there must be insufficient money to pay for the funeral, and you must be receiving *Income Support* or *Housing Benefit*. From Social Security you can get two very useful free leaflets *What to do after death* and *Help when someone dies*.

If the deceased has left a straightforward will leaving everything in a small estate to the caring relative and appointing that person as executor, it is quite possible to execute the will within a few weeks and without a solicitor. Telephone your local District Probate Office for the application forms for probate. Complete these and take them, together with the will, the death certificate, the birth certificate and maybe the marriage certificate, to the Probate Office. If the documents are in order, the executor will take the oath confirming the facts stated in the application. You will then state how many copies of the grant of probate you require. If the deceased's assets are invested in several places you will want one copy grant for each. Each grant will bear the seal of the court, so photocopies may not be used, and there is a small payment for each. The copies of the grant will be sent to you within a week or so, after which the deceased's assets may be realised and distributed by the executor.

You can also get advice from a CAB or a *DIAL*.

Dental Care for Disabled People

Because of the nature of their disability or because they have problems with access, some handicapped people have difficulty in getting dental treatment. Your local *Community Health Council* will give you a list of dentists in your area which have accessible surgeries, dentists willing to make home visits, hospitals giving dental treatment, and some hospitals which have special dental surgeries for disabled people.

Information is also available from the **British Society of Dentistry** (O).

Diabetes

Diabetes is often dismissed (and sometimes by diabetics themselves) as a completely manageable complaint, and therefore not really a disability. However, there are a number of varieties and severity levels of this disease, and the truth is that for a few it can be a life-threatening condition – in fact, in the USA it is a major cause of death.

Known formerly as 'Sugar Disease', diabetes is, in very simple terms, the inability of the pancreas to secrete enough insulin to burn up the amount of carbohydrate eaten. The balance of the sugar level in the body is disturbed and, either way, too much or too little sugar in the body can be potentially dangerous. If left untreated this can lead to convulsions preceding diabetic coma. There is no known cure for diabetes, but in the majority of cases it can be controlled by rigid adherence to a prescribed diet, exercise and maybe, in addition, insulin and drugs.

The exact causes of diabetes are unknown, but it can be attributed to hereditary factors, to excessive weight gain, shock, general bodily deterioration, or possibly even a virus. A great deal of research is going into the causes and management of diabetes.

Diabetes can affect people of any age, from babies to very elderly people. The onset can be quite sudden, although it is generally believed that it can be present for many years before the individual becomes aware of it. In a health district of 250,000 there would be around 5,000 diagnosed cases, and maybe a further 2,000 people who have got it without being aware of it. Many children have diabetes and in Britain as a whole there are over 1,000,000 known diabetics.

A person suffering from diabetes will appear to be perfectly fit and may not show visible signs of any abnormality. This is because for most people diabetes can be well controlled – by insulin injections and a strictly controlled diet, by a diet and tablets, or even by diet alone. Diet for diabetics – even children – means a rigid selection of items, accurate weighing of portions to the nearest gram and precise times for food intake. Whatever the form of medication, if it is taken regularly together with the recommended monitoring of blood or urine, diabetes should have very little, if any, impact on the daily way of life. With most occupations there should not be any problems with employment.

There can, however, be considerable psychological problems for some people when they are first diagnosed as having diabetes. Some people try to conceal the fact although it is difficult to understand why, as there are no discernible changes in outward appearance. It makes least impact on those who go to some trouble to understand it. Clearly for everybody there is a fear of the need for regular self-injection, and worry too about the possible long-term effects of the disease.

The majority of diabetics live happy normal lives. However, for a few it has been known to cause blindness, heart or kidney disease or body ulcers. Wounds can take longer to heal and patients can go into a coma.

The parents of diabetic children have considerable problems. Each year about 1,500 children are diagnosed in the UK, and the conditions of hygiene and sterility necessary for using a hypodermic syringe, the precisely-timed meals, the accurately-weighed food, the thrice-daily urine tests, and the maintenance of records, can all cause complications.

The great majority of diabetics, including children, manage their own treatment and develop considerable powers of self-reliance in doing so. Lack of knowledge is one of the root problems and in some health districts there is a specialist diabetics health visitor. The British Diabetic Association is a very go-ahead organisation, busy with informing the public, sponsoring research, running childrens' holiday camps and supervising the work of many local branches. There are very active sections for children and teenagers.

For more information contact the **British Diabetic Association** (O).

The British Diabetic Association

The BDA was founded in 1934 to help all diabetics, to create greater public understanding about the disease, and to raise money to support research. The association now has over 100,000 members and handles hundreds of enquiries every day from diabetics, their families and those who work with them. It gives information and advice on all aspects of diabetes, helping sufferers to understand their condition and giving them the chance to lead as near a normal life as possible.

The BDA produces a wide range of helpful literature and books and all members receive the free *Balance* magazine every two months. *Balance* contains the latest medical news, recipe ideas, how personalities cope with their diabetes, local events and fund raising.

Educational and activity holidays are organised for both adults and children, plus weekends for families with diabetic children or teenagers.

There are over 300 BDA groups and branches providing support locally and regular meetings and social events are held. There are three professional sections – education, medical and scientific and professional services – all of which keep in regular contact with those working in the field of diabetes. The association acts as the national spokesman on behalf of diabetics in the UK, campaigning for better services, and making representations to the government on matters affecting the individual. It was due to active campaigning on the part of the BDA that plastic disposable syringes were made available on GP prescription to all insulin-dependent diabetics in 1987.

One important function of the BDA is to support diabetic research to find a way to treat, prevent or cure diabetes. Spending over £1,000,000 a year, it currently supports over 60 research groups and projects. Although dependent entirely on voluntary subscriptions and donations, the association is the largest single contributor to diabetic research in the UK.

DIAL

A DIAL is a Disablement Information and Advice Line – an office which gives information to disabled people. There are over 80 DIALs in different towns up and down the country, and new ones are opening up every month. Clients present their problems by letter or telephone or they call in to the DIAL office, where almost all of the staff are disabled unpaid volunteers. The best person to give advice is often one who has encountered the problem in coping with their own handicap and found a solution.

Each DIAL is different, responding to the particular needs of its catchment area, and each is independent and self-financing. However, there is much in common to all and minimum standards for setting up are laid down by **DIAL UK** (O), the national governing body. A DIAL caters for all disabilities, all ages of client and the service is free, confidential and fully documented. A typical busy DIAL handles 2,000 clients a year, and as well as disabled people these will include caring relatives and professional care-givers – nurses, therapists, social workers and health visitors.

A DIAL database comprises books, files, leaflets, catalogues, hard copy from information services, and one or more microcomputers. It is normal to 'press-cut' over 50 publications a week. Disabled people need information on social security, social services, employment, education, housing, transport, holidays, sex, sport, health and equipment. In practice, there is no problem which a DIAL cannot answer; if the answer cannot be found in the office the staff will know where to look for it elsewhere.

Lack of information is a major problem for disabled people for whom travel is difficult, and many public offices inaccessible. Many are unaware of their rights to benefits, equipment, and services. Each year there is over £1,000 million of uncollected social securities, largely because of the complexity of the system.

If you have a DIAL in your town it will be in the telephone book; otherwise, **DIAL UK** (O) will give you details of your nearest DIAL and you can write to them.

Dimpled Rubber

Many physically disabled people find that dimpled rubber attached to a variety of everyday pieces of equipment makes for easier use with weak, paralysed or arthritic hands. Dimpled rubber can be purchased in small sheets from sports shops or in the form of different-sized thimbles from stationery shops. Sheet dimpled rubber is used normally for covering table tennis bats. Remember to ask for the cheapest kind – about 50p a sheet.

Dimpled rubber thimbles are really intended for counting paper money but they can be used by disabled people on fingers or thumbs for turning pages, to help grip between finger and thumb, to press small control buttons, to help turn small knobs, and to cover joystick knobs on electric wheelchairs.

Dimpled rubber can be glued around small levers to give a better grip. Small squares attached to the underside of a telephone, cassette recorder, portable typewriter, reading stand or portable radio will prevent sliding in one-handed operation. The most-used keys on a computer or typewriter – such as the carriage return – can be covered with dimpled rubber. A piece about 2in (5cm) wide, glued to the underside of a transfer board, will stop it moving as you slide your bottom along it. In short, dimpled rubber can be used in any situation where you want to prevent one object sliding over another.

Disabled Drivers' Assessment Centres

The following centres offer disabled would-be car drivers assessment of driving ability with different types of hand controls and different types of vehicles. Normally there are enclosed private road circuits.

Banstead Place Mobility Centre
Park Road
Banstead
Surrey SM7 3EE
0737 351674

BSM Disability Training Centre
81 Hartfield Road
London SW19
01 540 8262

Derby Disabled Driving Centre
Kingsway Hospital
Kingsway
Derby DE3 3LZ
0332 371929

MAVIS
Dept of Transport
TRRL
Crowthorne
Berks RG11 6AU
0344 770456

Mobility Information Service
Unit 2A
Atcham Estate
Upton Magna
Shrewsbury SY6 6UG
0743 77489

Stoke Mandeville Hospital
OT Workshop
Mandeville Road
Aylesbury
Bucks HP21 8AL
0296 84111

Tehidy Mobility Centre
Tehidy Hospital
Cambourne
Cornwall TR14 0SA
0209 710708

Wales Disabled Drivers' Assessment Centre
18 Plas Newydd
Whitchurch
Cardiff
0222 615276

Vehicles for the Disabled Centre
Astley Ainslie Hospital
133 Grange Loan
Edinburgh EH9 2HL
031 447 6271

NICD
2 Annadale Avenue
Belfast BT7 3JR
0232 491011

Disabled Living Centres

For a couple of decades we had 'Aids Centres' – places where there was a large permanent exhibition of aids for disabled people. When the word 'Aids' took on a different meaning, the centres were renamed 'Disabled Living Centres'.

There are 21 Disabled Living Centres in the UK so there is one to about three or four counties. Your local Community Health Council will tell you where your nearest DLC is – normally it is necessary to book an appointment before making a visit. A DLC carries many aids, ranging from large items like electric wheelchairs, scooters and stairlifts to small items like cutlery, kitchen ware and a multitude of 'aids to daily living'. Nothing can be purchased, but you can get hold of catalogues of commercial items and lists of equipment available from statutory sources.

The *occupational therapist* in charge can provide a supporting information service on aids, techniques, financial benefits, services and facilities. The OT can also answer daily

117

living problems faced by those with disabilities and their care-givers. All items of equipment can be tried at leisure by the disabled client who may be accompanied by an OT or other adviser.

The DLC is a resource centre for medical professionals involved with disability and also for architects, planners and designers catering for the needs of handicapped people. Some DLCs run refresher courses for professionals on subjects which involve both equipment and technique, such as lifting.

The overall governing body is the Disabled Living Centres Council, TRAIDS, 76 Clarendon Park Road, Leicester LE2 3AD.

Disabled Living Foundation

The DLF is the leading UK source of information and advice on solutions to the problems of daily life faced by disabled people. The DLF was the first equipment and information centre to be established in Britain. Information is provided through enquiry services, the publication of books, serials and videos, the largest permanent standing equipment exhibition in the country, and by the identification of and research into areas of unmet need. Enquiry services are open from 9.30–17.00, Monday to Friday. DLF also runs training courses for professionals involved with disabled people.

The Information Service handles over 26,000 enquiries a year from individual disabled people, caring relatives and caring professionals. The computerised database (DLF–DATA) holds details of over 10,000 products from over 1,500 suppliers. The department also produces the *Information Service Handbook*, a ringbolt sectional work which is annually up-dated. This forms a part of a subscription service used by 80 per cent of health and local authorities in England and Wales, as well as all DIALs and the majority of national disabled organisations.

The Equipment Centre houses approximately 2,000 different pieces of equipment, ranging from wheelchairs to hoists to household appliances to items of personal care. Disabled people are welcome to visit the centre to see and try out items and discuss their requirements with the staff. Each year the centre has over 7,000 visitors and therefore it is strongly recommended that you phone for an appointment. There is good access with a parking bay and a wheelchair hoist at the rear of the premises. The Radio 4 *In Touch* kitchen is a part of the display.

In addition to the general services the DLF has specialist departments in clothing and footwear, incontinence, music and visual handicap. All services are free to individual disabled people.

For further information, contact the **Disabled Living Foundation** (O).

Story

Fame and Fortune despite Disability

Disability has struck across all levels of society and across history since the dawn of time. Many hundreds of years BC the Chinese were accomplished physicians and surgeons. The ancient Egyptians knew the value of copper in allaying the painful symptoms of arthritis and they used electric eels to reduce pain in the same way that we use TENS machines today.

Julius Caesar became the most famous general and statesman of ancient Rome, extending the boundaries of the Roman Empire to Britain and through Gaul to the Rhine. He became the dictator and supreme ruler of Rome for life. All his life Caesar was disabled with what in those days was called the 'falling sickness'. Today we

---

call it epilepsy. Other famous epileptics include the Russian novelist Dostoevsky, Edward Lear, the creator of the childrens' 'Nonsense' stories, of which the *Owl and the Pussycat* is the best known, and Leonardo da Vinci, master painter and inventor, 500 years ago, of a paddle boat, helicopter, ducted air central heating, cranes, and the forerunners of the tank and machine-gun. In more modern times who would realise that epilepsy was a problem for England cricketer Tony Greig, actor Michael Wilding, or composer George Gershwin?

Many people have found fame even after the loss of an arm or a leg. Admiral Lord Nelson lost an eye and his right arm long before he won the Battle of Trafalgar. Ace flyer Sir Douglas Bader had both his legs amputated but he learnt to walk, dance, play golf and squash on two tin legs, all before leading fighter squadrons in the Battle of Britain. Sarah Bernhardt performed around the world as an actress even after having her right leg amputated. Byron limped on a club foot. Pop star Ian Dury made the charts in spite of a withered arm. Norman Croucher climbed the Alps ten years after losing both legs – and then went on to make similar climbs in China, Peru, Argentina and Kashmir. Cole Porter wrote many of his famous hits after the amputation of his right leg.

Thomas Edison, inventor of the phonograph and electric light bulb, was deaf, and so is Jack Ashley MP, present-day champion in Parliament of the rights of disabled people. Ludwig van Beethoven composed brilliant works of music in spite of his deafness.

Franklin Delano Roosevelt had been confined to a wheelchair with polio for many years when he became President of the USA for the first of two terms.

Disability

The World Health Organisation definition of disability is 'Any restriction or lack (resulting from an impairment) of ability to perform an activity in the manner or within the range considered normal for a human being'.

Disability Equipment Assessment Programme

These assessments are carried out as funded projects by hospital rehabilitation centres. The DEAP reports indicate the advantages and disadvantages of existing equipment and the aim is to help disabled people, their caring relatives and caring professionals to choose what is best for their particular needs. There is also a valuable feedback for manufacturers, enabling modifications to be brought in to improve their products. Some reports give 'star ratings', matched for each product against selected characteristics.

Since 1981 there have been a couple of dozen DEAP reports on subjects including long-handled reachers, armchairs, kitchen equipment, wheelchair cushions, cutlery and leg dressing aids. A list of reports available and single copies are available free from the DHSS Store, Health Publications Unit, No 2 Site, Manchester Road, Heywood, Lancs OL10 2PZ.

Disablement Service Centres

DSCs are run by the **Disablement Services Authority** (O). They were formerly known as Artificial Limb and Appliance Centres (ALACs). There are 18 main DSCs and a number of satellite centres – roughly speaking, one DSC serves two or three counties.

Each DSC has two main functions – an artificial limb service and a wheelchair service. The artificial limb service provides, after assessment, artificial limbs made by independent prosthetic makers, ensures proper fit and gives walking training. The service also provides artificial eyes. There is close liaison with the surgeon both before and after the operation.

The wheelchair service provides *wheelchairs* on permanent loan and servicing through nominated agents. Referrals are made by consultants and family doctors. There are over thirty wheelchairs in the range with many different attachments and accessories, and the service also provides cushions and walking aids. Consultants and GPs may also prescribe wheelchairs for subsequent delivery to the patient's home. However, the permanent wheelchair rider will get a better service at the DSC where he can try a range of wheelchairs. In some cases technical officers visit the patient's home to advise on the best wheelchair for that dwelling.

Disfigurement

Facial disfigurement may be the result of congenital deformity, severe burns, port-wine stain, facial cancer, industrial or road accidents, or cleft palate. Treatments include surgery, drugs, therapy and radiotherapy. Some assistance may be derived from skin camouflage and cosmetics, and often considerable guidance and skilled counselling is necessary. The *Disfigurement Handbook* has many useful addresses and is available from the Disfigurement Guidance Centre, 52 Crossgate, Cupar, Fife KY15 5HS (03377 281).

Overcoming Disfigurement by Doreen Trust is published by Thorsons.

Down's Syndrome

This is a condition which results from a genetic accident at the point of conception. It can happen to anyone, regardless of social class or ethnic origin. There are a number of versions of this disability, but in the most common type each cell in the body has an extra chromosome – 47 instead of 46. Down's syndrome is not a disease and it cannot be cured, but much can be done to alleviate the effects, which include varying degrees of mental handicap, physiological problems and the well-known facial appearance. The level of handicap varies considerably. Some youngsters with Down's syndrome are able to attend normal schools, but the worst affected are very severely handicapped.

The Down's Syndrome Association gives practical advice and information to adults and to the parents of children with Down's syndrome. The association publishes a news magazine as well as a quarterly educational review, and there are over 100 local groups and 12 main branches. The main Resource Centre, in London, has a large library, and a standing exhibition of learning aids, toys and audio visual aids.

For more information, contact the **Down's Syndrome Association** (O).

Drinking

It is very important to take in an adequate amount of fluid each day, as failure to do so can result in constipation or kidney problems. For people who, because of physical disability, are unable to lift a cup or have difficulty in doing so, there is a wide range of aids. These may be found in 'disabled' *mail order* catalogues or, if you have one near you, you can try them out at a Disabled Living Centre. Boots also carry a range of special mugs.

Disabled people who cannot lift a cup at all have to drink

everything through a straw. Because you have to suck up a column of air before you come to the liquid, this results, in the course of a day, in a large amount of air collecting in the stomach. At best this can give dyspepsia, and at worst the accumulation of gases in the chest cavity can be dangerous for a person with heart problems. The Saunders Straw has a small ball-valve at the lower end so once the liquid is drawn up the straw it stays at the top. No more air is taken in and the drinking is much the same as drinking from a cup. The straw is semi-permanent with a life of perhaps a year. It can be boiled clean or cleaned with denture cleanser daily. The Saunders Straw is available from **Medipost Ltd** (M).

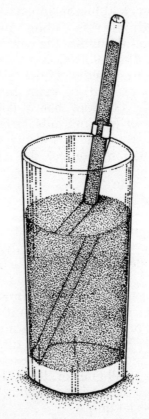

Pat Saunders' Drinking Straw.

Dyslexia

This is a specific disability which is far more widespread than is generally supposed. Dyslexia should be suspected if a child in early years at school confuses right and left, up and down, east and west, has difficulty with telling the time, or with arranging things in sequence, confuses letters similar in shape (such as d and b, u and n) reverses words (was, saw), misses out vowels, or foreshortens words (rember instead of remember). They may also have difficulty with arithmetical tables and often they are *left-handed*.

Many people are unable to read or write properly when they leave school – they are often unaware that they may be suffering with this learning handicap and that with the correct training they can be helped to overcome their frustrating problem. This training may be provided for dyslexics of all ages – from children of primary school age with reading difficulties to students at university, businessmen and people in all walks of life.

Many people at the upper levels of their profession have discovered late in life that they are dyslexic. When Susan Hampshire, three times winner of the Best Actress Award, was young, she knew she did not find it easy to read and write. Only later did she realise that she was dyslexic and she then learned, through sheer determination, to overcome the problems arising from it. In addition to acting, she has written books, including *Susan's Story*, a best-selling autobiographical account of her struggle against dyslexia.

For more information write to the **British Dyslexia Association** (O) or the **Helen Arkell Dyslexia Centre** (O).

E

Electronic Equipment Loan Service for Disabled People

This is a free loan service of second-hand electronic equipment no longer needed by the original user. The stock changes frequently but usually includes microcomputers, communication aids, cassette recorders, typewriters and printers. Application may be made for the current list of items available or for a particular item. In either case, a large stamped addressed envelope must be enclosed. Write to Electronic Equipment Loan Service for Disabled People, Willowbrook, Swanbourne Road, Mursley, Milton Keynes, Bucks MK17 0JA.

Employment

The general level of unemployment has fallen over the last few years but, whatever the level is for able-bodied people, for disabled people it can be as much as twice as high. The Tomlinson Report produced during World War II led the way for the 1944 Employment Act which is still the basic legislation underpinning the employment of disabled people. This was followed in 1946 with the Quota System which has been with us to the present day. In essence, this said that any employer with 20 or more employees must have at least 3 per cent registered disabled workers. At that time 3 per cent of the overall workforce was made up of registered disabled people. However, over the years registration has lost popularity and today fewer than 1.5 per cent of the workforce is registered disabled. Many disabled people regard the green registration card as a stigma – something which makes them different from their fellow workers. However, under the Wages Act of 1986 the law no longer allows a disabled person to be employed on terms less favourable than someone who is not disabled.

In 1981 the Manpower Services Commission recommended that the Quota System be replaced by a 'statutory general duty on employers requiring them to take reasonable steps to promote equality of opportunity in employment for disabled people'. At the end of 1984 the MSC published the *Code of Good Practice on the Employment of Disabled People*. This informative document, which is aimed at employers, gives useful definitions of disabilities, lists of relevant addresses and summarises the legal position. It sets out the basic objectives and tries to allay the concerns of both employers and workers over the real or imagined problems relating to the employment of disabled people. However, this is simply a document of persuasion; there is no force of law behind it.

Amendments made in 1980 to the Companies Act require a company with more than 250 employees to publish a clearly defined formalised policy on the employment of disabled people, but, overall, few companies pay more than lip-service to this legal requirement. Theoretically, under the law the Quota System stands. In practice it is rarely invoked.

The Manpower Services Commission is now called the Training Commission and they can be contacted through any Jobcentre. The Employment Service, which is a part of the Department of Employment, offers a wide range of services to help a disabled person to get a job and to monitor his welfare thereafter. Disablement Resettlement Officers (DROs) are specially trained officers based at larger Job-centres who offer a free advice service. The ES publishes a wide range of leaflets about their services and there is a list of these in their leaflet *Employing Disabled People – Sources of Help*.

Free, indefinite loans of special tools and equipment to enable a disabled person to take up or continue with a job are available. Typewriters and word processors, telephones and office equipment can be adapted, and flashing lights added to audible warnings. Braille micrometers, computers with special input systems and custom-built work-stations are also available. Grants of up to £6,000 may be made towards the cost of 'disabled' toilets, lifts, ramps or adapting premises to give mobility space to a wheelchair rider.

Severely disabled people who cannot use public transport can get financial help amounting to 75 per cent of the taxi fares. In some cases help is given if the disabled person is taken to work by a friend or colleague.

The Job Introduction Scheme run by the ES offers an employer a grant of £45 a week towards the cost of employing a disabled worker for a trial period. Usually this period is 6 weeks but it may be extended to 13 weeks.

The Training Commission runs a national network of Employment Rehabilitation Centres (ERCs). These provide a realistic work environment within which a disabled person may be assessed over a course lasting 6–8 weeks. A weekly allowance and travelling expenses are paid and help is given with securing employment at the end of the course. Job Rehearsal schemes enable a potential employee to have a three-week trial with a firm during which their allowances and travelling costs are paid. In some cases a complete change of career is indicated, in which case the Training Commission may arrange residential or non-residential courses, in some cases lasting over a year.

There are four residential colleges for disabled people without sight impairment:

Finchdale Training College at Durham
Portland Training College at Mansfield
Queen Elizabeth's Training College at Leatherhead
St Loye's College for Training the Disabled at Exeter

The **RNIB** (O) have extensive employment training schemes for blind people.

'Individual Training Throughout with an Employer' is a scheme in which the worker is paid an allowance whilst training on the employer's premises, and after the thirteenth week the employer makes a gradually increasing contribution. A minimum of six months' employment is guaranteed after training.

Sheltered workshops are run by local authorities or voluntary organisations for severely disabled people unlikely to obtain open employment. Sheltered workshops are run on a very wide scale by Remploy Ltd for disabled people who are capable of working regular hours with a reasonable productivity level.

Papworth Village Settlement and Enham Village Centre provide both sheltered housing and sheltered employment for physically disabled people to enable them to lead lives which are independent, self-supporting and as full as possible, with their families, in a village setting.

There are a number of useful books on employment for disabled people, including *The Employer's Guide to Disabilities* published by **RADAR** (O), *Fit to Work* published by **SIA** (O), and *Employment for Disabled People* published by Kogan Page.

Home-based employment has many attractions for physically disabled people. There is a saving of time, energy and travel costs, and the absence of distractions gives a higher productivity rate. For the person who may have varying levels of fitness, a home-based job means they can work to suit themselves – when they feel well. However, solo working without supervision requires a high level of motivation, and there is a loss of the social contacts found in a normal work place. Home employment can be self-employment and many disabled people turn hobbies such as wood carving, glass engraving, knitting or needlework into profitable enterprises. The products can be sold through **Countrywide Workshops** (M). Accountancy, book-keeping, tax consultancy, and computer programming are all possible. Through **IT World Ltd** (M) the Department of Trade and Industry sponsors remote work units in which disabled people work at home, using computers and data transfer equipment to work for employers located many miles away. Jobs such as stock control, personnel records, research and design, data assembly and storage, can all be done using information technology.

By and large, disabled workers have a higher performance level than their able-bodied colleagues. This may be because they are less mobile, or perhaps economic necessity gives them greater fear of losing their jobs. A survey conducted by Dr Melvyn Kettle showed that of a large group of disabled employees 76 per cent produced at a rate as good as or better than ablebods doing the same job; 91 per cent were rated as average or better on job performance; 79 per cent were better than ablebods in attendance; and 93 per cent were better on turnover. All this makes the disabled worker an attractive proposition to an employer.

The DRO is the key person who can provide advice and a wide range of free literature on careers, retraining and employment in blue- or white-collar jobs. He is also the contact for home-based employment under the DTI.

Centre on Environment for the Handicapped

CEH (O) is the national voluntary organisation concerned with the physical environment and disabled and elderly people. It is committed to the shaping of environments which enable everybody to participate in and contribute to their community. CEH operates as an information service on design and technical matters, such as building and fire regulations, and publishes design guidance (among other things), and a journal, *Design for Special Needs*, which appears in April, August and December.

The CEH Architectural Advisory Service is a register of architects. Enquirers to CEH receive (free) details of local architects who have experience of designing for disabled people.

Visitors are welcome to use the CEH library which contains the most comprehensive collection in Britain of books and periodicals about the environment and disabled peole. Seminars and conferences are organised which bring together consumer representatives and building providers to discuss and debate, to resolve conflicts, and find ways forward.

CEH provides the base for the Access Committee for England, the national focal point on issues of access for all disabled people.

Epilepsy

In Britain there are over 350,000 people who have epilepsy, and of these 100,000 are children. Epilepsy is a fault in the chain of electrical impulses transmitted by the brain. There are millions of cells in the brain, each capable of transmitting impulses and each sharing responsibility for particular human activities – speech, balance, movement, memory, the senses, thought, emotion and behaviour. Seizures or fits can occur when there is a sudden disorganised release of electrical activity in the brain. These seizures can take many forms, but overall 85 per cent of people can control the condition once the right drug regime has been established. The vast majority of people with epilepsy are able to live perfectly ordinary lives. Epilepsy is not a disease and it cannot be 'caught' by other people.

There are several types of epilepsy and many kinds of attack. Some, known as *grand mal*, are major and involve collapse, convulsions, incontinence and loss of consciousness. Afterwards there may be a period of confusion. However, most attacks are mild, involving only momentary loss of awareness or some twitching in a part of the body. Most attacks are over quickly and require no special attention. Many people have attacks only during the hours of sleep.

Although a major fit can be frightening for the onlooker the 'first aid' is simple. Leave the person where they are to have the attack and move them only if there is a danger from something sharp or hot. Keep calm, be reassuring and, if possible, loosen clothing around the neck. Do nothing to the mouth and do not give anything to drink. After the jerking movements stop, turn the person on to their side. If the attack lasts more than five minutes, call a doctor.

Epilepsy has no impact on intelligence or physical strength; in fact, history abounds with people of high achievement who had epilepsy – Julius Caesar, Tchaikovsky, Byron and Dostoevsky. Tony Greig's superb cricketing ability brought him the captaincy of England and who knew he had epilepsy? Michael Wilding's acting on stage and screen made him world-famous – he had epilepsy from the age of 19 but he was still able to pursue his chosen career.

The biggest problem for people with epilepsy is the attitude of people around them – friends, teachers, work-mates, employers. Adverse attitudes usually arise from ignorance which in turn breeds fear. Epilepsy gives rise to no continuing handicap and you can work alongside a person with epilepsy for years and be unaware of it.

People with epilepsy do have problems with obtaining employment, not because the condition affects their ability, but because of prejudice on the part of employers and an undefined fear on the part of possible colleagues. It is a simple fact that a mention of epilepsy on an application form can prevent selection for a job interview. Epileptics are banned by law from certain occupations. They may not drive heavy goods vehicles or public service vehicles; in most counties they may not work as PE teachers, nor in nursing under some health authorities. A driving licence may be held by a person who has been free of seizures, during waking hours, for two years. For people who have seizures only during their sleep, there must be a period of at least three years when sleep seizures only have been experienced before a licence can be granted.

The **British Epilepsy Association** (O) was founded in 1950 as a national registered charity. It is a well-structured organisation, with six regional offices and local groups in most towns. Through its 'Action for Epilepsy' campaigns it has done much to dispel many of the myths and superstitions associated with epilepsy. There are professional advice and counselling services available to individuals and their families, education through seminars and lectures and a 'Teachers Package' for schools. Advocates will attend appeal and industrial tribunals in support of epileptics with employment problems. In certain cases financial help will be given with the cost of holidays. BEA publishes a wide range of helpful leaflets and books as well as *Epilepsy Today*, a quarterly magazine.

For more information, contact the **British Epilepsy Association** (O).

Equipment for the Disabled

This is an excellent series of illustrated books on equipment for disabled people published by *Mary Marlborough Lodge*, Nuffield Orthopaedic Centre, Headington, Oxford OX3 7LD. There are a dozen or so titles in this series, which is continuously up-dated.

Eyes

Eye care becomes progressively more important with advancing years, and also to disabled people who read a lot or who regularly use a computer. Two useful leaflets are available free from the **Association of Optical Practitioners** (O): *Eye Care after Sixty* and *Making the most of Your Eyesight*. Both are in large print and each has a useful list of addresses. Write with a large sae to the association.

'I think I need glasses miss'.

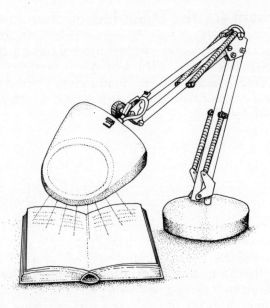

Illuminated magnifying glass.

Eye examinations are free to certain people, who are eligible for an examination once a year. If you need visual correction then the examiner is bound to give you a prescription on the statutory form which you should file carefully for future use. Certain groups of people – including those who need complex lenses, those on certain forms of social security, and children of school age – may qualify for financial help towards glasses in the form of a voucher.

Only 'ophthalmic opticians' are qualified to give eye tests and write prescriptions for spectacles; 'dispensing opticians' are permitted only to supply glasses, but for them the law no longer lays down particular qualifications. This means that spectacles may be purchased from a wide range of outlets and, since the cost of frames varies considerably, it pays to shop around. Once you have your prescription you can take it where you like to buy your glasses, and you can use it as often as you wish so long as it is less than two years old.

For more information write to the **Optical Information Council** (O).

F

Facial Paralysis

Facial paralysis is a cause of misery and embarrassment to over 25,000 people in Britain. There are a number of causes of permanent facial paralysis, the most common being Bell's Palsy, which is the result of a virus attack. The sudden loss of the use of facial muscles brings many problems. No longer can you smile or show any emotion. Clarity of speech may be difficult and drinking may only be possible using a straw. If an eye cannot be closed even during sleep, soreness and infection can set in, unless particular attention is given to monitoring the surface of the eye. About one in five of those who suffer with Bell's Palsy do not recover and must face a lifetime of hiding the affected side of the face; many refuse to leave their homes and the condition is especially distressing to young people.

There is a relatively new electro-genetic nerve stimulation technique offering some prospect of successful treatment. Hundreds of patients without previous expectation of recovery from facial paralysis have regained movement and a normal appearance. The use of an electrical neuro-stimulator to feed wasted facial muscles with the correct nerve impulses restores them to a healthy state. In turn the muscles feed the nerves and a survival loop is set up.

The pioneer in this field is a British company called **Neuro-Tech Ltd** (M) who make the electronic equipment and run seminars to train physiotherapists. Patients are treated only by a specially trained physiotherapist who initiates treatment and decides on the placement of the rubber electrodes. Patients are taught to use the equipment which is programmed for their needs and they continue the treatment at home.

For more information write to Bill Mackay at **NeuroTech Ltd** (M).

Fair Trading

Consumers of services and purchasers of goods are well protected by the law these days and often just a mention of the Office of Fair Trading is sufficient to make a shopkeeper see the error of his ways! Any goods sold should be 'of merchantable quality' – this means that an article should do what it is designed to do. A lawn mower should cut grass; a newly-tiled floor should not have tiles curving up; and the hotel in a package holiday should be completely built. For help with problems like these, contact in your local area the Trading Standards Office, the Consumer Protection Department, Consumer Advice Centre, CAB or *DIAL*. All of these offices carry a range of over 20 leaflets with titles like *How to put things right*, *Home Improvements* or *Car Repair and Servicing*. Alternatively you can write to the **Office of Fair Trading** (O).

Family Credit

See under Social Security.

The Family Fund

In 1973, in the wake of national sympathy with the families of thalidomide children, the Family Fund was set up with an initial grant from the government of £3,000,000. The Joseph Rowntree Memorial Trust was asked to administer the fund and has done so ever since. Successive governments have given support with annual grants of around £2–3,000,000 and the fund receives about 150 applications a week.

The Family Fund exists for families caring for a child who is handicapped by a very severe disability, such as functional

136

loss of two or more limbs, serious deformities, mental handicap, visual impairment, deafness, multiple handicaps or hyperactivity. With a few exceptions, grants are available only to children under the age of 16 years.

Families with a severely handicapped child who normally lives at home may be eligible for a grant, even though the child has to spend periods in hospital or if he is at school in term-time. They are not eligible if the child lives permanently in a residential home or hospital, apart from limited visiting expenses. The family is not eligible if the disabled child is in the care of a local authority.

Help may take the form of a grant of money for some definite purpose related to the care of the handicapped child. It is intended mainly to help in situations which are not at present covered by other services. The sort of help that has been given includes assistance in a variety of ways with transport problems, repair or replacement of essential household equipment (such as washing machines or refrigerators), adaptations to houses, respite care or holidays to relieve stress in the family.

There is no means test as such, but the fund is intended to help with needs arising directly from the care of the handicapped child, which are beyond the resources of the family, and each grant must be justified in the light of a family's social and economic circumstances. Help cannot be given towards any equipment or service which is available from statutory sources.

For more information contact a *DIAL* or the **Family Fund** (O).

Farmers

Farmers and their families suffer badly if physical disability strikes because of the rugged nature of the terrain around their house and their place of work. There is a disabled agricultural service which analyses these problems and produces tailor-made solutions. There is even a lift which will transfer a man from a wheelchair to the driving seat of a tractor. Write to George Kinghorn, Fairfield Industrial Estate, Louth, Lincolnshire.

Foreign Languages

For most of us who venture abroad, foreign languages can be a problem. These problems are worse for the wheelchair user, for whom a simple thing like a flat battery or a flat tyre can be a disaster on holiday. *The Disabled Traveller's International Phrasebook* solves this worry by providing a vocabulary of 200 specialised words and over 50 phrases of importance to disabled people. The contents are listed under 'The Human Body', 'Parts of a Wheelchair', 'Medicaments', 'Sources of Help', 'Aids and Appliances', 'Access', 'Wheelchair Motoring', and 'Repairs'.

Book 1 contains the following languages: English, Spanish, French, Portuguese, German, Swedish, Italian, and Dutch.

The Disabled Traveller's International Phrasebook is £1.50 (plus 19p postage) from Disability Press Ltd, 21 Davenham Avenue, Northwood, Middlesex HA6 3HW.

There is also an electronic hand-held communication device called a 'Brainbank' which gives an instant translation into one foreign language of whatever is played on the keys in English. There are nine additional plug-in modules giving a choice of languages. Contact **Quest Educational Designs** (M).

Friedrich's Ataxia

This is a relatively rare disorder caused by an abnormal gene which produces the symptoms only if it is inherited from both parents; this is called 'autosomal recessive inheritance'. The disease, which usually starts before adolescence, affects about one person in 48,000 in the UK. There is some loss of muscular control, difficulty with balance, tremor in the hands and slurring of speech.

The **Friedrich's Ataxia Group** (O) use most of their funds for research, but there is also a network of local branches and contacts offering support to sufferers and their families. Occasionally they make grants towards items of equipment or holidays – subject to the applicant's means.

G

Gardening

Gardening is an excellent, absorbing hobby for disabled people, particularly wheelchair riders. It gives exercise and fresh air, and may be practised outdoors, in a greenhouse or indoors. Outdoors, many wheelchair gardeners use raised beds made with brick or stone walls, or out of old baths, concrete drain pipes or disused water tanks. For those who prefer to work on a conventional garden there is a wide range of special lightweight garden tools available from **Homecraft** (M). In the greenhouse, planting seeds, pricking out seedlings, grafting and potting are pleasant jobs for the wheelchair gardener. Indoor and window box gardening can keep flowers in the home for much of the year and bonsai gardening (cultivating miniature trees) is a hobby in itself.

Horticultural Therapy (O) is a charity which supports disabled and elderly people through gardening and horti-culture. They have an extensive library and information service; they provide tools, aids, and publications at reduced cost; they give on-site advice on designs for new 'disabled' gardens; they give talks and demonstrations; and they run training courses at different venues around the country. There is an excellent quarterly magazine called *Growth Point*.

Gardening for Blind People

For information write to the Advisory Committee for Blind Gardeners, 55 Eton Avenue, Swiss Cottage, London NW3 3ET (01 722 9703).

Gardening without Sight by Kathleen Fleet is full of useful tips and gadgets for blind gardeners. It is available free in print or braille from the **RNIB** (O).

Gardens for the Disabled

The Gardens for the Disabled Trust was formed in 1967 to give practical help and, in some cases, funding to allow disabled people to adapt their garden and their gardening to suit their disabilities. The Trust has formed the **Garden Club** (O). There is an information service giving free advice on labour-saving gadgets and ideas for re-planning your garden for easier working, and a quarterly magazine for members. For details contact the Garden Club.

Graduates' Careers Information

The Disabled Graduates' Careers Information Service offers careers advice to disabled graduates and students in higher education. The computer databank contains over 600 examples of case histories which can be used to assist disabled students to plan their careers and find satisfactory employment. Contact **Disabled Graduates' Careers Information Service** (O).

Greater London Arts

GLA aims to promote the practice and enjoyment of the arts for people in London and for those able to pay the occasional visit to the capital. It is a development agency, working closely with local authorities, national funding bodies and other agencies, by influencing, complementing and supplementing their policies and programmes.

The encouragement of the arts through financial support is an important part of the work of GLA, and its funds are provided mainly by the Arts Council, the British Film Institute and the London boroughs. Their priorities are black arts, people with disabilities, women, the spread of arts provision, education and training. They are particularly interested in encouraging arts where little or no arts provision currently exists. GLA has a staff of specialist officers who can give advice and information both to the participant and to the spectator.

Artswork is the two-monthly GLA newsletter which provides current news and information about the arts scene. Contact Greater London Arts (01 837 8808).

Guillain
-Barré
Syndrome
Support Group

Guillain-Barré Syndrome

GBS is a paralysing condition, sometimes known as 'Royal Free Disease' or 'Iceland Disease'. All are variants of poly-

141

neuritis which means 'damage to many nerves'. Little is known about the causes and there is no agreed form of treatment. It is usually a 'one-shot' attack and often the invading virus has left the body even before the patient arrives at the hospital. One theory is that the patient's body produces antibodies that attack the nervous system, and this results in partial or complete loss of the motor nerves and then paralysis. Sometimes the sensory nerves are damaged too, so that the sufferer is unable to feel pain, hot and cold, hard and soft or texture. The absence of preliminary symptoms, coupled with the speed of the initial attack, means that the effect is devastating.

The extent to which a person recovers from polyneuritis depends largely on age. People in their twenties would recover to apparent physical normality, although they may not be athletic. In his forties a man may have a residual limp or walk with a stick. If the person is in his fifties or older he may become a tetraplegic in a wheelchair with severe loss of the use of all limbs. It also seems that many patients have led competitive athletic lives up to the point of the attack. About 90 per cent of patients recover to 90 per cent normality, while between 2 and 5 per cent die from direct or indirect causes. Average recovery time is from two to five years and is normally from the extremities – toes and fingers – inwards.

In the initial attack, the maximum level of paralysis, which may be total, may be reached with frightening speed – perhaps a matter of a few hours. In severe cases the patient will be put on a life-support machine.

When sensory nerves become damaged the effect can be extremely uncomfortable. Sometimes the skin surface becomes super-sensitive, so that even the tiniest speck of dust can cause intense itching – this is made worse when your paralysis prevents you from reaching the offending spot. Some sensations are completely beyond normal experience. Alongside the usual pins and needles, feelings of heat or cold, cramp and pain, many people have areas of skin beneath which worms or spiders seem to be moving. This is not a figment of a fevered imagination – just a scrambled message to the brain from damaged sensory nerves.

What is now defined as polyneuritis was described as far back as 1859 by a French doctor named Landry. He wrote of a disorder of the nerves that 'paralysed the legs, arms, neck and breathing muscles of the chest'. Because the paralysis starts in the feet and rapidly travels up the body, it was then known as 'Landry's Ascending Paralysis'.

In 1916 three physicians in Paris – Georges Guillain, Jean Barré and Andre Strohle – put together research, resulting in a definition of what became known as the Guillain-Barré Syndrome. Since then research has added to what is still a meagre store of information. Doctors have several names for the syndrome, the most common being 'acute (rapid onset) idiopathic (of unknown causes) polyneuritis'.

Coming to more recent times, it seems that the Americans are ahead of the rest of the world, currently identifying over 3,000 cases a year and with an excellent support group, started by Robert and Estelle Benson in Philadelphia in 1980. They welcome letters and you can write to them at the Guillain-Barré Syndrome Support Group, R and E Benson, PO Box 262, Wynnewood, Pa. 19096, USA. They publish an excellent quarterly magazine and, for new patients, an invaluable 30-page booklet called *Guillain-Barré Syndrome – an Overview for the Lay Person*.

The British Guillain-Barré Support Group was founded at Guy's Hospital, London in 1985 by Mrs Glennys Sanders and now has over 300 members. For details write to Mrs G Sanders, British Guillain-Barré Support Group, 45 Parkfield Road, Ruskington, Sleaford, Lincolnshire NG34 9HT (0526 832046).

H

Handicap

The World Health Organisation definition of handicap is 'a disadvantage for a given individual, resulting from an impairment or a disability, that limits or prevents the fulfilment of a role that is normal (depending on age, sex, and social and cultural factors) for that individual'.

Handicapped Adventure Playground Association

HAPA was established in 1966 and has built and equipped five adventure playgrounds for handicapped children in the London area. The playgrounds are staffed by experienced play workers and they are also open to the brothers and sisters of the handicapped children.

The HAPA has an information service which includes information packs on how to start a playground, staff training, play activities and children with special needs. They also have photographs, slides and a video, which is very useful for selling the idea to fund raisers. They publish a journal and visits to their existing playgrounds can be arranged.

For more information contact the **Handicapped Children's Adventure Playground Association** (O).

HANDIDATE

This is a friendship agency for people with disabilities. It is a register of people wanting either pen-friends or actual introductions. Contact HANDIDATE, The Wellington Centre, 52 Chevallier Street, Ipswich, Suffolk IP1 2PB (0473 226950).

Handihols

This is a register of names and addresses of families with a disabled member who wish to exchange their homes for holidays. **Handihols** (O) try to match up exchanges so the dwellings have roughly the same disability facilities. There is an annual registration fee of £3 plus a fee of £3 for each party in an exchange.

Story

Handicap

Handicap is a word with many many meanings. We handicap horses with different weights. Golfers are handicapped by strokes and yachts and racing dinghies by time. Handicapping systems give all competitors an even chance. The best carry the highest handicaps.

From my wheelchair, I take comfort in knowing why I am handicapped – it's to give all my able-bodied colleagues an even chance!

Healthcall

See Telephone Services.

Healthline

See Telephone Services.

Look after your Heart

The Coronary Prevention Group publishes an excellent series of booklets with titles which speak for themselves –

You and Your Heart, Blood Pressure and Your Heart, Healthier Eating and Your Heart, as well as a periodic bulletin called *Heart to Heart.* Some of the leaflets are free. Heart disease is the leading cause of premature deaths in Britain, accounting for 180,000 fatalities a year. However, simply by understanding the working of the heart, and taking sensible precautions, a level of prevention is possible.

Write to the **Coronary Prevention Group** (O).

Help for Health

This large information service was set up ten years ago by Wessex Regional Health Authority to answer questions on self-help and self-care in health, illness and disability. The service receives enquiries from health and social services staff as well as directly from disabled people, carers and the wider public. During 1987 over 8,000 enquiries were answered.

Operating from an information centre at Southampton General Hospital, Help for Health offers a service by telephone, by letter and to personal callers. Most enquiries come from within Wessex (Hampshire, Isle of Wight, Dorset and Wiltshire), but because there is no other service quite like it many enquiries are also received from other parts of the UK.

Resources include a reference library of popular medical books, an extensive collection of leaflets on almost every health topic, subscriptions to 150 magazines and journals, and a comprehensive database of self-help groups and publications. The database, which runs on IBM PC-compatible equipment, contains details of over 3,000 self-help groups and over 2,500 publications. It is now being made available on subscription to other organisations.

Contact **Help for Health** (O).

Holidays

The main purpose of a holiday is recreation – and by this is meant *re-creation* – the making of a new you. A holiday will also benefit your care-giver, often your spouse. Even if it pours with rain and you look forward to coming home for the last few days of your holiday, the change will have done you good and given you something to talk about for weeks.

The able wife, caring for a newly severely handicapped husband, works three times as hard as she did before he was disabled. Each day she has to do all the housekeeping chores, plus all that the husband did before he became disabled, as well as a full day of nursing. She will not admit, even to herself, that her man is a bit of a burden, and she could do with a couple of weeks alone to 'recharge her batteries'. When you are disabled there is little enough you can give your spouse at the best of times, so let this be a way of showing your love and consider taking your holidays apart occasionally.

A holiday involving a disabled person requires a great deal of careful planning. When you have decided how much you can afford and roughly where you want to go, write to possible venues enclosing a comprehensive list, including your actual handicap, need for ground-floor room or a lift, toilet and bathroom needs, diet, whether you need care at night and how level you need the vicinity of the hotel to be. You should also note your travel capacity. Can you ride in a car, coach, train, or plane? What is your travel time limit? Can you get travel insurance? Do you need medical certificates?

It is wise to keep the travelling distance as short as possible. There is no point in enduring hundreds of miles of traffic jams just to sit on a beach identical to one only an hour's drive away from your home. In Britain there are, in broad terms, two types of holiday available. The first is a group holiday, in which a number of people with the same disability go on holiday together. Such holidays are organised by social services or voluntary associations and they are limited to certain dates. In the second type of holiday the disabled person chooses a venue which is designed for handicap. Most of the national 'disabled' associations make provision for members' holidays, so it is worth writing to **MSS** (O), **British Epilepsy Association** (O), the **Spinal Injuries Association** (O), **RNIB** (O), **RNID** (O), the **Spastics Society** (O), **MENCAP** (O), and **MIND** (O). Some of these have considerable capital invested in hotels, caravans, self-catering chalets, narrow boats and custom-built respite care units, and they do not limit their holidays to their own members. If you cannot afford a holiday, contact your local social services for help.

There are a number of 'across-the-board' organisations which provide holidays for disabled people, including the **Scouting Association** (O), **PHAB** (O), **John Groom's Association** (O) and the **Winged Fellowship Trust** (O). Some of these use volunteer carers so they can take unaccompanied disabled people.

Many disabled people prefer to use conventional holiday facilities and a number of agencies, such as the RAC and AA, publish lists which indicate places supposed to be suitable for handicap. These do need to be checked with care – disabilities vary so widely that few hotels could possibly be suitable for all handicaps. To avoid disappointment it is essential to be honest and detailed about your needs.

Some thought should be given to the travelling arrangements both *en route* and at the holiday venue. The main things are parking, food and toilets. Disabled toilets are listed in the *AA Guide for the Disabled*, and it is worth buying a key giving access to any one of hundreds of disabled toilets up and down the country. These are available from many local authorities and from **RADAR** (O), who publish an up-to-date list. Most towns also publish a local guide for disabled people, and this gives parking as well as accessible places to eat and for entertainment. These are available at information offices or **RADAR** (O).

For people who are interested in a particular sport or hobby there are a number of organisations and venues which make special provision. The Ashwellthorpe Hotel at Norwich, run by the **Disabled Drivers Association** (O), offers holidays for disabled people interested in classical music, chess, photography, or Scrabble. The **Calvert Trust**

Adventure Centre (O) provides angling, sailing, canoeing, bird watching, archery and swimming.

Canal cruises make splendid holidays because the whole family or a group of friends can go. The narrow boats are fully accessible for wheelchairs, having special ramps to embark, lifts at both ends and large toilets. Try **SIA** (O), or **Staffordshire Narrowboats Ltd** (O).

Caravan holidays are pleasant because these are normally on ordinary holiday sites, some of which provide entertainment. The caravans are custom-built and fully wheelchair-accessible, having a long ramp for entry, a balcony, mains water, electricity and colour television. Try the **Scouts** (O), **SIA** (O), **MENCAP** (O), or **Oxford Caravans for the Disabled** (O). SIA also have a 'disabled' motorised caravan.

A number of organisations run holidays for unaccompanied handicapped children. These are of immense value to hard-pressed mothers. Try **BREAK** (O), **Buckets and Spades** (O), **APHASIC** (O), or **Holiday Care Service** (O).

For disabled people holidaying abroad, most airports have leaflets outlining the special provision made – write to **British Airports Authority** (O). Normally a medical certificate is required. Gradually new aircraft are coming into service with wheelchair-accessible toilets. To get the best service write well ahead of your journey. Electric wheelchair batteries cannot be carried but sometimes it is possible to hire a pair at your destination. Disabled people going abroad should also check with their local social security office on any action necessary to protect their benefits. Insurance for travel abroad can be difficult to arrange as many policies exclude people with disabilities, and medical care abroad or ambulance evacuation can be very expensive. From your local social security office obtain Leaflet SA 30 which explains reciprocal 'NHS' arrangements. For insurance try **RADAR** (O), **CR Toogood & Co Ltd** (M), or **Europe Assistance Ltd** (O). Most countries in Europe and North America have national and international disability guides, often available at embassies. *Europe for the Handicapped Traveller* is an excellent book published by **Mobility International** (O).

Discounts on ferry fares to Europe are available through the **DDA** (O) or the **DDMC** (O). Normally disabled people are required to leave their vehicles when at sea, but all the ferries have lifts and are fully accessible. Write for *Access at the Channel Ports* from **Pauline Hephaistos Survey Projects** (O). The **ACROSS Trust** (O) provides holidays in several European countries for unaccompanied, very severely disabled people, including the terminally ill. **Threshold Travel** (M) provides holidays in Europe and the Mediterranean countries for accompanied physically handicapped people. Disabled people who have difficulty with finding the fare for a care-giver may apply for assistance to the **IYDP Holiday Fund** (O). **Thomas Cook's** in Portsmouth (M) in association with DIAL Hampshire, offers an excellent service to disabled people wishing to go on standard package holidays, and hopefully this will be available in most towns by the end of 1989. The **Jubilee Sailing Trust** (O) offers cruising holidays on their square-rigged sailing ship *Lord Nelson*.

"You get a good view of the sea from this room!"

151

Most *DIALs* offer an information service on holidays and travel, and there is a holidays officer at **RADAR** (O), from whom you can also obtain *Holidays for the Physically Handicapped* and *Holidays and Travel Abroad*. The *Directory for the Disabled* by Ann Darnbrough and Derek Kinrade has two very comprehensive chapters on holidays; this is published by **Woodhead-Faulkner** (M).

Holiday Care Service

The **Holiday Care Service** (O) is a registered charity which provides free information and advice on holidays for people with special needs – those who are elderly, disabled, one-parent families, or people whose circumstances make it hard to find a suitable holiday.

Disabled people, their families, friends or caring relatives can write or telephone, explaining their problem and what sort of holiday they are looking for. The Holiday Care Service will provide them with details of what seems most appropriate to their needs, and the enquirer can then make their reservations direct.

The service holds information on accommodation, transport, publications and guides, inclusive holidays in the United Kingdom and abroad as well as possible sources of financial help. All types of holidays are covered – from commercial inclusive holidays, to specialised holidays run by voluntary associations and catering for specific handicaps.

To assist disabled and elderly people who need a care-giver or companion for their holiday there is a scheme called 'Holiday Helpers'. Experienced volunteers can be introduced to make an independent holiday possible.

Home-based Employment

There is a very useful newsletter issued bi-monthly for people involved in home-based employment. It is called *Homebase* and it is an excellent forum for the exchange of ideas and experiences, particularly as much home-based work now involves computers. Write to Chris Oliver, Homebase, 56 London Road, Millborne Port, Sherborne, Dorset DT9 5DW (0963 250764).

Home Helps

The provision of home helps to elderly and handicapped people is a function of the Social Services Department. Most home helps are female and, although the traditional role continues to involve housework, it is slowly changing to include a more personal and caring type of work. Home helps may do shopping or wash a client's hair, but they may not give blanket baths or any form of nursing. The rate charged is subject to the client's means, the minimum being £1.90 a week and the maximum £2.70 an hour.

Homelink

Homelink buildings are factory-engineered portable buildings which arrive on site fully fitted out, ready to link to a house or be positioned nearby in a garden. Standing on simple pad foundations, the buildings can be easily removed, if the need arises, to be sold or relocated elsewhere. The buildings are delivered on a flat-bed truck, and can normally be positioned by one man using the patented jacking system. Where access is difficult they can be craned into position. These features make attractive options for local authorities, for whom housing provision for elderly and disabled people has always been time-consuming and expensive. Homelink means that a family can provide for a newly-disabled member at short notice without permanently extending their home.

There are eight different buildings in the Homelink range. The largest comprises a double bedroom, bathroom (including washbasin and toilet), living room and kitchen. Other variations include just a bedroom, a bedsitting room, a bedroom with adjoining toilet, or a bedroom with a bathroom. The buildings are completely maintenance-free, and they have a high level of thermal insulation. They arrive complete, needing only attachment to drains, water and electricity and then furniture. From the date of ordering to occupation can be as little as two months, but planning permission is needed.

The internal decor is pleasant and the level of fittings is chosen to suit the user's needs – this may include support rails, lever taps, 'disabled' WC, waist-level electric power points, alternative forms of heating, including oil-filled radiators, choice of floor coverings, shaver point, kitchen waste bin, fridge, cooker and curtain fittings. All of the buildings are internally suitable for a wheelchair occupant.

Homelink buildings are a modern solution to the need for special living accommodation for disabled people, particularly where the need is urgent because the family home is too small for a wheelchair, or the only toilet is upstairs. Write for catalogues to the Marketing Manager, **Portakabin Ltd** (M).

Horticulture

The Society for Horticultural Therapy and Rural Training is a Somerset-based charity which offers a service throughout the United Kingdom. They provide advice on all aspects of horticulture and gardening as a therapeutic activity or as a pleasant hobby for disabled people. Technical training for staff and help with new schemes can be given, and they publish *Growth Point*, an excellent, well-illustrated magazine. There are now raised gardens for wheelchair riders, 'touch and smell' gardens for blind people, indoor gardens and a wide range of special 'disabled' gardening tools. Write to **Horticultural Therapy** (O).

Housing Benefit

See under Social Security.

Huntington's Chorea

This is a hereditary disorder of the nervous system which gives uncontrollable muscular movements. It takes its name from Dr George Huntington, an American family doctor who published the first paper on the disability in 1972.

Huntington's Chorea (HC) affects males and females equally. It is passed by genetic inheritance directly down the family line, with any son or daughter having a 50/50 chance of inheriting the gene. It does not skip a generation, so if a child does not have the gene, then neither will the grand-child. It tends to appear between the ages of 30 and 45 and much more rarely in childhood.

As well as varying levels of involuntary movement, HC can cause falls through poor balance when walking. In some cases there may be psychological problems, such as lack of concentration, short-term memory loss or depression.

There are drugs which will alleviate or eliminate the symp-toms, and there is some hope that research may lead to the identification of the actual HC gene.

The **Association to Combat Huntington's Chorea** (O) was founded in 1971 with the aim of promoting research, assisting affected families, and increasing public awareness of the disease.

Hydrocephalus

This is a condition commonly known as 'water on the brain'. In fact, the liquid is cerebrospinal fluid, which should flow from the brain down the spinal chord, after which it is absorbed into the bloodstream. If the flow is obstructed, the fluid accumulates in the brain and in babies the head will enlarge.

. Hydrocephalus may be a congenital condition, and premature babies are at risk. Most babies born with spina bifida also have hydrocephalus. In later years it may be caused by brain tumours, or meningitis. Hydrocephalus may cause problems with vision, perception and muscular co-ordination. Write to **ASBAH** (O) – the Association for Spina Bifida and Hydrocephalus.

I

Identity Systems

See Medical Identity Systems.

Ileostomy

Ulcerative colitis and Crohn's disease are both 'inflammatory bowel diseases' for which there is no known medical cure. Sometimes the damage to the large intestine (colon) is so severe that it has to be removed. This is a modern surgical operation called an 'ileostomy'. In an ileostomy the lower end of the small intestine is brought out through the wall of the abdomen, so that bodily waste matter can be collected in a lightweight, externally-attached bag. The patient has to gain experience in draining the contents of his bag four or five times a day. The contents are semi-liquid and there is little need to limit eating habits. With the special modern adhesives a good seal is maintained, and skin problems are rare since the complete bag should need changing only every three to seven days.

With modern techniques, equipment and clothing, a person with an ileostomy soon learns to cope with it in such a way that it makes little impact on their normal way of life, or that of their family. There is no reason why an ileostomy should affect employment, social life, sexual activity or many sports. However, it is a condition for which there is a great need for counselling, advice and up-dated information, and this is where the **Ileostomy Association** (O) comes in.

There are over 20,000 people in Britain with a permanent ileostomy. The Ileostomy Association is a registered charity founded in 1956 which has 9,000 members in over 70 local groups. Each local group is backed by its own medical president, and a stoma nurse who attends meetings to give confidential advice to individuals. There is a constant flow of new products and equipment exhibitions are staged at local meetings. Hospital visits are made both before and after operations. The IA sponsors medical research and publishes a wide range of informative leaflets, as well as a quarterly journal, to keep members abreast of new developments. There is an advisory service on employment, housing, insurance, marriage and pregnancy. 'Stoma-Care' clinics are found in many hospitals, and IA members often give counselling and practical help. Holidays can be arranged through the Kingston Trust.

Impairment

The World Health Organisation definition of impairment is 'any loss or abnormality of psychological, physiological or anatomical structure or function'.

Income Support

See under Social Security.

Incontinence

See under Continence.

Centres for Independent Living

The CIL movement began in the USA in the early 1960s. A group of severely disabled students at the University of California, Berkeley, had spent their undergraduate lives in the University Hospital and felt it was time to realise their need to live and work in the community, away from the restrictions of institutional life. Over the years, by organising themselves and involving themselves directly in finding solutions to their problems with federal, state and private funding, they transformed Berkeley into a completely access- ible area, with accessible transport and a care attendant scheme controlled by the disabled individuals. This move- ment spread throughout the USA, with disabled people joining together to become recognisable consumer groups.

At the same time, disabled people in Britain were realising the need for self-determination. They began to form organisations to work within the framework of statutory services, in order to 'de-segregate' disabled people, and allow them to take an independent role in society. This led, in 1981, to a group of disabled people setting up the British Council of Organisations of Disabled People, a national forum of disabled people bringing together many organisations with widely different interests.

CILs are now growing slowly but steadily in Britain. There are considerable variations in the functions of those CILs set up so far. Most are involved in housing and care attendance, transport, education and employment, and awareness training. A common aim is the promotion of independent living in the community for young disabled people currently living under institutional conditions.

For more information contact CILP, Victoria Buildings, 117 High Street, Clay Cross, Chesterfield, Derbyshire.

Information

One of the most common utterances of disabled people must be 'If only I had known that years ago . . .'. When someone becomes disabled, they enter a whole new world of strange jargon; of people who have a great impact on your life but whose job titles mean little to you; of social security, baffling in its complexity; and of equipment – everybody seems to know about it, but nobody knows where to get it. To achieve a happy and fulfilled life a disabled person needs access to a regular supply of accurate, up-dated information. Most information is of a transitory nature – we find it, use it and then discard it. The rules and amounts of benefits and allowances change from time to time; every week new 'disabled' items of equipment appear; there is a constant stream of events for disabled people – sport, concerts, music, theatre, group meetings. Without information the life of a disabled person would be that much poorer, and their care-giver would have to work much harder.

Apart from the element of choice, the transition from being able-bodied to riding a wheelchair is much the same as taking up a new hobby or a *sport*, such as golf or sailing. First, you go on a basic training course, then you buy some books and start subscribing to the relevant magazines. Thinking it will improve your personal performance, you may invest in the latest expensive equipment. You join a club whose members play this sport, and there you get advice, and maybe a coach will give you more intensive training. In following a sport or in coping with disability you will be happier if you have a positive approach to making yourself an expert, and to do this you need information.

Information is not all that easy to come by but the book you are now reading will give you the main signposts. These are the national and local information services, certain statutory bodies, the media (radio, television, newspapers and magazines), national and local organisations devoted to specific disabilities, associations devoted to 'across-the-board' disabled activities such as *sport*, education, *writing* or *sex*. Information is said to be 'passive' if it requires little effort on the part of the recipient, and this sort of information comes through the letter box on a regular basis in the form of *magazines*, bulletins, information services and newsletters. Such information is important because it keeps the disabled person up to date. 'Active' information is that which the handicapped user has to seek out by telephone, letter or personal interview, and is often the means of solving a specific problem.

Addresses may be found in Appendix II and there are details elsewhere in this book about the following main national sources of information:

RADAR	*Disabled Living Foundation*
NCVO	*DIAL UK*
BSAD	*Centre on Environment for the Handicapped*
SPOD	*Disability Alliance*
GLAD	*Multiple Sclerosis Society*

DIG   *Help for Health*
SIA   *Spastics*
King's Fund
  Centre

Help is available from these by telephone or by letter. Also listed elsewhere are the specialised *telephone services*, from the large general services such as Healthline, to smaller services such as BACUP.

With one person in five having a daily intimate contact with disability, there is a disappointing output from the popular media devoted to the interests of disabled people. Not one of the major national daily newspapers has a regular feature for handicapped readers. Most magazines are tied to national voluntary associations and you have to pay a year's subscription in advance. *Caring*, now in its seventh year, is one of the few magazines for disabled people which can be purchased at any bookstall or which you can have delivered with your daily paper. There are disability-based programmes on radio (*Does He Take Sugar?*) and on television (*Link*) but there are too few and they are put out at off-peak hours. The number of regular disability programmes on local radio has actually declined, and only a few local newspapers carry regular features for disabled people.

The monthly bulletins of RADAR and the Multiple Sclerosis Society are excellent but they reach comparatively few people. Both cover every aspect of disability and they lead the field for 'small-ads' for second-hand equipment·and vehicles. There are a number of 'disabled' societies whose publications are of value to the disabled world at large. *Disability Now* is a very informative newspaper published by the **Spastics Society** (O). The SIA newsletter is published quarterly for members and is the best source of up-dated information for wheelchair riders.

At local level the main sources of information are *DIALs* (Disablement Information and Advice Lines), Citizens Advice Bureaux, and public libraries. Information is also available from local branches of national organisations for disabled and elderly people.

Insulation

Help the Aged has a free information sheet on home insulation and the grants available from your Town Hall. They also have a special telephone 'hot line' – 01 280 3399 – for queries about winter warmth. Write to FREEPOST, **Help the Aged** (O).

Invalidity Benefit

Invalidity Benefit follows on after Statutory Sick Pay or Sickness Benefit if you are still incapable of work after 28 weeks. To qualify you must have paid sufficient National Insurance contributions. The benefit is made up of up to four parts – basic invalidity pension, additional invalidity pension, invalidity allowance and an element for dependants. Normally, a disabled person whose condition does not improve stays on Invalidity Benefit until retirement age or at five years later. At retirement age you have the choice of remaining on Invalidity Benefit or going on to Retirement Pension. Invalidity Benefit is not taxable but you cannot work full-time, while Retirement Pension is taxable but you can work at the same time if you wish.

To claim, you will need to get Form SSP1(E) from your employer, about two months before the end of your 28 weeks. Complete this and send it to your local Social Security office. You will be told in writing if your claim is successful, and if it is refused you can appeal. You need Leaflet NI 16A which is available in the Post Office, Social Security offices and *DIALs*.

Invalid Care Allowance

This is a taxable benefit for people who have to give up work to stay at home to care for a disabled or elderly person. It is not necessary for them to be related and there is no requirement for National Insurance contributions. The care-giver must work for the disabled person for at least 35 hours a week and be aged between 16 and 65 (male), or 16 and 60 (female). The disabled person must be drawing Attendance Allowance or Constant Attendance Allowance. Married women are not excluded from ICA.

You cannot get ICA if you are already drawing the same amount or more from any National Insurance income maintenance benefit. While you are drawing ICA you are credited with NI contributions. The required leaflet is NI 212 and you send the form from this to the **Invalid Care Allowance Unit (O)**. If you are turned down you can ask for an *appeal tribunal*. The carer cannot get ICA if their earnings exceed £12.00 a week, but they are allowed up to 12 weeks' 'holiday' in any six-month period without the allowance being affected.

J

Roger M Jefcoate MA

Roger Jefcoate is an adviser on electronic aids. His work is entirely independent, and he is often sponsored by charity to travel throughout Britain visiting severely disabled people at their home, their place of work or education, and to give advice on the practical application of electronic technology to increase independence. This visiting advisory service is free to disabled people, and Roger is often able to obtain financial help towards the cost of appropriate equipment through various charities. He specialises in environmental controls, reading aids, writing aids, communication aids and computers. Write to Roger Jefcoate, Willowbrook, Swanbourne Road, Mursley, Buckinghamshire MK17 0JA.

The Jubilee Sailing Trust

The trust was formed in 1978, based upon a concept put forward by its founder and first secretary, Christopher Rudd BA, with the object of providing a point of contact for disabled and able-bodied people in the unique setting of a sailing ship at sea. The success of the scheme lies in the opportunity it gives to a disabled person to test himself or herself to hitherto unimagined limits. The sea has always provided a challenge to the able-bodied; now through the Jubilee Sailing Trust, it becomes available to the handicapped would-be sailor. It does much for the morale of the wheelchair rider if he enjoys his breakfast bacon and eggs while his able-bodied colleague is parting with his over the side of the ship! The sea can be a friend or a ruthless enemy, but it is a great equaliser; on it able-bodied and disabled can be mutually supportive.

In the years from 1983–85 the trust chartered the brigantine *Søren Larsen*, well known for her television appearances in the *Onedin Line*. She was a square-rigged sailing ship taking an amateur crew on cruises varying between a weekend and fifteen days. Up to half of the crew of 22 on each voyage were disabled, including three in wheelchairs. Each season comprised around ten cruises, including the Tall Ships Race in which the crew included people with polio, blindness, muscular dystrophy, cerebral palsy and speech impairment. These cruises demonstrated the effectiveness of Christopher Rudd's original concept, and provided a proving ground for the development of both systems and equipment. The *Søren Larsen* was fully equipped for disabled sailors. She had track around the deck, to which wheelchairs could be attached to stop people going over the side when the ship heeled, and there was a special helmsman's seat, electric lifts, wheelchair toilets and tactile compasses.

The experience gained during those early years was used to custom-build the trust's own training ship, a 400-ton barque named *Lord Nelson*, designed by Colin Mudie. The 135ft-ship, costing over £2,000,000, was designed to give maximum access to wheelchairs, so the wheel, chart room, engine room and even the flat-topped bowsprit can be reached. She has an amateur crew of 44 and among the half which are handicapped there can be up to eight wheelchair users. There is a permanent crew of 6–8, including a doctor and a nurse/purser. In her first season in 1987 the *Lord Nelson* did 31 voyages, involving 996 voyage crew of whom 394 were physically handicapped. It is not necessary, but disabled people usually sail with an able-bodied partner or friend, and previous sailing experience is helpful but not essential.

The programme of voyages for the following summer season is published each year in August.

The trust is a registered charity which needs to raise substantial funds every year in order to keep fees for the amateur sailors within their means. Many hundreds of local supporting groups throughout Britain, and even in Europe, make up a very large fund-raising network.

For more information contact the **Jubilee Sailing Trust** (O).

K

Kidneys

The human body has two kidneys which are located high at the back of the abdomen on each side of the spine. A kidney is a complicated purification plant which filters out waste products from the blood, which then goes back into circulation. The waste products are water-borne as urine along two tubes to the bladder, from here the urine leaves the body via a single tube, the urethra. The body can make do with one kidney, and some people voluntarily have a kidney removed to give to a blood relation.

In Britain about 7,000 people have some form of kidney failure each year. In addition there are kidney disorders due to infection, physical damage in an accident, or an obstruction in the kidney, ureter or bladder – most of these cases respond quickly to hospital treatment. Kidneys are said to fail when they stop functioning. This is called 'renal failure' and it causes an accumulation of water and waste matter, which in turn upsets the balance of the constituents of the blood. This may go on for years before the symptoms become apparent. Kidney failure may be suspected in people who become anaemic, over-tired, run-down, or have loss of appetite, but sudden kidney failure is relatively rare. Any kidney failure is potentially dangerous, and in some cases damage to the kidneys may be so serious that no recovery is possible.

Most health districts have one hospital with a renal department but overall the provision meets only about half of the demand, so there are waiting lists. There are two main forms of treatment – dialysis and kidney transplant. One reason for the limited provision is the acute shortage of kidney donors.

Dialysis is a method of purifying the blood artificially, and there are two systems. Peritoneal dialysis is carried out in a renal unit in hospital. A very small plastic tube is inserted into the wall of the abdomen, and a special fluid is passed through it and then pumped out again, carrying the waste products. A new modified version of this enables patients to carry on with normal activities at home whilst dialysing. This is called Chronic Ambulatory Peritoneal Dialysis (CAPD). Haemodialysis is the better-known method in which the patient is joined on to an artificial kidney machine by tubes inserted into the arm or leg. Blood is pumped into the machine, purified and then returned to the patient. The process takes four or five hours and has to be repeated two or three times a week. It is also possible to have a dialysis machine at home but a room must be allocated for this only, or an extension built. Normally the Health Authority will meet the entire cost as well as training the caring relative.

Treatment through dialysis does limit life style, but many people are able to stay employed and enjoy a fairly normal social life. Diet is important and foods containing potassium – some fruits and coffee – should be avoided. Problems can arise from loss of interest in sex or from male sexual disfunction, and in this case it is worth while consulting a sex therapist or **SPOD** (O). It is possible for a person to stay on dialysis for many years.

The alternative to dialysis is a kidney transplant, which these days is considered to be a fairly straightforward operation with a 70 per cent success rate. Successful transplants bring a rapid and quite spectacular improvement in the health and fitness of patients, many of whom return to active sport. A successful transplant depends upon the availability of a donor kidney and the matching of the donor tissue with that of the recipient.

Self-help associations include the **Renal Society** (O), the **National Federation of Kidney Patients' Associations** (O) and the **British Kidney Patient Association** (O) which has three holiday centres providing dialysis, including one in Majorca. They also provide financial aid, help with education, and information and advice.

The King's Fund

King Edward's Hospital Fund for London was founded in 1897, largely as a result of initiatives put forward by the Prince of Wales. The Fund took its name on the Prince's accession to the throne. It became an independent charity incorporated by Act of Parliament in 1907, and its current assets top £85,000,000.

The original objective was to provide grants to hospitals and this has continued to the present day. The current London Programme, which is concerned with health care in the inner-city areas, has already made well over £1,000,000 available.

Today the activities of the King's Fund have diversified to take in all aspects of health care, hospital management, acute services, quality assurance, community care and services for people with long-term disabilities. These are channelled through four organisations: The Grants Committee, which from a budget of over £800,000 makes grants for objectives ranging from art in hospitals to setting up a pain management clinic; The King's Fund College, which provides courses, seminars and consultancy services concerned with the improvement of management in the health-care field; **The King's Fund Centre** (O) which is located in purpose-built premises in Camden, London, and which has a large library, an information service and superb conference and exhibition facilities – the main aim of the centre is the development of new ideas for the delivery of health care, but much work is being done on long-term community care, and the provision of services for disabled and elderly people. The Centre also publishes many books, papers, reports and leaflets; lists are available. Fourthly, there is the King's Fund Institute, formed in 1986, which is located at the Centre. The main aim of the institute is to produce research papers and analyses to contribute to discussions on health policy. To this end they bring out publications, set up conferences and maintain contacts with the media.

The National Health Service is under public scrutiny; attempts are being made to address the needs of disabled people, and the proportion of elderly people in society is increasing – it is against this background that the unique role of the King's Fund is seen to be of increasing importance.

L

Laryngectomy

The removal of the larynx or voice box is called 'laryngectomy' and people who have had this life-saving operation are called 'laryngectomees'. They have to learn to breathe through a hole in their neck and they also have, under a speech therapist, to re-learn how to speak, using either the oesophagus or an artificial speech aid. The voice will always be a little strange, but most laryngectomees live perfectly normal lives.

The **National Association of Laryngectomee Clubs** (O) helps with rehabilitation, forms new local clubs, and provides advice and information. The clubs for laryngectomees are set up in association with hospital speech therapy departments. Membership is made up of patients who, with relatives or friends and caring professionals, meet regularly to try their new voices and work to achieve fluency.

Left-Handed

Equipment and all kinds of aids are available from:

Anything Left-Handed
65 Beak Street
London W1R 3LF
(01 437 3910)

Legal Aid

With any legal problem where a solicitor may be needed, it may be possible to get legal aid, and this means that the state may pay part or all of your legal fees. Normally, if you are on Income Support you qualify for legal help automatically, otherwise there is a means test for both capital and income. For information, call at any CAB or Law Centre, or contact the **Legal Aid Head Office** (O).

Legislation for Disabled People

Copies of Acts of Parliament are published by the Stationery Office and may be ordered from any large bookshop. Most public library reference sections, Citizens' Advice Bureaux, *DIAL*s and law centres hold selections of Acts of Parliament which may be studied on the premises. The following legislation relates completely or in part to disablement:

Disabled Persons (Employment) Act 1944
Employment of registered disabled persons.
National Assistance Act 1948 Part III
Residential care and welfare for disabled people.
Health Services and Public Health Act 1968
Services for elderly people.
Chronically Sick and Disabled Persons Act 1970
Assessment of needs for services and statutory provision; information on services; provision of services; adaptations to dwellings; orange badges; access to public buildings; special needs housing.
Education (Handicapped Children) Act 1970
Discontinuance of classifying children as 'ineducable'.
Road Traffic Act 1972
Disability and driving.
Housing Act 1974
Improvement and intermediate grants.
Rating (Disabled Persons) Act 1978
Various reliefs from rates.
Residential Homes Act 1980
Registration, inspection and conduct of residential homes.
Education Act 1981
Based on the Warnock Report; special education needs; integration.
Transport Act 1982
Refusal or withdrawal of orange badges.
Health, Social Services and Social Security Adjudication Act 1983
Joint finance; registration of homes; charges for local authority services.
Building Act 1984
Building regulations.
Disabled Persons (Services, Consultation and Representation) Act 1986
Social Services/education to assess needs of disabled child before completion of education. Right of disabled person to

171

appoint a representative; needs of disabled person under CSDPA 1970; regard to be taken of abilities of carer; duty to inform of relevant services; co-option on to local authorities of people with special knowledge of disability needs.

National Association for the Limbless Disabled

Formed in 1981 to promote welfare for disabled people who have lost a limb and to advise on the rehabilitation of those who have had a recent amputation, NALD runs a nation-wide counselling service, and provides social activities through local branches. They publish an interesting quarterly magazine and campaign for much-needed improvements in the limb fitting service and the design of prosthetics. Contact **NALD** (O).

Look after Your Legs

Combatting pressure sores and leg problems is a part of a daily way of life for physically disabled people who have limited mobility. Poor circulation in the legs can lead to oedema, liquid accumulation giving the characteristic thick ankles, night cramp pains, and sores that may never heal – if they become ulcerated this can result in ampuation being necessary. There is every good reason to take all the preventive measures possible and one of the most important is exercise.

However, if you are paralysed, it is difficult or impossible to exercise your legs. The Powex is an electrically-powered, variable-speed leg exerciser which can be used by anyone with limited or no mobility, from a wheelchair or an ordinary chair. The rotation of the pedals is electronically controlled from 5 to 30 revs per minute. The pedals can also be rotated manually without assisted power, and the pressure that has to be applied to rotate them can be adjusted to suit the user's capabilities. Instead of just receiving treatment once or twice a week, with a Powex you can have a little exercise every day in the comfort of your own home. This exercise increases the blood circulation, reduces swollen ankles and relaxes the muscles. It would be of value to tetraplegics, paraplegics, people with *multiple sclerosis, arthritis, muscular dystrophy* or some *stroke* victims.

I have used a Mark 1 Powex more or less daily for five trouble-free years. My legs are totally paralysed and the daily exercise has been an important factor in warding off problems. The Mark 2 Powex pedaller is similar in appearance to its predecessor but is lighter in weight (22lb (10kg)), and has adjustable feet. In addition, there is now a heavy-duty model, the Mark 3, which has a more powerful motor. This has been designed for use in day centres, nursing and residential homes, clinics and hospitals.

For a catalogue write to **Cleeve House Products** (M).

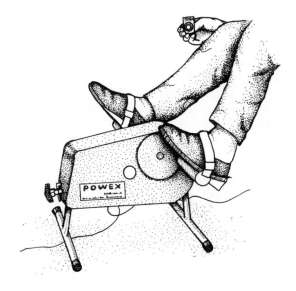

Powex electric leg exerciser.

M

Magazines

Magazines represent a useful way for a disabled or elderly person to keep up to date with new products, services, Social Security, holidays, sport and leisure. The following are but a selection of the many that are available:

RADAR Bulletin – monthly from **RADAR** (O)
MSS Bulletin – monthly from **Multiple Sclerosis Society** (O)
SIA Newsletter – quarterly from **Spinal Injuries Association** (O)
Disability News – monthly from 12 Park Crescent, London W1N 4EQ
Contact – quarterly from **RADAR** (O)
Caring – monthly from AE Morgan Publications Ltd, Stanley House, 9 West Street, Epsom, Surrey KT18 7RL
Which? Way to Health – quarterly from the Consumers' Association Ltd, 2 Marylebone Road, London NW1 4DX

The two bulletins have excellent 'small-ad' pages of second-hand products, from adapted motor cars to electric wheelchairs. The *SIA Newsletter* is the best for wheelchair users. *Which? Way to Health* is for people who actively preserve their health. *Caring* is the only magazine for disabled people available from any newsagent.

Make-up

The Red Cross Beauty Care Service is available to day-care centres, hospices, psychiatric wards, people of all ages recovering from an operation, and blind and partially-sighted ladies. The Beauty Care Service is free.

The Red Cross Cosmetic Camouflage Service can be of great help to people with permanently disfigured faces. They advise and teach disabled people how to camouflage or cover scars or birth marks with special cover creams, most of which are available on prescription. This service is also free. Those who need help should find out from the Red Cross whether the service is operating locally. They must then obtain a letter of referral from their doctor or medical consultant. For more information contact:

The National Organiser
Beauty Care and Cosmetic Camouflage Service
British Red Cross Society
9 Grosvenor Crescent
London SW1X 7EJ

Mary Marlborough Lodge

This is an NHS unit where the physical, psychological and social needs of severely disabled people are assessed and where they, and their care-givers, can get advice on all aspects of equipment, independence training and follow-up care.

The centre has 18 beds for patients and 3 for caring relatives, and there is a specially-equipped flat for training for independent living. Admission is by letter of application from the patient's GP to the Medical Director, Mary Marlborough Lodge, Nuffield Orthopaedic Centre, Headington, Oxford OX3 7LD (0865 64811). Normal length of stay is 1–3 weeks. The assessment includes a full medical examination, identification of problems, trial and choice of equipment, wheelchair provision and modification; and advice to the caring relative. Through the Oxford ALAC, which is on the premises, advice is given, and provision is made of mobility aids and artificial limbs. There is a bio-engineering workshop and a research unit.

MAVIS

The Mobility Advice and Vehicle Information Service was set up by the Department of Transport to help disabled people with practical help and advice on driving ability, car adaptations and car choice. Anyone with a disability who would like to visit MAVIS should first obtain a provisional driving licence if they are not already qualified. For full information contact **MAVIS** (O).

Medical Advisory Service

See Telephone Services.

Medical Identity Systems

Many disabled and elderly people have medical conditions which should be taken into account in their treatment in the event of their being rendered unconscious in illness or accident. Clearly, it would be helpful for a doctor or medical rescue team to have instant access to the victim's medical history, and to show that this is available the casualty should be wearing some instantly identifiable symbol.

Three of the best-known systems are:

Medic-Alert There is a one-off registration fee (about £15.00) for which your full medical history is stored at Medic-Alert HQ. You are issued with a wrist bracelet or necklace chain with a double-sided disc, on which is your personal registration number and the telephone number of Medic-Alert, which is manned 24 hours a day. On receipt of a call they will provide full details of your medical history. This is

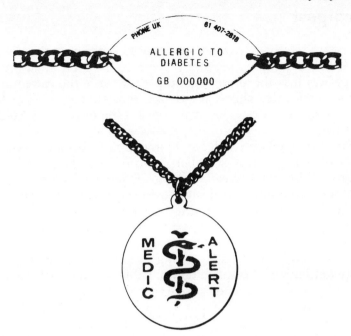

backed up by an abbreviated version on a card which you carry on your person. Write to Medic-Alert Foundation, 11/13 Clifton Terrace, London N4 3JP.

SOS Talisman   With this system you write your medical history on a piece of paper which is sealed inside a case worn as a pendant, bracelet or wristwatch attachment. Prices are from £8.00 upwards. The SOS Talisman can be bought in many jewellers or you can get details from Talman Ltd, 21 Grays Corner, Ley Street, Ilford, Essex IG2 7RQ.

Medvis International   For a one-off fee (around £6.00) your full medical history is stored at Medvis International HQ. You are given a credit-card-sized 'emergency medical card' into which is laminated a microfiche of your medical history – this can be read by a doctor with an ophthalmoscope. You keep this with your credit cards, which is where medics usually look to establish your identity. For details, contact Medvis International, PO Box 28, 207A Stamford Street, Ashton-under-Lyne, Lancs OL6 7QF.

177

Medipost

There are relatively few shops devoted entirely to the needs of disabled people, so many have to rely on mail-order shopping. It is therefore a good idea to have the catalogues of the mail-order shops which are most likely to cater for your needs at a price you can afford. One of these is **Medipost** (M).

There are well over half a million people in Britain who use a wheelchair but few suppliers who offer a range of high-quality clothing, footwear, and wheelchair accessories. These products have all been designed in the last twelve months and are continuously monitored for improvement.

Mullipel is a very popular artificial fleece used extensively in situations where *pressure sores* might occur. Mullipel is an excellent support surface, giving weight distribution with good ventilation. It is machine washable, has a very long life, and is available in a wide range of patterns and colours.

Included in the Medipost range are: a wheelchair set, comprising back and seat pads and arm covers; slippers and heel protectors; square and rectangular sheets for armchair or bed; and Mullimittens, which keep hands warm whilst leaving fingers and palms uncovered for controlling an electric wheelchair.

In the range also are brightly-coloured track suits, the Pat Saunders drinking straw, and wheelchair attachments, including a cup and holder, an ash-tray, and a sun parasol. Many items are zero-rated for VAT, subject to completion of the form supplied by Medipost with their catalogue.

Mobility Allowance

Mobility Allowance is an untaxed benefit for physically disabled people who have difficulty with walking. It does not normally affect other forms of Social Security but accumulated Mobility Allowance may be taken as part of your capital in assessment for *Income Support* or *Housing Benefit*. Initial application may be made between the ages of five and 65. Those people who are already drawing Mobility Allowance may continue to do so to the age of 80.

To qualify for Mobility Allowance your physical condition must be such that you are unable to walk, you are virtually unable to walk, your life is at risk if you walk, or walking causes severe pain. You must be able to go outdoors. Normally a DHSS doctor will assess you at home and this will be with any aids you normally use – sticks, crutches, walking frame or artificial limbs. He will consider your method of walking, how far you can walk, how fast you can walk and evidence of distress, such as heavy breathing, pulse rate or perspiration. If you are unable to rise unaided from a sitting to a standing position, this should be taken into account. It helps if you can get letters commenting on your walking ability from a consultant, GP, physiotherapist, care attendant or community nurse.

Assessment for Mobility Allowance has nothing to do with the fact that you live on a steep hill, that you need a motor car, that you cannot ride on public transport, or the strength of your caring relative. It is only about your inability to walk.

The required leaflet NI 211 contains the application form, which should be sent to the **Mobility Allowance Unit** (O). If you are refused you can ask for an *appeal tribunal*.

If you get Mobility Allowance you become entitled to exemption from road tax, exemption from rates on your garage, an *Orange Badge* for privileged parking, help from Motability with leasing or buying a car or wheelchair, or, if you are otherwise qualified, Severe Disablement Allowance.

Mobility in the Home

Of all the handicaps arising from physical disability, loss of personal mobility is the greatest. The house in which you are living when you become physically disabled was probably not designed for disability; come to think of it, families are not designed to cope with it either. Both will have to change and adapt – hopefully not too much – to provide for the newly-disabled member. The majority of disabled and elderly people are members of family units – spouses, children, parents, or grandparents – and we should concentrate on the disabled family rather than the disabled individual. Re-organisation of the family home is inevitable as a consequence of the introduction of a severely disabled member, but a careful analysis of the needs can produce a compromise acceptable to all.

Major physical disablement may mean that a person is confined to a manual wheelchair; very severe disability may necessitate the use of an indoor electric wheelchair. A less severe condition may leave a person able to walk using a walking frame, crutches, or sticks. So there are disabled people who are wheelchair users and there are those who are ambulant – local authority 'disabled' housing is classified as either 'wheelchair' or 'mobility' housing. Although we do tend to think of 'disabled' housing in terms of the degree of walking ability, the same general principles also apply to those without hearing, sight or speech.

The first thing to decide is the range of action which the disabled person wants – where does he need to go to maintain a reasonable life? A wheelchair pilot may be content to live entirely on the ground floor, but there will need to be access to a bedroom, toilet, bathroom, the family living room and the garden, while others may need access to a kitchen, tailored to their needs.

Mobility or wheelchair council housing may be available, although the level of provision varies from place to place. Mobility housing is suitable for people able to walk with an aid and it may also be used for able-bodied people; wheelchair housing enables a wheelchair rider to live a full life – to sleep, bath, use the toilet, cook, eat, telephone, clean the house, enter and leave – if possible unaided. A number of national voluntary 'disabled' associations also have wheelchair flats and houses for rent, although their waiting lists may be long.

Families living in their own houses may find an extension

to the house is the answer and for this there are intermediate or improvement grants for which you contact your local *Social Services* or the council Housing Department. In some towns one extension may attract grants from both departments.

The first choice you have to make is whether to move or stay. If you become wheelchair-bound and your house has more than one floor you are faced with your inability to get upstairs. One answer is to move to a bungalow or flat; this may be all right if you intended to move anyway, but if you do not want to leave your friends (and when you become disabled you soon find out who they are), or if you love your garden or your pub, or if your spouse threatens divorce, then you may prefer to stay where you are and modify the house. The cost of moving from one £40,000 house to another is at least £5,000 and the additional trauma, on top of new disability, may be too much for the caring spouse.

Having chosen to stay, your next decision is whether to have a ground-floor extension or to provide the means for the disabled person to get upstairs. A ground-floor extension can range from a single room, like a bathroom, to a complete living unit providing for sleeping, toilet, bathing and leisure. A built extension of this kind involves assessment by the domiciliary OT, securing grants, planning permission, equipment from Social Services and Health, estimates from builders . . .in other words, a long, daunting task over 12 to 18 months. A better solution is *Homelink* – factory-engineered portable buildings made by the **Portakabin Group** (M). These arrive on site fully fitted out, to link on to the house, or to be positioned nearby in the garden. Standing on simple pad foundations, the buildings can easily be removed if the original need disappears, and they have a resale value. Homelink is a way of providing for a disabled person at short notice without permanently extending the house.

There are eight different buildings in the Homelink range. The largest comprises a double bedroom, bathroom, wash basin and toilet, living room and kitchen. Other versions include just a bedroom, a bedsitting room, a bedroom with a toilet or a bedroom with a bathroom. The buildings are completely maintenance-free, and they have a high level of thermal insulation. Homelink buildings arrive complete, needing only attachment to drains, water and electricity. Although planning permission is needed, occupation may take place within two months of placing the order. The internal decor is pleasant and the level of fittings is chosen to suit the user's disability needs, and may include support rails, lever taps, waist-level electric power points, and a 'disabled' WC. Shaver point, fridge, waste disposal, cooker and curtain fitments are included, also to choice.

There are some advantages in making it possible for the disabled person to go upstairs. If the means of sleeping, toilet and bath are already upstairs, and usable by the disabled person, you save the considerable cost of alterations; secondly, the ground floor is largely untouched, so your home seems less 'disabled'; thirdly, if attention is needed during the night the caring relative is near at hand.

If an ambulant person can walk a little they may be able to get upstairs using a simple aid made from a wooden cigar box attached to the end of a walking stick. This halves the height of each stair and makes 12 steps into 24 smaller steps. For wheelchair riders who can transfer unaided you can use a stairlift with a seat; alternatively, you can install a small vertical lift which will take an occupied wheelchair, and there are also *stairlifts* which will take a loaded wheelchair upstairs. There are portable devices for moving a disabled person from one floor to another. The Escamatic Mobile Stair Rider is a battery-powered device operated by the care-giver, and it requires little physical effort. The NM52 is complete with a seat whilst the NM66 is designed to move the person seated in their wheelchair. Both models will travel upstairs, down stairs or on the level. Write to **Baronmead International Ltd** (M).

Space is essential for the wheelchair rider living at home and some sacrifices have to be made in the way of moving of furniture, or even getting rid of a few pieces. Over the years most of us accumulate too much furniture anyway, and your critical eye should light first on the largest items. Settees should be replaced by *armchairs*; a refectory-type table with a circular draw-leaf table. Floor space is at a premium, so hang things on the wall, rather than clutter up the floor. Where possible, use sliding doors or rehang them so they open flat against the wall. Ensure all doors and windows can be operated from the wheelchair, and train the family not to leave things lying about in the path of the wheelchair – especially their feet!

The disabled person, for both social and safety reasons, must be able to leave and enter the house from both front and back unaided. Patio doors are available which are specially designed for use with wheelchairs. A 2m (6ft) square porch at the front door enables a transfer to be made from a wet and muddy outdoor wheelchair to a clean indoor chair. All steps and sills should be removed from the front entrance, and internal door sills can be replaced with plastic ones which deform as the wheelchair passes over them. Externally all steps should be replaced with well-made concrete ramps and concrete paths should give movement around the garden. A car-port wide enough to give car/wheelchair transfers in wet weather is very useful.

There is some virtue in reducing the need of the disabled to move around the house. A cordless telephone or simple intercom may give communication which obviates the need for movement. **Possum** (M) and other environmental controls (**QED** (M)) can provide communication with the front door. If the house is large enough, it is a good idea to provide one room for the disabled person to sleep and live in – if possible near the front door. This will tend to concentrate all the 'disabled' paraphernalia in one place and save wear and tear on the nerves of the caring relative. It will also enable the disabled person to imprint their own personality on the room and give privacy for visitors.

The disabled person is very dependent on his *caring relative*; her health is his health, her failure his failure. The more mobile the disabled person is within the house, the lower the work-load on the care-giver. The house is home for all the family; the more it can remain 'undisabled' the better for all. There is no reason why a private house should look like a hospital just because a member of the household is disabled. Mobility is essential and possible for a disabled person in his own home – it just takes time, patience and seeking the right advice.

E TENEBRIS LUX

Mobility Trust

Formed in 1986 with the broad objective of helping the most severely disabled people who have mobility problems, the trust also promotes research, design and development of mobility aids, particularly where these are not available on the open market or from statutory sources. The trust will lend equipment or mobility aids to disabled individuals or organisations, and will try to bring back on to the road disabled drivers who could drive only a vehicle with very sophisticated controls.

The trust will advise on the choice of personal electric vehicles and motor cars and also on sources of finance. They will purchase, on behalf of a handicapped client, a particular piece of equipment, aid or technical device, and applicants may be deaf, dumb, blind or physically or mentally handicapped.

Contact the **Mobility Trust** (O).

Motability

In 1977, government backing enabled the setting up of Motability with the aim of helping disabled people to use their *Mobility Allowance* to achieve the best value for money in securing their chosen aid to mobility – anything from a wheelchair to a motor car. The first car was supplied in 1978 and since then 95,000 cars and 5,000 wheelchairs have been provided, with the scheme proving more successful, and greater interest shown, each year. Motability has arranged special terms with motor manufacturers, wheelchair makers, insurance brokers and others, so that today a variety of schemes can be offered to help disabled people become mobile.

Under the leasing scheme operated by Motability, disabled people can get a new Austin Rover, Fiat, Ford, Renault, Nissan, Peugeot-Talbot or Vauxhall car for three years. They have to pay all or most of their Mobility Allowance for the whole of the three-year period, together (in some cases) with a deposit and a contribution towards a specially arranged insurance premium. For some of the cheaper cars offered through Motability there is no initial deposit and the insurance is included. There are over 200 different car models available, with deposits ranging from nil upwards, depending on the size and specification of the cars. More expensive models also represent good value if the disabled person is looking for a comprehensive hire package, under which maintenance and repair costs, AA membership, and a 'loss of use' insurance is all covered by the rental.

For people who prefer to buy their car, Motability offers a hire purchase scheme under which finance can be provided towards new and used cars in return for all, or part, of the Mobility Allowance. Motability has arranged good discounts for new cars with a number of motor manufacturers, but if people want a car which is not on Motability's list they can negotiate their own discount, and then ask Motability if finance can be provided towards the cost. The difference between the cost of the car and the finance provided in return for the Mobility Allowance has to be paid as a deposit at the start of the agreement. Number plates, delivery charges, maintenance, repairs and insurance are costs which the disabled person has to meet under the hire purchase scheme. The finance provided towards the car is offered on very favourable rates of interest, and in some cases is sufficient to meet the cost of the car without any deposit being required.

Cars supplied on both lease and hire purchase arrangements can be adapted to suit the needs of the disabled person, but the type of adaptations which can be made to leased cars is limited because the car has to be returned at the end of the three years. If required, Motability can provide the names and addresses of professional organisations which can assess the needs of the disabled person and advise them whether or not they might be capable of driving, and what sort of car and adaptations they might need.

The Motability *wheelchair* scheme now has 18 wheelchair manufacturers participating, offering good discounts and service on powered and non-powered wheelchairs, 'buggies' and scooters. Models are available for indoor and outdoor use, and many are suitable for local shopping and visiting friends.

The only credit rating required is whether the disabled person receives *Mobility Allowance* for a long enough period of time to cover the leasing or hire purchase agreement. The disabled person does not need to be able to drive to take advantage of one of the schemes, and can even be a child if someone elses receives the Mobility Allowance on their behalf. War pensioners with Mobility Supplement can also use the Motability Scheme at special rates.

Motability is a registered charity and if a disabled person cannot meet the cost of putting a car on the road, including any adaptations, and the cost of driving lessons, Motability may be able to provide financial help from its special funds.

Full details are available from **Motability** (O).

Motoring

There are many people who are so severely disabled physically that they will never be able to drive a car. In many of these cases, therefore, all the car driving is done by the caring relative. A little planning will be necessary to take care of any emergencies.

Whilst the needs of the disabled passenger must be considered in the acquisition and running of a car, those of the driver/carer are equally important – he or she has the responsibility for two lives. Taking a severely disabled person on a long car journey is a task which is demanding, both physically and mentally. The disabled person may have to be toiletted, wheeled out to the car, lifted on to the front seat, the wheelchair folded and stowed in the boot, and the front door locked. There may be a need for drugs or special equipment – even if the disabled person is only spending a few hours with friends. All this is before the journey starts.

Often disability comes part way through life so a fairly common situation is one where a family already owns one or more cars, and where an adult member becomes severely handicapped. In most families, it has been the tradition for the man to 'manage' the car with everything from insurance to topping up the oil, and whoever becomes the driver may need advice.

When disability comes, it will be necessary to consider whether your existing car is still suitable – or, for that matter, whether you need (or can still afford) a car. In fact, life for a wheelchair rider would be very limited without a car, and you may need to get one even if you did not have one before your disability. In choosing a car, much will depend on finance, followed by the 'disability' aspects.

If the carer is going to have to lift a *wheelchair* into the back of an estate car or hatchback frequently then you should look for a low loading height – around 17in (45cm) – and a straight-in entry; avoid cars which involve lifting the wheelchair up, leaning in and lowering. Try to acquire a second wheelchair which can be left in the car; often the Disablement Services Centre will supply a lightweight chair for this purpose. The Autochair is a stream-lined container for the car roof. With the touch of a button it will hoist your folded wheelchair from beside the car and stow it safely out of sight on the roof. Write to **Mobility Techniques Ltd** (M).

The method of transfer from wheelchair to car front seat needs working out. If the seat is about the same height as the wheelchair seat, a transfer board may be used. A stout belt around the passenger's waist helps the driver to pull him into the seat. In some cars the edge of the seat is a long way in from the door sill and this makes it difficult getting your bottom on the seat if you do a standing transfer. In some families the driver/carer may also be handicapped, in which case you should look for hand controls, automatic gears, powered steering or power-assisted brakes. Powered steering and automatic gears are now available on many small cars. If a driver has to lift a disabled passenger in and out of a car then this should be tried a number of times before you decide to buy the car. Often the suitability of a car for a disabled person is unrelated to the cost – it either works for you or it does not.

Of the wide range of specialised 'disabled' vehicles on the market, the 'popemobiles' are probably the best known. The earliest of these was the Mini, which is still available, and there are now larger versions based upon the Metro, Ford Escort and the Vauxhall Astra. All of these cars have a raised roof with a windscreen for the seated wheelchair rider and rear entry for an occupied wheelchair up a small ramp. There is room in addition for two seated passengers. Write to **Mobility International** (O) or **VW Ponting** (M). Relatively new is the Volkswagen Caddy which helps rear entry since it can be lowered between its own back wheels. The VW Caravelle is a small van offering a sliding side door with an electro-hydraulic wheelchair lift, and seating for five passengers. Write to **Invatravel** (M).

One of the best vehicles for the permanent wheelchair rider is the Brotherwood conversion of the Nissan Prairie which, as a station wagon, has proven its reliability over a number of years. This is a sort of 'poor man's Range Rover', which nevertheless gives a very high level of comfort and finish whilst offering features not found in any other car. The rear bumper is attached to the tailgate giving a very low loading level of 35cm (16in). The back doors slide towards the rear so when both doors are open, as there is no door pillar, entry from the side is very easy. All the seats fold right down, forming a double bed. For the seated wheelchair passenger, entry is from the rear up a shallow ramp and, as the floor is lowered, the wheelchair rider is at the same 'head height' as the seated passengers. A slightly raised roof conversion is available for the taller wheelchair rider. On either side of the wheelchair rider are two single seats so the car can take five passengers in comfort. A rotating slide-out seat for the front passenger and optional extras include automatic gears, power steering, electric windows and electric sunroof. Write to **Rod Brotherwood** (M).

If a vehicle is in a taxi fleet that says something about its reliability and low running costs. Such a vehicle is the 1200cc Renault Trafic which provides for one, two or three occupied wheelchairs, and some seated passengers. Visit your nearest Renault garage.

Some disabled passengers can get into car front seats using an aided 'stand-turn-sit', but in the long run this can be bad for the helper's back. It is better to use a transfer board or other mechanical means. Roof-mounted or internal hoists are available for lifting people in and out of the car using slings (**S Burville & Sons** (M)).

A very good system is the 'Car Chair' in which the front car seat is replaced by a wheelchair which may be powered, manual or pushed. The chair is reversed on to a small fork lift built into the car and it is then lifted, the wheels retracted, rotated into the car and lowered – all by pressing buttons. Write to **Car Chair Ltd** (M). If a person is paralysed from the waist downwards it is very difficult to rotate them on a front seat and put their legs in the car. This problem is solved by using a rotating seat from **Elap Engineering Ltd** (M).

On short journeys the two main essentials are parking and an accessible toilet. An *Orange Badge* will help with parking and you apply for this from your local *Social Services*. If the town you are in has a 'Guide for Disabled People' you will find in it a map showing the unisex disabled loos.

Touring and long-distance holiday travel by car is quite feasible for a disabled passenger, given careful planning. Comfort is essential, so sit on a piece of Mullipel, and avoid backache with an inflatable lumbar cushion (**Medipost** (M)). Try to arrange a stop about once an hour; roll on your side for ten minutes to give your bottom a rest. If your seat belt is uncomfortable, get one of those plastic gadgets for holding it slightly loose. It is very important to support the feet properly; the ideal is a wedge-shaped cushion filled with polystyrene beads and covered with sheepskin. It is a great help to the driver if the passenger can navigate on a long run and it pays to have a good, up-to-date road map, and the route written out beforehand. You may need a street map of your destination town.

Toilet stops must be planned carefully for the disabled

passenger who cannot readily nip out of the car and go behind a bush. It is worth buying a key and a national toilet list from **RADAR** (O). For those unforeseen bladder problems when you are caught in a ten-mile motorway tailback, carry a 'Convenient' – a disposable urine collection device which can be used in the car by males or females (**CC Products** (M)).

Safety is of greater importance in any car carrying a relatively immobile disabled person, so membership of a 'get-you-home' organisation is desirable – RAC, AA, or National Breakdown Recovery Club. If you do break down you can attract attention with an illuminated flashing 'HELP' sign (**Handi Kontrols Ltd** (M)) or a 'HELP' pennant from **Cleveland Spastics Work Centre** (M). For emergencies, carry a few bars of chocolate or biscuits and one dose of any essential medication. It is always worth while carrying a quantity of clean water to drink, wash with or top up the radiator with.

Mobility Allowance is a benefit essentially for people who are partially or totally unable to walk; if you think you may qualify, contact your nearest *Social Security* or *DIAL* office. **Motability** (O) is a government-sponsored organisation offering certain makes of cars on a four-year lease if you make over your Mobility Allowance. They also offer a hire purchase service. AID – Assistance and Independence for Disabled People – is the alternative method of getting a car. They give advice on all aspects of car purchase including hire purchase over five years, and inclusive package deals including vehicle costs, adaptations, accessories, insurance and delivery to your door. For cars under a certain price there is no deposit and they will consider part exchange. Write to the **AID Centre** (M). **The Mobility Trust** (O) will provide advice and, in certain cases, material help to those with problems.

Quite large discounts – from about 5 to 18 per cent – are available to disabled buyers of new cars. Car tax and possibly VAT may not be payable on a car substantially modified for use by a disabled person. The rules are quite complicated so it is well worth while getting the leaflets from your local VAT office before you part with any money. If you have *Mobility Allowance* you could be exempt from road fund tax.

There are a number of publications which no disabled

motorist should be without. Top of the list is *Motoring and Mobility for Disabled People* by Ann Darnbrough and Derek Kinrade, published by **RADAR** (O). *Door to Door* is a useful book available free from most *DIALs* and the annual *AA Guide for the Disabled* has a very comprehensive list of 'disabled' loos and accessible hotels.

The best source of information is probably the **Mobility Information Service** (O) which produces an excellent series of leaflets on every aspect of motoring – car discounts, road tests, ferry concessions, hand controls, and the problems of motoring with certain disabilities. There is a very good free telephone information service, and they have a new driver assessment centre with private roads.

Any *DIAL* will provide you with catalogues and advice and useful leaflets are available from **RADAR** (O) and **DLF** (O). **Banstead Place Mobility Centre** (O) offers information on any mobility problem. Here also there is a private road facility for assessment, training and trying out types of road and pavement vehicles, and they have a free telephone advice service. **MAVIS** (O) – Mobility Advice and Vehicle Information Service – was set up by the Department of Transport to give practical advice on driving, car adaptations, and car choice – both for passengers and for drivers.

Information can also be obtained from the disabled motorists' organisations and if you do a lot of motoring it is worth joining one of these. Write to **Disabled Drivers Association** (O), the **Disabled Drivers Motor Club** (O), or the **Disabled Motorists Federation** (O).

Motor Neurone Disease

This is really a group of related diseases affecting the motor neurones – nerve cells which control muscles – in the brain and spinal cord. Damage or destruction of these causes weakness and muscle wastage. Loss of movement is followed by paralysis in all the limbs, difficulty with breathing and swallowing, and loss of speech. This is a tragic progressive disease for which there is no known cure, and the gradual deterioration is extremely distressing for both the sufferer and the family. It results in a terminal condition and everything possible should be done to preserve a high quality of life for as long as possible.

In this the **Motor Neurone Disease Association** (O) can help with the welfare of the patient. Assistance may take the form of the provision of equipment to help with day-to-day living, financial help, or practical and moral support for the caring relative. In all they do they are aware that time is running out, so they act with a sense of urgency.

The MND Association promotes research and provides information on coping with the disease. There are many local branches.

Mouth and Foot Painting

Any person who has lost the use of his hands and paints by holding the brush in his mouth or in his toes should apply to join **Mouth and Foot Painting Artists Association** (O). However, the quality of their work should compare favourably with that of an able-bodied artist. Disabled artists can join as student members by submitting six paintings, together with a medical certificate stating that they are unable to hold a brush in their hands. A panel will judge the merit of the work and the potential of the artist. Even if the work does not reach the required standard, the applicant may be awarded a grant to pay for home tuition or a scholarship at an art college. The student's work is reviewed periodically with a view to granting full membership, which can provide a monthly salary.

When the association was founded in 1956 there were only seven members. Now it is a body with over 230 member artists in 40 different countries. For further information contact the **Mouth and Foot Painting Artists Association** (O).

Multiple Sclerosis

This disease, which used to be called 'Disseminated Sclerosis', is the most common of the diseases of the central nervous system, and at present there are over 80,000 cases in Britain. Imagine a telephone network with underground cables, each carrying hundreds of thin wires and each taking a message to a different place; or the electric cables in a house or a motor car. Now suppose the insulation on some of those wires becomes worn away and the wires touch. Chaos results with things happening but none of them right. This is what happens in MS; myelin – the protective sheathing of some of the nerves – becomes damaged. 'Multiple Sclerosis' means 'many scars'. The messages from the brain do not reach the intended muscle, either because they are stopped or because they are re-routed to the wrong muscle. In time, the unused muscle can waste away or the nerve may become damaged. MS may be the result of a breakdown in the body's auto-immune system, which, for reasons unknown, temporarily changes its role from defence against viral or bacterial attack, and attacks normal body tissue – in this case the myelin.

It is said that you could line up a thousand people with MS and they would all be different. Often there is muscular weakness which can eventually result in varying levels of paralysis. A feeling of excessive fatigue is common and this may be worse in hot environments. In some people sight or speech may be affected. The onset of MS is very gradual and often some of the symptoms mimic those of other diseases, so doctors are very reluctant to give definite diagnoses. This is exacerbated by the frightening 'incurable' label that is attached to the condition. There are no mental effects so most MS patients understand exactly what ails them, and this makes it that much more difficult to bear. However, once it is arrived at, the final definitive diagnosis initiates a period of emotional shock when counselling is essential. This may come from a local branch of the **MS Society** (O), from **Action for Research into Multiple Sclerosis** (O), or from a **DIAL** (O). Diagnosis of MS is not the end of the world. For many people the disease remains in such a mild form it goes unnoticed; in some cases it goes away. Peer counselling from a physically handicapped person can be of great value.

MS occurs between the ages of 15 and 45. Tragically, most victims seem to be between 25 and 30 – just when they are likely to have young families, big mortgages and busy lives. It could not happen at a worse time and sometimes the spouse may not be able to cope. Of all disabilities, MS holds the record as the worst marriage-breaker of all.

It is generally accepted that Multiple Sclerosis is a growing problem. In the northern 'white' countries – Britain, Scandinavia, Holland and North America – the figures are rising by the day, and in the USA alone there are 350,000 victims. At the beginning of the century there was no sign of MS in China, and now it is a growing problem there. There is some suspicion that this could be the result of changing to a 'western' diet. The incidence of MS is three times higher in the Orkney Islands than in the rest of the UK – this could be to do with their diet, or there could be some undetected environmental factor. It is a fact that the incidence of MS is very low in tropical countries on either side of the Equator, and this may point to 'civilised' stress being an underlying cause. MS might well stand for 'Mystery Sickness', because it is neither contagious nor infectious, nor is there any proof that it can be passed from parent to child. There is also a strong theory that there is a link between MS and sinusitis in childhood. There may be as many as 200,000 people with MS who have no symptoms at all.

MS is characterised by a distressing pattern of relapses and remission, and its unpredictable nature can tear lives apart. Millions of pounds have been spent on research but, to date, there is no known cure. This being the case, the MS person, once he or she has been given a clear diagnosis, must first grapple with the emotional effects, and then address themselves to adapting to coping with the symptoms.

A common emotional response is anger, followed by a 'why me' phase. Family and friends will bear the brunt of this phase and will need to exercise great patience until the next phase, which is one of grief and depression. These two phases are often associated with loss of sleep, appetite and self-esteem. Finally comes acceptance, and with it peace and relaxation, when the sufferer realises that there are problems but most of them can be overcome.

The first symptoms of MS are mild and vague – a little numbness, tingling, perhaps bladder problems and a feeling of weakness. As time goes on there may be difficulty with walking, dressing, continence, obesity, sexuality, speech and vision. These symptoms may take years to appear. Most MS people carry on working for many years after diagnosis and there is no indication of a shortened life, given careful management. Eventually a MS person may find their ability to walk so reduced that they have to use a wheelchair. By now they will have developed an aggressive policy towards the management of their condition, and they will see the wheelchair as just another tool in maintaining normality. There are many MS wheelchair riders who not only continue successful lives, but reach the top of their professions, and some have children too.

From the start, expert advice is necessary about equipment. You have to know what you need and where to get it. Some items will be free from Health and Social Services or the Manpower Services Commission; others you will have to buy. Because of the 'up and down' nature of MS you have to provide for the worst conditions that could come about. Your armoury of aids for coping with the symptoms of MS will increase as the years go on and you never stop learning. Look for advice from other people with MS; from local branches of **MSS** (O) and **ARMS** (O); from **DIALs** (O) and **Disabled Living Centres** (O); from health visitors and district nurses; from domiciliary *physiotherapists* and *occupational therapists*. Many of the problems of partial or severe paralysis are shared with other disabilities and, as with them, great care must be exercised to avoid peripheral medical problems associated with pressure sores, bladder and bowels, vital capacity, weight control, diet, exercise and circulation. Equipment will start with simple items such as walking frames, sheepskins and support rails for the *toilet*. After twenty years it may include an electric bed, armchair, toilet and wheelchair, a converted motor car or even a special sailing dinghy.

Much has been written about special diets for treating or curing MS, but no evidence has emerged that any of them are effective. Most of these special MS diets are based upon a simple comparison of the eating habits of those parts of the world where MS is prevalent and those parts where it is not. We consume wheat, rye, fats, sugar, coffee and alcohol and we get MS; the people living in the tropics do not and they do not get MS. However, although there is no diet that will cure MS, it is wise for a physically handicapped person to follow a diet that will keep bowels and bladder working, that will keep weight down (to help your weak muscles when you stand up), and produce healthy flesh (to avoid pressure sores). So do take the advice of a good dietician.

There is a common misconception that exercise is bad for MS people. In fact, if exercise is correctly programmed for the individual, if the right exercises are selected, and if the individual monitors himself carefully, exercise is possible and will promote good health. The old-fashioned physiotherapist's 'No pain, no gain' philosophy is absolutely the wrong approach to exercise for the MS person. Suitable exercise may involve walking, a static cycle, or mild aerobics. During any exercise the individual should be able to stop and speak a sentence clearly to show he or she is not out of breath. First exercises must be slow and gentle and subsequent progression must be at a very shallow rate and always monitored by a caring medical professional.

In the early stages most people with MS continue with their normal employment and this may go on for years. However, the unstable nature of MS may, without warning, mean an hour, day or week when the person is only partly productive or even off work. This may or may not fit in with the type of work. Stress should be avoided, as MS people often tire more quickly than others, and this may need a change of job, perhaps within the same organisation. Other solutions may be reduced hours, flexible hours or part-time working. Severe cases of MS may involve some loss of co-ordination or there may be impaired vision or speech. MS rarely affects intelligence, so an experienced and bright person, even limited by MS, could have a lot to offer his employer. Since the progress of the disease is very gradual, it gives both employer and worker time to plan ahead for future problems.

In the last ten years, the *microcomputer*, sometimes with data transfer by telephone, has been behind a wide expansion of *home-based employment*, which in many ways is good for MS people. In home-based work the individual can work at any time and only when he feels well; all he has to do is to reach a pre-determined target within a given time. Travel to work, which is both tiring and expensive, is avoided, and absence of interruptions means a higher productivity rate. On the other hand, the worker loses important social contact with his colleagues and also needs to be highly motivated to work without immediate supervision. Home-based employment can include professional jobs such as writing, journalism, personnel management, stock control, tax consultancy, accountancy, programming, tachograph checking and word processing.

It must be remembered that the onset of MS has a traumatic effect on the able-bodied spouse, and it can be the last straw to find that the disability of one partner means that sex is either impossible or indescribably difficult. Pain, inability to attain or maintain certain positions, and loss of sensation can all put added strain on a marriage already under stress.

Fortunately, this previously overlooked aspect of the disease has now been recognised, and there are very helpful leaflets available from **SPOD** (O) – Sexual Problems of the Disabled. Sexuality is and should be an important part of life for MS persons. Sexuality affects one's basic feelings of self-esteem, provides pleasure in a new world which will not afford much relaxation, and is an important part of the relationship with the spouse since the ability to make love happily strengthens the attachment between parners. However, the problems are large; skilled counselling is needed and should be made available in the years ahead.

Probably the most significant development in the treatment of MS is the use of hyperbaric oxygen chambers – large metal compartments similar to the decompression chambers used for divers with the bends – which will be found at a number of branches of **ARMS** (O). No final conclusions have yet been reached about this treatment, and the best that can be said is that it does bring an improvement in some cases and that there are no significant side-effects. A world-wide test on hyperbaric oxygen involving 3,000 MS people showed improvement in enough cases to carry on trials. Eyesight especially often improves with HBO treatment.

Multiple Sclerosis is a disability in which it is very necessary to seek all the advice and information possible – not just at the start but for ever more. The best sources are the two main national organisations, both of which have large networks of local branches. The Multiple Sclerosis Society was formed in 1953 with two main objectives – to conduct intensive research into the causes of MS and possible cures, and to help in all ways possible those who have to live with it. The society has put over £10 million into research and there is good reason to believe that one day the long-awaited breakthrough will come. MSS has over 350 local branches all run by volunteers, many with MS. House-bound members are visited regularly and care is taken to see that they receive all the aids and benefits to which they are entitled. 'Crack MS' is the young arm of the society, providing newly-diagnosed people with information and advice.

The MS Society has a number of short-stay and holiday facilities, as well as a new respite centre at Horley in Surrey. MSS publishes an excellent quarterly magazine and a monthly bulletin.

Action for Research into Multiple Sclerosis (O) (ARMS) was formed in 1974; today it has over 7,000 members and raises £500,000 a year for a co-ordinated research programme which has involved 3,000 of its own members. There are around 60 local centres and most offer physiotherapy and hyperbolic oxygen therapy, as well as advice on nutrition. ARMS runs three telephone services:

London (24 hrs daily)   01 222 3123
Glasgow (day and evenings daily)   041 637 2262
Birmingham (day and evenings daily)   021 476 4229

Multiple Sclerosis is incurable but it is controllable. Coping with MS is one long series of challenges. You should not try to do it alone, but really you only have yourself to beat.

Muscular Dystrophy

Muscular dystrophy is a neuro-muscular disease which results in progressive wasting of the muscles, leading eventually to almost total paralysis. It is an inherited condition and carriers of the muscular dystrophy gene can be identified with blood tests. It is found in many different forms.

The **Muscular Dystrophy Group of Great Britain** (O) was founded in 1961 with the twin objects of providing support for sufferers and their families, and promoting research into the cause, treatment and cure of the disease. There is a strong regional organisation supporting 450 voluntary branches, which give practical support and advice to affected families on a local basis.

The group publishes a wide range of pamphlets, handbooks and guides as well as a quarterly journal. At headquarters a Patient Care Co-ordinator is available for advice and there are eight Family Care Officers around the country.

Music in Hospitals

The **Council for Music in Hospitals** (O) was founded forty years ago and currently arranges over 1,500 performances each year in hospitals, nursing and *residential homes* and hospices throughout Britain.

The concerts are given by professional artists, chosen for their ability to relate to their audiences. The concerts take place in halls, chapels, tea bars and on the wards. The warmth and high level of artist/patient interaction makes these concerts into memorable occasions.

For information write to the **Council for Music in Hospitals** (O).

Myalgic Encephalomyelitis

This is a disease which can attack individuals or it may be the result of an epidemic. ME usually starts with flu-like symptoms – running nose, giddiness and possibly gastric problems. The initial symptoms may clear up under treatment but the patient is left with profound fatigue, muscle weakness and spasm, and pain. Positive diagnosis is very important to persuade the person that he is not 'putting it on', and also to convince statutory bodies who can help with benefits, equipment and services. If a family doctor is convinced these symptoms are no more than the aftermath of flu, it may be necessary to ask for a second opinion.

The **Myalgic Encephalomyelitis Association** (O), formed in 1976, now has over 2,500 members. There are a number of local groups offering support, information and advice. The association brings the disease to the notice of the medical fraternity and raises funds to support research. There is a confidential telephone line, called *Listening Ear*, available three evenings a week.

N

National Association for the Limbless Disabled

See under Limbless.

National Council for Voluntary Organisations

The **NCVO** (O) is an information service for voluntary organisations, national or local, large or small. It provides advice on fund-raising, legislation, trust law, management, project development, community care and job creation. It identifies and publishes solutions to management problems facing national organisations, and runs seminars and conferences. The work and problems facing the voluntary sector are projected to the media, to Parliament and to the public.

The publications work for the NCVO is carried out by Bedford Square Press, which prints many books and leaflets on subjects relating to the voluntary sector. There is a large library and an information unit which runs a. library, provides a public enquiry and referral service, and is responsible for alerting other NCVO departments to external events. Support is provided to voluntary groups involved with YTS schemes and with local community health initiatives. The Voluntary Action Group produces *Voluntary Action* which is published as a supplement to *New Society*. For details contact **NCVO** (O).

National Health Service

DEPARTMENTS OF HEALTH AND SOCIAL SECURITY
The departments have overall responsibility for Social Security, the National Health Service and for Social Services. Contact at Alexander Fleming House, Elephant and Castle, London SE1 6BY (01 407 5522).

Social Security – benefits, allowances and pensions – is operated through regional and local offices.

The National Health Service is structured in 'regions' and 'districts'.

Social Services is a local authority function funded and run by county councils but within departmental rules.

REGIONAL HEALTH AUTHORITIES
There are 14 Regional Health Authorities in England. Each region comprises two or three counties, although sometimes a regional boundary cuts across a county. They are responsible for planning health services and setting priorities in each region. They allocate resources to the District Health Authorities.

DISTRICT HEALTH AUTHORITIES
There are 192 District Health Authorities, each health region being divided into between 8 and 22 districts. The DHA is responsible for the management and development of local health services.

FAMILY PRACTITIONER COMMITTEE
FPCs are independent of DHAs and do not usually have the same boundaries. The FPC is responsible for administering the services of local NHS family doctors, dentists, opticians and pharmacists. These people are not NHS employees but they contract their services to the FPC, which then remunerates them for services provided. The FPC produces a list of local GPs. Patients may contact the FPC if they wish to change their GP or if they wish to register a complaint.

LOCAL AUTHORITIES
These are county and district councils which provide local services such as social services, housing, environmental health and education. Boundaries of DHAs rarely coincide with districts.

JOINT CONSULTATIVE COMMITTEES
JCCs are set up in many areas to co-ordinate NHS and local authority services in matters such as care of elderly and disabled people. JCCs do not deal directly with the public.

COMMUNITY HEALTH COUNCILS
There is generally one CHC for each DHA. The CHC represents the interests of the public within the health district. It

provides a check on Health Authority plans, monitors the quality of local services and has a right of comment on proposed closures. It advises members of the public, including those who wish to make complaints. Each CHC must include members from the local authority and local voluntary organisations.

Story

Wheelaway

At a conference to discuss the McColl Report on the supply of wheelchairs and artificial limbs, a wheelchair-borne speaker recalled that he had been solemnly instructed by a DHSS clerk that he must inform the authorities if he was taking his wheelchair abroad. 'Now,' he asked, 'who do I tell about taking my NHS spectacles overseas?'

(With acknowledgements to *Therapy*.)

National Key Scheme

Over the past few years there have been many problems with vandalism and mis-use of free public toilets for disabled people. Originated and run by RADAR, the National Key Scheme has now been adopted by over 230 towns and there are over 1,500 toilets available to key-holders. These include a number on *British Rail* stations.

The scheme involves the fitting of a standard lock to 'disabled' toilets which can be opened only with a special key. Keys may be purchased from local town halls or for £2.50 from **RADAR** (O) who will also supply a full location list of the toilets.

Neighbourhood Energy Action

Recent winters with prolonged spells of exceptionally cold weather have placed at great risk large numbers of disadvantaged people, and there has been an increase in deaths of elderly people from hypothermia. Neighbourhood Energy Action provides advice and services related to draughtproofing, loft insulation, the efficient running of heating appliances, and how to get grants from local authorities. Disabled and elderly people take priority for energy-saving projects and they should make maximum use of all grants and services available. A copy of the NEA leaflet may be obtained free from Neighbourhood Energy Action, 2–4 Bigg Market, Newcastle-on-Tyne, NE1 1UW (Freefone 0800 234800).

O

Occupational Therapy

Occupational therapy may be defined as 'the treatment of physical and psychiatric conditions through specific selected activities in order to help a disabled person reach a maximum level of function and independence in all aspects of daily life'. The occupational therapist is a member of a team of professionals whose collective aim is the rehabilitation of the disabled person. The team will vary in its constitution but usually includes OTs, *physiotherapists*, social workers, GPs, nurses, speech therapists and Disablement Resettlement Officers.

OTs may be found in hospitals where they work on the wards, in their own department, and maybe in an industrial therapy unit or a day centre. Out in the community, domiciliary OTs work under the local authority as part of the Social Services department.

For the person who becomes severely physically disabled through illness or injury, first contact with an OT may well be in the Intensive Care Unit, in the provision of the equipment for reading. As the patient progresses, sessions of occupational therapy will increase to three or four hours a day. Much activity will be directed towards coping with the personal tasks of daily life – transfers, dressing, *toilet*, washing, eating, *drinking* and *mobility*. Later the disabled person will become motivated towards higher ambitions – communication, sport, employment, sex and education – and the rebuilding of a life, within the constraints imposed by disability, will begin.

The domiciliary OT is mainly concerned with providing the means for a disabled person to live a full life at home. Careful assessment will determine the equipment, services or house modifications needed. Under the 1986 Disabled Persons Act the disabled person must be given this assessment in writing and they may be advised by an advocate of their own choice. The OT will provide training for both the disabled person and their caring relative in the skills needed to achieve a normal life, in spite of the constraints imposed by the disability. He or she should be a source of information and advice (thereby providing the disabled person with the means of making decisions about his own future), and the focus of the rehabilitation team. The domiciliary OT is contacted at your local social services.

Orange Aids

This is a system of inter-connecting rods, clamps and gadgets to help physically disabled people, particularly wheelchair riders. The essence of the system is a small piece of steel, rectangular, and about 15cm (6in) in length, which is screwed or clamped to the edge of a desk, bench or kitchen work-top. Round holes and slots in the metal bar enable a wide range of aids to be attached with thumb-screws. Because the standard clamp is permanently fixed to the edge of the table, aids and tools can be attached with ease and speed, using fingers only. There are similar clamps for attachment to a wheelchair or bed.

The Orange Aids system was originally invented by Trevor Baylis, an engineer, in 1982. It has since expanded, and now there are many parts available in this unique system, which is sold world-wide. It is a kind of 'Meccano' set for physically disabled people – you can do anything with it from opening an envelope to whisking an egg.

The applications of Orange Aids are almost limitless and the number of inter-connecting pieces runs into hundreds, from tiny metal items to a bench over 6ft (2m) long. There is an excellent illustrated catalogue and also a user guide. In broad terms there are items for personal care (mirrors etc), the kitchen (egg-whisks, graters, mixing bowls, colanders, bread-cutters), the work-shop (benches, vices, saws, drills, planes), the office (desks fitting around the wheelchair, computer holders, lecterns, angle-poise lights), for the bed (a double-deck computer table), and for hobbies indoors and out (magnifying glasses, clamps for cameras or binoculars, easels for painting or tapestry). Many items are designed for one-handed use by hemiplegics.

The Orange Aid concept first identifies the problem, then items are selected from the existing range which, when joined together, provide the solution. Because Orange Aids are made from the highest quality materials – stainless steel, aluminium and phosphor-bronze – and the engineering is to a very high standard, all the parts are likely to have an indefinite life. Although the system is widely used by *occupational therapists*, social workers, the Manpower Services

Commission and the Department of Trade and Industry, many disabled people simply get the catalogue and order what they want through the post.

Write for a catalogue to **Orange Aids Ltd** (M).

Orange Badge Scheme

This is a national arrangement providing parking concessions (on-street only) for disabled people who may be drivers or passengers. The Orange Badge is for the use of one designated disabled person only, and can be used in any vehicle (including a taxi) provided it is displayed correctly. It may not be lent to any other person.

The Orange Badge authorises the holder:

- To park free of charge and without time limit at parking meters on-street.
- To park for as long as they wish where others may park for a limited time only.
- To park on single or double yellow lines for up to two hours provided the orange parking disc is displayed also showing the time of arrival.

Even with an Orange Badge, parking is forbidden:

- Where there is a ban on loading or off-loading. This is indicated by one, two or three yellow marks on the kerb.
- Where there is a double white line in the centre of the road.
- In a bus lane.
- On zig-zag markings.
- On crossings or their approaches.
- On a cycle lane.
- Where it could cause danger to other road users.
- Where emergency vehicles – ambulances, fire engines – exit or enter.

To qualify for an Orange Badge you must be:

Blind
or
Getting *Mobility Allowance*
or
Using a vehicle supplied by a government department
or
Getting a grant towards your vehicle
or
Your doctor confirms you have a permanent substantial disability which means you are unable to walk or you have considerable difficulty with walking.

Application should be made to your local *Social Services Department*. You may be directed by your GP. There is no right of appeal against their decision.

When in use the Orange Badge must be displayed on the near side of the car windscreen. It must be removed by the holder when the period of use is ended. Badges are issued for three years, towards the end of which you should re-apply.

Some authorities providing off-street parking may have 'disabled' reserved spaces. Sometimes these are marked 'Orange Badge Holders Only'. Some authorities waive charges for parking on these spaces.

The Orange Badge Scheme is often abused, mainly by the

disabled holders, and consequently ordinary motorists tend to have little love for it. The badge should never be left on the car, particularly where the holder is a non-driver. It is illegal for an able-bodied person to use a badge and the holder can be fined up to £400 for allowing this to happen. It is also illegal for a disabled person to sit in the parked car using privileged parking while the able-bodied driver is elsewhere. The Orange Badge Scheme is not operative at Heathrow or in certain London boroughs.

Normally a vehicle displaying an Orange Badge cannot be wheel-clamped. In some towns there are marked on-street 'disabled' spaces; access is allowed to town centres where no other vehicles are permitted; there are exemptions from tolls – for example, for bridges.

The Orange Badge Scheme is covered by the Disabled Persons (Badges for Motor Vehicles) Regulations 1982. Leaflets are available from the Department of Transport, from *Social Services Departments* or *DIALs*.

Story

Orange Badge

Therapy Weekly's gossip column, 'Ultrasound', recorded this infuriating item for those of us who battle unceasingly against the abuse of Orange Badges. A particularly cheeky fake Orange Badge was spotted on a Mini outside a West London recording studio. 'Disabled' it said, 'Deafened by the Funk'.

Osteopathy

This is a type of manual treatment for the structural and mechanical problems of the body. It deals with mechanical faults and pain in bones, joints, muscles, ligaments and other soft tissue. On an initial visit to an osteopath a full examination will be given and a case history taken. If necessary, an X-ray may be taken. At this first visit the patient will be told whether his condition will respond successfully to osteopathy, and if not, medical or surgical treatment may be recommended.

Osteopaths use their trained, highly-developed sense of touch to detect minute stresses within the structure of the body, and to release them gently. Rhythmical movements may be used to stretch contracted tissues to restore limb movement to full range. Head or facial pain may be helped with the application of gentle pressure to the head or neck.

Osteopathy is a treatment by manipulation but often special exercises are prescribed to be carried out at home. About half of the problems presented to osteopaths are concerned with back pain, and for this problem osteopathy is very good. Osteopaths have a lengthy training and are qualified by the **General Council and Register of Osteopaths** (O) from whom further information can be obtained.

The Outsiders Club

The Outsiders Club (O) is an organisation for people who are socially or physically handicapped, those who are lonely, and for people who find it difficult to form relationships. They issue a confidential membership list and a useful booklet giving practical ways to find new friends, and possibly romance. Members are encouraged to ask personal questions, by letter, telephone or in person, at one of the club's social functions.

Anyone over eighteen can join and there is no upper age

limit. About 50 per cent of the members are physically disabled. Some members offer help such as driving, emotional support and organising all kinds of activities. Most, but not all, of the social events are in London. There is a quarterly magazine and an up-dated mailing list, and those who are nervous about revealing their address in the membership list can use the club's forwarding service.

Oxygen

A surprising number of disabled people need, on a regular basis, a supply of oxygen for emergency use. A few years ago this meant living with one of those enormous oxygen cylinders not more than a couple of feet away, day and night, indoors and out. Since then we have seen neat portable cylinders which could be refilled at most hospitals, and some people are lucky enough to have expensive oxygen-making machines in their homes.

One lightweight cost-effective alternative is available from **Safelab Systems Ltd** (M). The OXYFIT weighs less than 1lb (0.5kg) and comes in a neat case together with two spare cartridges, each capable of providing up to 15 minutes of medical oxygen. The oxygen cylinders are disposable when empty and the whole outfit is small enough to fit into a medical bag – in fact it will go into a coat pocket. It will be very useful to *asthmatics*, people with *heart* conditions or anyone who needs an occasional 'top-up' of oxygen from time to time.

Contact **Safelab Systems Ltd** (M).

P

Pain

Pain is a dominating factor in the lives of many disabled and elderly people and by and large the NHS does not help too much. Many people suffer pain permanently, believing there is no answer, but any 'new' pain should be treated as a warning signal that something within the body has gone wrong, and advice should be sought immediately from the family doctor. It is unwise to disguise this warning with a pain-killing drug without dealing with the underlying cause. Pain is a subjective sensation which defies comparison between one person and another – one man's twinge may be another man's unbearable agony. Only the most severe pain causes observable signs such as sweating, incoherence, a cramped attitude or shock.

Pain is a secondary result of many physical disabilities which limit limb movement. A *wheelchair* rider seated for many hours may have cramp pains in the knee joints or in the back, especially if his chair is not set up correctly. *Arthritis* can cause severe and prolonged pain in almost any part of the body, as can torn muscles or ligaments. Headache and migraine can cause pain in the head, and chest pains can be the result of wind, *angina* or over-stretching the vital capacity of the heart or lungs. A doctor should always be called for sudden, severe, 'first-time' chest pains.

Pain is often referred from one part of the body to another so that the cause is in one place and the pain sensation is in another. For example, heart pain may be felt as a sensation in the tip of the shoulder. Physically disabled people may feel *'pressure sore'* pain in their bottom, heels or elbows.

The relief of chronic pain by electrical stimulation of the nervous system has a long history which goes back to Roman times, when the electric ray fish was used to alleviate *gout* pain and headaches. In 1745 Galvani used a Leyden jar as a means of producing a small electric charge for the same purpose. The Duchenne de Boulogne made the earliest known type of electric stimulator in 1830, and this was followed in the next year by Faraday's electro-magnetic generator which produced the first alternating current. Since then much has been written about the technique, but interest waned until relatively recently. Originally, electrical stimulation was used only for the functional stimulation of muscles, but around 1965 two things re-awakened interest in the technique: the first was a paper by Mellzack and Wall called *The Gate Theory of Pain*, which suggested that electrical stimulus could relieve pain; and the second was the appearance of the transistor which led to solid state electronics giving the first portable electrical stimulators.

In the 1980s we have seen increasing use of TENS – Transcutaneous Electronic Nerve Stimulation. This works in one of two ways – it can block the pain messages to the brain, or it can activate the body's natural pain killers. There are dozens of these TENS devices on the market, and such is the wide variety of size, shape, weight and price that any would-be purchaser should take expert advice before parting with his money.

In essence, a TENS stimulator is a small plastic box about the size of a cigarette packet with a couple of rubber contacts on the ends of thin wires. There is an on/off switch and a couple of small control knobs. The device is battery-operated and there is no electrical danger or side-effects, neither is it addictive. Often the box is provided with a clip so it can be worn on the belt or clipped in a pocket. The contacts are usually small circular rubber discs, which are placed on the skin, allowing the current pulse to reduce or eliminate the pain by blocking the ability of the sensory nerves to send pain messages to the brain. The best place for the contacts is determined by the user by trial and error, but most people would start by putting a contact either side of the pain location. All TENS machines are sold with detailed and illustrated instructions.

TENS machines range in price from £60 to £300. Any disabled or elderly person who thinks a stimulator would relieve their pain should either call in their community *physiotherapist* or ask their GP for a referral to the nearest pain clinic or hospital physiotherapy department. An assessment will be made and a stimulator lent for trial at home over a period of weeks. For some, stimulators have little effect, but without doubt TENS does relieve pain for many thousands of people. Most people buy their own stimulator and manufacturers will supply the device on loan prior to purchase. This is essentially a user-operated technique and there are so many variables that it requires a lot of time and patience to achieve the best result. There are many possible locations for the electrodes and these are closely related to the points used by acupuncturists. There is a variety of electrodes and, depending on the price of the stimulator, controls for pulse amplitude, pulse width, pulse rate and maybe more than one channel.

An attractive feature of TENS is that if it does no good at least it does no harm, so there is every good reason to try it. The worst that can happen is a mild burn from a dry electrode, and a warm sensation should give adequate warning. Some stimulators provide several different types of electrode, and all give clear instructions.

The average hospital physiotherapy department will give a short assessment and training course and if, as in 90 per cent of cases, the treatment appears to be effective, they will lend the patient a stimulator on trial for several weeks. At the end of this time they will advise on the most suitable machine and where it can be purchased. The NHS does not provide machines free, but some *Social Services Departments* will help, and so do some hospital Leagues of Friends. Another possible source is the **Joan Seeley Pain Relief Memorial Trust** (O).

The TENS system has been used successfully for all forms of *arthritic* and rheumatic pains, for low *back pains*, for phantom stump pains in amputees, birth pains, *sciatica*, headaches and cramp. American research has shown a 60 per cent success rate for the relief of low back pain. A stimulator should not be used except under the general supervision of a medical adviser, and there are a few types of patient who should not use a stimulator at all – for example, people who use heart pacemakers. For everybody, too, there are certain positions on the body where the electrodes should not be placed. Most people will find a simple and relatively in-expensive model satisfactory. The stimulator is powered by a PP 3 dry battery, and it is wise to buy a couple of recharge-able batteries and a charger. The contacts are small rubber pads used in pairs; most machines have one pair, but it may pay to look for a machine with two pairs, particularly where two limbs are involved. A special gel is available to give good electrical contact with the skin, and failure to use this may result in mild burns or a lack of stimulation. The gel is not obtainable on prescription and it is sold by relatively few pharmacists. The leads from the machine to the electrodes are available in different lengths.

Some pain clinics keep in permanent contact with patients and supply gel, electrodes, and maintain equipment, even though the user has to make the initial purchase. Most manufacturers require a doctor's note from any purchaser and VAT is not payable if the right declaration is signed.

Some people obtain adequate pain relief by using the stimulator for an hour a day; others use it permanently; others 'cure' their pain and leave off using the machine for weeks. Most people find that not only does the stimulator stop pain when it is in use, but also that the pain does not return for anything up to twelve hours afterwards. It must be said that the user of TENS needs considerable patience to get the best out of it. It does take time to find the right contact points (which to start with should be marked with an indelible pencil). For example, a patient with low back pain may need to place one electrode on his back and the other on his leg.

For information on TENS machines and to obtain cata-logues write to **Spembly Ltd** (M), **Dow Corning Wright** (M), **Eurocraft** (M) or **Neen Pain Management Systems** (M).

'Intractable pain' is defined as 'that which is unrelieved for 30 days or more'. Pain clinics were started around 17 years ago, but they have been recognised by the NHS for only about seven years, and they are not very well known to the general public. You cannot take your aching back straight into a pain clinic – you must be referred by a GP or a consultant. There are now about 150 pain clinics in Britain and your local *DIAL* or *Community Health Council* will tell you where your nearest clinic is. Patients are divided into two groups – those with a normal life expectancy and those with less than a year or so to live. The first group may be treated with analgesic drugs, *acupuncture*, psychotherapy, TENS, hypnotherapy, neurosurgery, *relaxation*, yoga or a combination of these. The second group have life-threatening ailments – severe organic disease, *cancer*, MS and similar illnesses. For these the relief of pain may involve more drastic methods, possibly the destruction of nerves or even the replacement of spinal fluid with water. Information may be obtained from the **Intractible Pain Society of Great Britain** (O) or from the **Pain Relief Foundation** (O).

It is said that 60 per cent of depressed people are in pain; 40 per cent of all people in pain are depressed. The emotional stress arising from this can have a drastic effect upon the family of the person suffering permanent pain.

Parkinson's Disease

This is a condition which has three main effects – tremor, stiffness of the muscles and difficulty of movement. These are distressing symptoms which may occur alone or in combination. Tremor is the dominant characteristic, and this can occur in any part of the body, including the face. Usually only one part of the body is affected, but this is an embarrassing handicap giving rise to anxiety which, in turn, makes the tremor worse. Stiffness of the muscles produces an expressionless face, immobile posture, and poor control of any function requiring precise manipulation. The typical Parkinsonian has difficulty with dressing, shaving, feeding, speech, balance and walking. They can be rooted to the spot and have difficulty with turning around. Dribbling is common and speech may be very quiet and slurred.

In isolation Parkinson's Disease does not diminish the intelligence, so the sufferer is well aware of his condition. This makes it very frustrating and this should be understood by those around him who must refrain from treating him as though he lacks understanding.

Parkinson's Disease is the result of a failure of a small group of cells in the brain, due to the reduction in the production of certain chemicals. The condition is irreversible but it can in some cases be improved with drugs. Normally the disease never goes away but the progression is very slow so, as new handicaps arise, there is time for adjustment for both the individual and his family. Some of the symptoms can be reduced with drugs, but a close watch must be kept for adverse side-effects. Parkinson's Disease is incurable but it is manageable and there is good reason to believe progress in treatments will accelerate.

Considerable benefit comes from a positive attitude to self-help in understanding the nature of the disease, in the acquisition of suitable equipment in the home, and in the arrangement of your daily life style. Seek the advice of your domiciliary *occupational therapist*, Health Visitor or local **DIAL** (O) about equipment. Difficulty with standing can be over-come with an electric riser armchair and with support rails around the toilet. Suitable clothing helps problems with dressing and the toilet, and information is available from the **DLF** (O). It is important to use one of the many aids to walking, as Parkinsonians develop the dangerous habit of lurching from one piece of furniture to another. Difficulty with *drinking* can be overcome by using a straw. Good general health should be maintained and weight should be monitored – exercise is good but should not be taken to the point of fatigue. Constipation needs a doctor's advice.

Parkinsonians can be a great strain on their families, but they do need to be treated as normal people and given assistance only when they ask for it. In all things they will be slow and it is necessary to exercise much patience, particu-larly at meal times. They will tend to be withdrawn and want to 'just sit', but they should be coaxed into going out to maintain social contacts. Much help and practical advice is available from the **Parkinson's Disease Society** (O) which publishes a useful range of leaflets and a regular newsletter. There are local branches in most towns.

Story

Too Bad

The eminent consultant was feeling quite pleased with the progress of a lady with Parkinson's Disease, having spent a considerable amount of time on getting her medication balanced properly. One day she asked 'Do you mind if I ask you a personal question? Do you do brain surgery?' He replied that he did not, and she said, very kindly, 'Well, don't feel too bad about it – if you cannot do something it is much better to admit it and just get on with your life.'

(Professor D L McLellan, Southampton University.)

PHAB

The **PHAB** (O) concept started in 1957 when the National Association of Youth Clubs, which for some time had assisted individual disabled members, ran a residential course for equal numbers of physically handicapped and able-bodied young people (hence the name). During that week of shared sports, hobbies and social events, the barriers of fear, ignorance and embarrassment were systematically identified and broken down. A situation had been created in which, without artificial means, with only unwritten rules, disabled and able-bodied young people could work, play and be entirely normal together. The next fifteen years saw the development of these ideas with more combined courses and holidays each year. Clubs were established with joint membership of physically handicapped and able-bodied youngsters, and in 1974 PHAB was set up as an independent charitable trust. It

218

retained its links with the youth clubs, and now also works in close association with the *Scouts* and Guides, and the Duke of Edinburgh Award Scheme.

Every PHAB club is independent, self-financed and responds to the needs of its particular area. The club is both sustained by the national organisation and contributes to it. There is an excellent quarterly magazine, and for those setting up a new PHAB club a very comprehensive 'Starta-kit'. There is even a training course leading to a Royal Society of Arts qualification.

The national body also runs a wide range of over 50 holidays a year, both at home and abroad, and has a nationally-negotiated comprehensive insurance scheme.

PHAB is unique among disabled organisations in having a 'Working Party on Spirituality' to consider the problems of the disabled person in relation to any religion – Christian or otherwise.

PHAB continues to expand with the planned objective of 1,000 clubs by the year 2000. There are no bounds of age or culture and your friendly PHAB club needs you, your time, your money, or all three. Write to **PHAB** (O).

Phobias

The word 'phobia' comes from a Greek word meaning 'fear'. In the UK there are around 4 million people with phobias.

The great majority are only mildly affected, or find it easy to arrange a lifestyle which avoids the relevant anxiety situation. Acrophobics fear heights – it is easy to avoid standing on cliff edges, but less easy to move out of a tower block. Many mild phobias, such as a fear of birds, snakes or mice, are life-long conditions which can be 'lived around'. Of the 120,000 people with severe phobias, the majority receive no treatment, largely because they do not ask for it, thinking it is an untreatable condition.

Fear in a situation of real or imagined danger is a normal human reaction often accompanied by physical symptoms. The pulse increases, the heart beats faster, breathing speeds up, sweating starts, hairs rise on the back of the neck, the palms moisten – these are normal anticipatory reactions of a body preparing for fight or flight. However, in a phobic person these physical symptoms can occur when no real danger is present, and a cycle of fear can be set up so the person becomes 'afraid of fear'.

There are over 375 classified phobias and they are more prevalent than most doctors realise. Many of these phobias may affect a person only slightly and are under control, but in other instances the phobia becomes a real handicap, affecting not only the sufferer but also the immediate family. Many phobic sufferers keep their fears secret because they are afraid of being laughed at, and a lack of understanding on the part of relatives and friends increases the misery of phobic persons. No matter how absurd these fears may appear to the non-afflicted, the terror of the sufferer is genuine.

There are three main groups of phobias:

- Fears of specific objects such as dogs, cats, mice, snakes or birds.
- Fears of situations, such as going outdoors, enclosed spaces, flying, heights, school or places of employment.
- Fears of specific illnesses, such as cancer or AIDS, or of hospitals or death.

Fear of specific objects can often be traced to a frightening experience in childhood. Fear of illness or death often follows such events happening to friends or relatives. It is not always necessary to find the cause for a phobic condition, but it is possible to set up a programme to reduce the symptoms gradually.

Agoraphobia is the name given to a fear of going out. In severe cases the individual may be confined to his or her house for many years, and others will be afraid even to go out into their own garden. Agoraphobia is by far the most serious and handicapping of the phobic illnesses and probably represents, in its various forms, over 50 per cent of all clinical presentations of primary phobic neurosis. The onset of agoraphobia is almost imperceptible, starting perhaps with sandwiches in the office because of a vague feeling of discomfort in the canteen. In the final stage employment has to be given up and self-imprisonment in the home becomes a way of life. It is characteristic of agoraphobics that they continuously limit their range of action by avoiding the situations that cause anxiety.

Typically agoraphobic people suffer with inexplicable panic attacks which are accompanied with hot and cold sweats, rapid breathing, palpitations and a feeling of faintness. In many cases, it appears to be the memory of such attacks that causes the sufferer to fear going out alone, in case they are overcome by these symptoms again with no one to help them. Probably the most important factor is the reaction of the family. It is necessary to strike a balance between 'Pull yourself together' and over-protectiveness. Some people find yoga or other relaxation techniques a help.

The **Phobics Society** (O) was founded in 1970 by Katherine Fisher who had suffered with agoraphobia for twenty years. The Society is a non-profit-making registered charity manned by ex-phobics, working very closely with all the research agencies and treatment units in the UK. The society has local branches throughout the country whose members will give tangible help, advice and information. Practical help is given wherever possible, and self-help papers are sent to each member on joining.

Physiotherapy

One of the most important of the remedial therapists serving disabled and elderly people is the physiotherapist, sometimes known in America and other countries as a 'physical therapist'. The physiotherapist treats injury and disease by improving and assisting the natural healing mechanisms of the body, with the ultimate objective of restoration to full active life.

There are 23,000 chartered physiotherapists in the UK of which about half work in the *NHS* and around 2,000 are in private practice. The majority of physiotherapists (95 per cent), are women. The term 'physiotherapist' is not a protected title and there are people practising physiotherapy who do not have the same training, knowledge and experience as a Chartered Physiotherapist. If private physiotherapy treatment is needed, it is important to use only a Chartered Physiotherapist who will have the letters MCSP (Member Chartered Society of Physiotherapists) or SRP (State

Registered Physiotherapist) after his or her name. All chartered physiotherapists have spent a minimum of three years in full-time study and hold a diploma or degree.

Physiotherapists work in hospitals, rehabilitation centres, the community, schools, industry, sport and in private practice.

In hospitals, physiotherapists work on the wards (including intensive care units) with breathing and mobility exercises; in the remedial gymnasium on general rehabilitation after major surgery, strokes, viral attack and paralysing accidents and diseases; in the paediatric department treating children with *cerebral palsy*, *cystic fibrosis*, *muscular dystrophy*, *spina bifida* or *asthma*; in the out-patients' department working on recovery from hip operations, *back pain*, neck and shoulder problems and sports injuries.

In the community, physiotherapists may work from hospitals, health centres or clinics. Treatment and advice is

223

given in the patient's home and often a schedule of exercise is given for him to do daily – perhaps under the supervision of the caring relative. Some of the larger nursing homes have a physiotherapist on the staff.

Physiotherapists work in both special and mainstream schools with teachers, nurses and care attendants, looking after handicapped children and enabling them to gain the maximum benefit from their education. They also help less severely handicapped children, such as those with asthma, to enjoy normal sporting activities.

In industry, physiotherapists play an important part in advising shop-floor workers how to avoid injury, by teaching correct lifting and handling techniques, and recommending the right seating and equipment for office staff. The physiotherapist in a private practice will function both from his or her own premises and in patients' homes.

Physiotherapists are to be found caring for the protagonists in many *sports*. Most professional football teams have a full-time staff physiotherapist; in other sports they may be employed just for particular events, or be on call for high-flying athletes. In sport the physiotherapist has a dual role – to maximise individual performance and to treat injuries.

In the early days physiotherapists were mainly concerned with rehabilitation and the treatment of acute 'curable' conditions. Nowadays there is a certain amount of 'maintenance' treatment for severely physically disabled and elderly people. Physiotherapists help elderly people regain and maintain their independence, in teaching strengthening exercises and helping with stairs, walking and general mobility exercises. This is also extremely important for the *wheelchair* rider – to avoid problems with legs, circulation, bowels, bladder, heart and lungs, and general health.

There is an acute shortage of physiotherapists but every physically disabled or elderly person will probably need preventive physiotherapy from time to time. Many GPs can now refer you directly to a Chartered Physiotherapist at your local NHS hospital or to a community physiotherapist who can treat you at home. For information write to the **Chartered Society of Physiotherapists** (O).

Story

Instant Recognition

Paul, a comprehensive school teacher, broke his back in an accident and, after a long spell in hospital, he found himself in the rehabilitation centre following an intensive daily routine of physiotherapy. Paul was completely paralysed – unable to walk or even stand – in fact, his body was as floppy as a rag doll's.

Each morning Paul was taken from his ward in his wheelchair to the hydropool. There, in the changing room three attendants would remove his pyjamas, and put on his bathing trunks. After being wheeled to the hydropool, he was lowered into the warm water with a hoist. Half an hour later, he would be lifted out of the pool and, back in the changing room, two attendants would hold him up by the armpits while the third would remove his trunks. He was showered, dried, and wheeled back to the ward.

One morning one of the changing-room ladies was absent when, soaking wet, Paul was returned to the changing room. The other two tried to hold him up and, at the same time, bend down to remove his trunks but each time he collapsed. So they called the first person to pass the door in to help. This was Mavis, who had just finished her training as an occupational therapist. Mavis, quite used to seeing human bodies, did not hesitate. She bent down in front of Paul, held up by the attendants, and peeled down his wet trunks. Then she blushed crimson, looked up and said 'Hello Sir'.

The last time Mavis had seen Paul was three years before when she was a sixth-form student in his 'A' level biology class.

Plumbing

Plumbing Services for the Disabled Community is a nation-wide service providing specialists in plumbing, central heating, water services, special *toilets*, showers and *baths*. They will also do surveys, provide drawings and supervise work. Contact on 01 468 7767 or 01 859 4186.

Poliomyelitis

There are around 10,000 people in Britain disabled with polio, although vaccination has now almost eliminated the disease from Europe. Polio, which used to be called 'infantile paralysis', is caused by a virus entering the body through the nose or mouth, which attacks the motor nerves and causes some level of paralysis. The degree of severity varies between weakness in the extremities, such as the fingers, to total tetraplegia and possibly the need for special equipment to help breathing. Many people with polio live permanently on crutches or in wheelchairs.

Polio does not affect intellectual capacity and the majority of polio people go through mainstream education and enter normal employment. Contact **British Polio Fellowship** (O).

The Portage Scheme

This is a system of educating handicapped children under the age of five, which was introduced into this country by Dr Albert Kushlick, who studied its working pattern in the town of Portage in America. There are now over 100 Portage schemes operating in Britain. Each scheme varies slightly in its approach.

The Portage Scheme is available to the parents of children under five who are showing signs of being a year or more behind what would be considered to be normal development. Any mother who is worried about the progress of her child may contact the **National Portage Association** (O) direct or through a health visitor, doctor or social worker.

Volunteers, mostly from associated professional backgrounds, are trained on a series of courses, and in each area overall supervision is exercised by educational psychologists. Each home volunteer visits on a regular basis, often weekly, normally for one hour. At the first visit a check-list is made summarising the child's ability level, and this is used to monitor subsequent progress. This check-list, which is in a standard format used all over the UK, includes infant stimulation, socialisation, language, self-help, motor development and cognitive development. In partnership with the parent, a card-index system is devised giving problems and suggestions for their solution.

The Portage Scheme is a well-tried positive method enabling parents to help their child; it can be rewarding for both and the regular visits of the volunteer keep things moving. Usually each family is set one or more tasks, depending on progress, and each task is broken down into achievable steps. To the child the practice is playtime and it takes place in the relaxed environment of his own home. This is undoubtedly a successful method of educating young handicapped children, but it does demand a high level of motivation from the parents.

Possum Trust

The main purpose of the Possum Trust is to provide equipment on loan to disabled people for a specified period, normally between one and five years. Existing equipment is being improved and new equipment constantly appears, so it is necessary to have a loan system to ensure that no old or obsolete equipment remains with a disabled person, and to give them the use of the most up-to-date items available.

Each disabled applicant is visited by a 'Possum Assessor' who advises on the equipment available, and where severe physical handicap presents problems with coping with a typewriter-type keyboard, other input methods are suggested. If, after a period of use, the input system provided proves to be unsatisfactory, it will be changed.

The Trust will meet half the cost of the loan of any equipment and it may well be that the local District Health Authority or *Social Services* will contribute the other 50 per cent to any disabled person who is in need of the equipment but cannot obtain it under the present *NHS* rules. Should the original user cease to need the equipment, it can then be transferred to another suitable applicant nominated by the District Health Authority for the unexpired portion of the loan period.

If no help is forthcoming from statutory sources, then assistance will be given to contact local charities such as the Lions, Round Table, Rotary Club and so on, and the local *DIAL* will normally help too. For more information write to Ken Winter, Administrator, **Possum Trust** (O).

Possum Users Association

Now known as SEQUAL; *see* under 'S'.

Prader-Willi Syndrome

The Prader-Willi Syndrome is a complex medical condition that affects boys and girls alike and continues to affect them throughout their lives. People with this syndrome have multiple handicaps, including an uncontrollable appetite, poor muscle tone and balance, emotional instability and maybe some learning difficulties. People are born with this condition and there is no known cure. Usually only one child in a family is affected.

The **Prader-Willi Syndrome Association** (O), which is a registered charity, provides support for parents and care-givers, promotes knowledge and awareness among caring medical professionals as well as the general public, and seeks to improve the quality of life of Prader-Willi people.

The charity is promoting research into the provision of special residential accommodation. Because of the obsessive food-seeking habits of the sufferers, many normal disabled placements are unsuitable.

For more information write to the **Prader-Willi Syndrome Association** (O).

Pressure Sores

A pressure sore is a skinless, open, bloody wound in which the tissues have died. It is likely to increase in size and it is highly susceptible to infection. A pressure sore the size of a 10p piece, given the best treatment available, can take six to eight weeks to heal, and a few people have been known to die from pressure sores. An otherwise healthy person can develop a severe penetrating pressure sore within 30 minutes, if they remain completely immobile seated on a hard surface. Of all the secondary medical problems to which a physically disabled person may be prone, pressure sores are the most expensive in cost, time and personal misery, and without doubt 'an ounce of prevention is worth a pound of cure'.

Pressure sores are caused by an interference with the blood circulation from a source close to the surface of the skin. Reduction or termination of the blood supply results in the death of the flesh. The most common causes of pressure sores are pressure and shear forces. Pressure is a force exerted on the skin more or less directly inwards and is caused by the force of gravity acting on the body; it is aggravated by lack of movement and poor support surfaces. This force stops the movement of the blood.

A shear force acts along the surface of the skin; it is a 'tearing' force which actually breaks down the flesh mechanically. Shearing forces act on the buttocks when a person sitting up slowly slides down the bed; when a person slumps in an armchair; when a paraplegic makes a sliding transfer from *wheelchair* to bed or car seat. Often pressure and shear will occur simultaneously at the same place.

Many physically disabled people spend the greater part of their time seated in a chair or wheelchair, or lying in bed. It is the weight-bearing parts of the body which are at risk – the buttocks, hips, elbows, heels, shoulders, and sometimes the back of the head. The smaller the weight-bearing point the higher will be the pressure. Many support surfaces – seats, *toilets*, and beds – are flat, but human bodies are so designed that most of their outer surface is curved. If you put a curved surface on a flat one then the area of contact is very small. If you can make the bearing surface conform to the shape of the contact part of the human body, the support area will be increased and the pressure reduced. Many of the anti-pressure sore cushions and bed mattresses go a long way to achieving this aim. Water is also a highly conformable medium giving the largest support area possible, and this is why high-risk pressure sore patients are nursed in hospital on water-beds.

At greatest risk from pressure sores are those people who are relatively immobile – elderly people who are unable or unwilling to move much, those who have been ill for a long time, and physically disabled people who are partly or completely paralysed. Some of the last group may be at higher risk through loss of sensory nerves; this may mean they feel no pain at the point where the tissue damage is imminent, so they do nothing to relieve it. For such people there are audible sensory alarms, such as those made by **Talley Medical Equipment Ltd** (M).

So how can the *wheelchair* rider avoid pressure sores? The

price of prevention is constant vigilence, the right equipment, good hygiene, exercise and sensible diet. Movement is essential – little and often. Reaching for a cup of tea will relieve the pressure on your bottom for ten minutes; if you type or use a sewing machine for a couple of hours, the movements you make will keep the pressure points changing. Every wheelchair jockey should lift his bottom clear of the cushion for fifteen seconds every quarter of an hour. Exercise is essential partly to change the pressure points and partly to stimulate the circulation.

There are scores of makes of wheelchair cushions and no one cushion is suitable for every disabled person or even the same person all the time. Wheelchair cushions may be filled with foam rubber, air, water, gel, or polystyrene balls. **Spenco** (M) Silicore cushions and mattresses are excellent, and, for those who can use them, RoHo cushions from **Raymar** (M) are probably the neareast thing to floating on water. Sheepskin is good for chairs and beds and **Medipost**

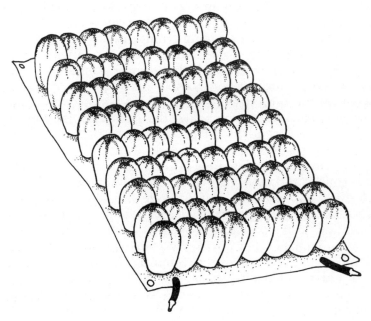

Ro-Ho cushion.

(M) supply an excellent Mullipel wheelchair set, comprising seat and back cushions and covers for the arms. Mullipel is a very good machine-washable artificial fleece which comes in a variety of attractive patterns. For many people the standard 3in (7.5cm) black foam-filled cushion is satisfactory, but do remember they get hard fairly quickly and the Disablement Services Centre will always replace it, even within a year. An excellent book is *Choosing the Best Wheelchair Cushion* by Peggy Jay published by **RADAR** (O).

Whilst pressure and shear are the two main causes of pressure sores, there are a number of contributory factors. Breakdown of tissue (flesh) is less likely to occur in a person who, although disabled, enjoys good health; we are what we eat and healthy flesh is less prone to pressure sores. As the most likely place for pressure sores is your bottom, a high level of personal cleanliness and social care is essential. For those unable to cleanse themselves after a bowel action the answer is a **Clos-o-Mat** (M) electric toilet with its 'wash and blow dry' system. A hot sweaty area is more likely to generate pressure sores than a cool, clean skin, so avoid tight pants and sit or lie on something which gives good ventilation. Look hard at your sleeping arrangements. Many people use ripple mattresses (**Talley** (M) or **Pegasus Airwave** (M)), which have tubes or cells which alternately inflate and deflate. Care of support surfaces is essential. Very skinny people are more prone to pressure sores because the boney protuberances are not far below the skin. People who are overweight will tend to get pressure sores because of the increased pressure. Use all the early warnings at your disposal; if your rear hurts, get off it; your care-giver should make a night and morning inspection of your buttocks, heels and elbows. Red marks may indicate the sites of incipient sores. For some, **Dermalux** (M) cream helps. Pressure sore prevention is a complicated business with thousands of products available. For advice try your nearest *DIAL*, write to **DLF** (O) or get a leaflet from **Spenco** (M) or from Alington Ward, Odstock Hospital, Salisbury, Wilts.

The avoidance of pressure sores is a 24-hour, seven-day business. Beware of relaxing your vigilance on the odd occasion. If you go to a football match or the theatre, take your cushion with you. If you make a long journey by car or coach, sit on a sheepskin and try to lie on your side every couple of hours to get the blood flowing through the pressure points of your bottom. If your girlfriend says 'Your place or mine?', take your Spenco mattress with you.

Protected Service Scheme

See under British Telecom.

Q

Queen Elizabeth's Foundation for the Disabled

This is a well-established voluntary organisation which provides a range of facilities for disabled men, women and young people from the age of 16 upwards, from all parts of the UK. Provision is made for assessment, vocational training and education, sheltered employment, improvement of personal mobility, holidays and convalescence.

Queen Elizabeth's Training College offers 194 places for residential training in technical, clerical and practical courses for disabled people of all ages above 16. All disabilities except blindness are accepted. There being no academic terms, students are admitted throughout the year and much of the tuition is given on a tutorial basis. Most courses are directed towards recognised qualifications, and training fees and personal allowances are paid by the Manpower Services Commission. Contact Queen Elizabeth's College, Leatherhead Court, Leatherhead, Surrey KT22 0BN.

Banstead Place is a residential centre giving assessment and continuing education for 35 school leavers. Each student follows a programme tailored to his needs. The staff includes teachers, nurses, care assistants, *physiotherapists*, *OTs*, and speech therapists. Write to Banstead Place, Park Road, Banstead, Surrey SM7 3EE.

Banstead Place Mobility Centre (O) covers all aspects of outdoor mobility.

Dorincourt is a workshop providing industrial employment for disabled people, both resident and non-resident. There is a purpose-built hostel and an Arts Centre. Applicants must be capable of working a normal week in a sheltered workshop. There are four sections – ceramics, printing in letterpress and litho, transfer design and packing and shrink-wrapping. Write to Dorincourt, Oaklawn Road, Leatherhead, Surrey KT22 0BT.

Lulworth Court provides holidays and convalescence for severely paralysed men and women, including those who are incontinent. The lower age limit is 16 and full nursing is available so guests can be unaccompanied. Outings and entertainment are arranged. Write to Lulworth Court, Chalkwell Esplanade, Westcliff-on-Sea, Essex SS0 8JQ.

Quest Educational Designs

QED (M) specialises in a broad-based range of communication aids designed for both children and adults with special needs. These cover in particular those with severe physical handicap and people who are unable to speak, or who suffer from speech impairment.

In recent years, new aids have been developed and others modified in the light of changing needs of disabled people, and this on-going work embraces important and valuable feedback from both users and therapists.

The QED range of communication aids is designed for practicality and ease of use and often further refinements can be applied to suit the particular needs of the user.

QED also distributes a wide range of products that are manufactured by other companies in the field of communication, and they are the sole UK distributor for Zygo Industries Inc., of Portland USA. Zygo make a very refined, highly-adjustable head pointer. Also supplied are computer products, including the BBC Master from Acorn, monitors from Microvitec, printers from Star, and Concept keyboards.

Other aids from QED include page turners, 'Scrolly' reading aids, a wide range of alarms and bleepers, a visuo-motor scanner to help with hand and arm control, rotary indicators, keyboard emulators, a wide range of input switches, the Vocaid, Orovox and Talking Notebook speech synthesizers, and the QED Memowriter communicator.

If your handicap problem has a micro-chip-based solution you would be well advised to contact QED who will always quote for one-off systems.

R

RADAR

The **Royal Association for Disability and Rehabilitation** (O) was founded in 1979, and it is the principal national umbrella organisation looking after the interests of disabled people in Britain. It is essentially the association of national associations. A staff of over 60 in the London headquarters is divided broadly into the following departments: Access and Mobility, Education, Employment, Housing, Welfare, Aids and Rehabilitation, Holidays, and Information. Problems may be put to any of these departments by telephone or letter.

RADAR publishes many leaflets and books as well as a monthly bulletin which gives details of new legislation, housing, holidays, aids and equipment and a quarterly magazine called *Contact*. RADAR has access to all relevant government departments, it represents the disability case in Parliament and provides secretarial services to the All-Party Disablement Committee. It is a member of Rehabilitation International and plays an extensive role in conferences and seminars abroad. Regional officers provide support to local voluntary associations.

Rail Travel

Most stations are accessible but some local stations may be unmanned, so, unless you have personal knowledge of a local station, it pays to travel only between main-line stations. For someone confined to a wheelchair it is usually essential to travel with a friend. Many of the larger stations have special car parking spaces reserved for disabled people. Main-line stations have unisex disabled toilets fully accessible to wheelchairs, and many of these are fitted with *National Key Scheme* locks. Bigger stations have portable ramps to help wheelchair riders to get on board the train, and wheelchairs for slow-walking ambulant disabled people. Booking office windows are fitted with induction loops for hearing aid users. Purple signs indicate special facilities for disabled people.

InterCity trains have wide doors, grab rails and, by removing a seat, provision for wheelchair-bound passengers to travel within the passenger saloons – this facility is available only if it is booked in advance. On some trains there is provision for people who can transfer from their wheelchair on to a train seat.

The latest local and suburban trains have wide, power-operated doors, low floors and wheelchair-bound passengers travel within the saloon. On all older trains wheelchair riders have to travel in the guard's van and should have a friend with them, although there will be no seating for that person.

A few trains have toilets adapted for wheelchairs. On long trips it is possible to break the journey at a station with toilet facilities and continue by the next train.

People travelling in their own wheelchairs are charged half fare for day return (this applies also to a friend), and there is one-third off standard fares. Permanently severely disabled people can buy a Disabled Person's Railcard for £12, giving reductions on most tickets; details are in the leaflet *Disabled Person's Railcard* available in main post offices. Eligibility includes blindness, Attendance or Mobility Allowance, SDA, Industrial or War Disablement Pensions or registered deaf. Wheelchairs and guide dogs travel free.

People confined to wheelchairs cannot travel on sleeper services but these are quite convenient for ambulant disabled people. Compartments are convertible for twin or single berth use, and communicating doors between pairs of compartments enable care-givers to travel with their charges. Guide dogs can travel in a single compartment with a blind person.

Any *DIAL* will help you with your travel plans and British Rail has much to offer the disabled traveller, but it is essential to book well in advance and advise them of all your needs. Look for their leaflet *British Rail and Disabled Travellers*.

Rare Disabilities

There is much benefit to be gained from making contact with someone with a similar disability to your own, and the usual method is to join the appropriate voluntary association. However, there are many very rare disabilities for which it is difficult to know whether an organisation exists. A solution is provided by **Share-a-Care** (O) which is a scheme which aims to put such people in touch with each other.

Reader's Digest

The *Reader's Digest* is available on standard cassette for blind, visually handicapped and physically disabled people. A selection from the magazine – three hours' listening – is recorded on two cassettes which can be played on any standard tape player or recorder. In 1987 a year's subscription was £5.00. Contact Talking Newspaper Association, 68a High Street, Heathfield, East Sussex TN21 8JB (04352 6102).

Rehabilitation International

This body, based in New York, is the recognised world authority on disability and is at the top end of the 'chain of command' in the world of disability.

At the lower end is the local 'disabled' association. This brings together people who have the same disability – *Multiple Sclerosis, epilepsy,* and so on – or people with the same interest – sport or art, perhaps – or groups seeking political action to improve things for disabled people, such as **DIG** (O) or **BCODP** (O). That local association may be a member of a town or county umbrella group or federation of local organisations. Each 'disabled' association will be a part of a national association. These national associations will be in membership with the **Royal Association for Disability and Rehabilitation** (O) (RADAR). RADAR is the top British organisation and it is a member of Rehabilitation International.

REMAP

Within the general guidance of **RADAR** (O), Rehabilitation Engineering Movement Advisory Panels use the voluntary services of engineers, doctors, occupational therapists, model makers and workers in plastic, metal and wood. The group's original objective was to restore to physically disabled people the basic mobility to live a normal life, but nowadays a REMAP will design and make any one-off device to solve the particular need of a disabled person. Often the device may be the result of the collaboration of several people, each an expert in his own field. There is a REMAP in most towns and they are to be found in the local telephone book. REMAP members give their time without charge, and if there is a cost in the materials used this can usually be recovered from *Social Services*.

Remote Work Units

A Remote Work Unit may be defined as an employer with a disabled worker who is doing a home-based job using a microcomputer provided (free) by the Department of Trade and Industry. Falling costs of computers, coupled with the rising costs of office space and travel to work, have made the system increasingly attractive to employers. For the severely physically disabled person it offers genuine gainful employment resulting in renewed self-esteem, which for many is a passport to better health. For someone with a disability like *Multiple Sclerosis*, involving unpredictable 'ups and downs' in well-being, the worker can arrange his tasks to suit. *Home-based employment* eliminates travel, which for the disabled person can be time-consuming, expensive and tiring. Usually people who work at home have a higher productivity level because there are few of the distractions found in a normal work-place. Against this must be set the lack of social contact, and the need for a high level of motivation due to the absence of immediate supervision.

Now in its fifth year, a recent review of the scheme showed that the most common disabilities were spinal injury (36 per cent) and Multiple Sclerosis (23 per cent) and about three-quarters of the workers were in wheelchairs. The majority were registered disabled and had some level of academic achievement – some had degrees and most had some typing skills. Three-quarters of the employers rated their home-based disabled workers' output as well above the average of normal employees, and the home-based workers also had a lower sickness record. Most of the work is sent to the employee in hard copy and in half the cases the distance is over five miles. (Two workers I know are coping well, although they are located over 100 miles from their employers.) The jobs cover a wide range of skills, including data manipulation, journalism, accountancy, tachograph analysis, tax consultancy and stock control. Word processing figures high on the list. In a few cases modems are used to provide workers with direct telephone-based data links with their employers.

The Department of Trade and Industry and the European Social Fund have jointly spent over one million pounds on computer-based work units and they have set up over 100 handicapped people in paid home-based jobs with real prospects. For more information write to **Department of Trade and Industry, Information Technology Division** (O) or **IT World Ltd** (M).

Remploy

Remploy was established in 1946 as a government-subsidised company to provide sheltered employment for disabled people, in accordance with Section 15 of the 1944 Disabled Persons (Employment) Act.

Disabled people seeking work in a Remploy factory must be registered as disabled with their local Jobcentre (green card). The DRO (Disablement Resettlement Officer) can send suitable applicants to their nearest Remploy factory for initial assessment. A three-month trial period is followed by assessment for the final job.

Whilst the majority of employees in a Remploy factory are disabled, it is a normal industrial environment with shop-floor disciplines, production targets, product design and levels of management. Jobs are provided for employees of all ages and for the widest range of skills, education and abilities, whilst at the same time involving the whole range of disabilities. Training facilities are excellent and disabled people may climb the promotion ladder right up to management. Many handicapped people spend their entire working lives with Remploy. All factories provide good facilities for sports and social activities and these are recorded in the Remploy newspaper.

Employing over 9,000 disabled people, Remploy provides real work for more disabled people than any other organisation in Britain. The thirteen trading divisions are involved with three main trading groups – furniture, packing and assembly, and leather and textile products. They make everything from fine chairs for royal occasions to wheelchairs. Remploy is the largest supplier of uniforms for the Armed Forces.

The company sponsors sheltered placement schemes in other companies enabling teams of disabled workers to work alongside able-bodied employees. The teams are employed by Remploy and the host company pays only for actual work done. Remploy also operates a number of home-based jobs for disabled people who are house-bound. The factory is responsible for the delivery and collection of the work.

Residential Care

There are many types of residential care homes, ranging from enormous institutions with scores of beds, to converted private houses catering for three residents or less. Some have age limitations; some are for children, and some for people with a specific disability; some you can enter as a young or middle-aged person and stay until you die; and some are for people with a particular work background – railway homes, homes for ex-servicemen, and members of certain other trades or professions. Regrettably there are still many disabled people permanently in hospital because there is nowhere else to put them.

The law relating to residential homes is complex, wide-ranging and some of it goes back a long time. Some or all of the following legislation applies: the National Assistance Act 1948, the National Assistance (Conduct of Homes) Act 1962, the Health Services and Public Health Act 1968, the Nursing Homes Act 1975, the National Health Service Act 1977, the Residential Homes Act 1980 and current fire regulations. Theoretically, any disabled or elderly person unable to cope (or whose *caring relatives* are unable to cope) should be offered a choice of home and their wishes respected.

A nursing home is any premises used for providing nursing for people suffering from any sickness, injury or infirmity. Such homes must be registered by the District Health Authority.

Residential homes, whether provided by the local authority, private individuals or voluntary associations, are registered by *Social Services*. Most of this comes under the 1948 Act and is known as 'Part III Accommodation'. There are considerable variations in the quality of provision, from time to time and from place to place – this can be very important if you are contemplating retiring to live in another town. There is no security of tenure nor any system of appeal against being forced to move; however, it must be emphasised that such instances are rare. It is possible for a home to have dual registration both as a residential home and as a nursing home. The fit elderly person entering a residential home eventually becomes the frail aged person needing daily nursing care.

If you decide to go into a residential home you should start planning a long time ahead – maybe as much as a year. Get a list of homes from your local **DIAL** (O), CAB or the Yellow Pages. Write for brochures and, taking a friend with you,

visit two or three. Try and get a feeling about the home by talking to some of the residents. Before you go make a list of the things you would like – a single room, your own furniture, a garden to sit in, nearby shops, library or park. Most homes are fully occupied and you may have to put your name on a waiting list.

Well in advance you should write to your local Social Security office to see what financial help, if any, you may get. You should also write to your local *Social Services Department*. Charges are fixed by the managing authority, and lower rates may be charged, subject to a means test. The minimum is prescribed by the government – currently £30.95 a week. For those on *Social Security* the residential care rate is £125 a week; for physically disabled people under pension age, £180 a week. In nursing homes these figures are £230 and £170. The rates change annually. Charges in private nursing homes vary over the country, but typically lie between £150 and £250 a week.

There are many excellent nursing and residential homes

but finding them is not easy, and time spent comparing one with another is a good investment. Try contacting **CARE-MATCH** (O), the **Council and Care for the Elderly** (O), **GRACE** (O), **Age Concern** (O), the **British Federation of Care-Home Proprietors** (O), or the **National Confederation of Registered Rest Home Associations** (O).

People are all different so it is difficult to generalise about what one should look for in a good home. Certainly, personal privacy comes high on the list, and for many a single room would be a must. In fact the majority of people entering a home have had a room to themselves to sleep in for years. Good food in adequate quantities is also essential and equally important is a daily regime permitting normal social hours convenient to the residents. Putting people to bed early in the evening to suit the staff is a relic of the days of Victorian nursing which unfortunately is still prevalent. Space is important – in the lounges to permit informal arrangement of furniture; in the dining room for wheel-chairs; in toilets and bathrooms for care-givers; and in lifts and passages to permit ease of movement for slow walkers.

Preservation of independence comes with the provision of intercoms, alarms, and the correct location of light switches, power points and telephones. The bedroom becomes the resident's entire home – the only place they have in the world. It should have a wash basin, television, radio, telephone jack, and somewhere to write. It should be a place where a person can be alone to do his own thing or entertain a visitor or another resident. It should also be a place where no one enters without knocking. In the residential situation disabled and elderly people should, within the limits of their ability, be able to organise their own lives.

Restricted Growth

Most people of unusually short stature are not disabled, but they do have considerable handicaps, all of which arise from living in a world designed for people of average height. The interests of people of restricted growth are the responsibility of the **Association for Research into Restricted Growth** (O), which believes that short stature should not be an obstacle to a full and satisfying life.

The association provides information on home aids, clothing and footwear. Typical of the aids is a briefcase which opens out to form a pair of steps and a gadget for reaching light switches. ARRG publishes a regular news magazine and a booklet called *Coping with Restricted Growth*. Social activities include parties, dances, dinners and holidays. Parents of children of restricted growth are welcome to join the association.

Retts Syndrome

This is a rare neurological disorder which affects only girls. It produces a regression in behaviour and some physical changes from the age of nine months onward. There may be a reduction in head growth, loss of manipulative ability and *scoliosis*. The incidence may be as high as one in 15,000 female births. These children obviously require considerable care and parents can draw support from other parents. Write for details to Miss AJ Clare B. Ed., **UK Retts Syndrome Association** (O).

Riding and Driving

Riding is a very good sport for physically or mentally handicapped people, providing a new experience and a stimulating challenge as well as an absorbing fresh-air hobby. It is of considerable therapeutic value, giving improved co-ordination and balance, a feeling of independence and greater self-confidence. Newly-discovered abilities begin to take precedence over long-accepted handicaps. Riding for disabled people is a social activity involving new relationships with the volunteer helpers – and with the horse! This may well be the first step from a sheltered, limited life at home to the outside world.

Riding or driving is enjoyed by people with *cerebral palsy, spina bifida, Multiple Sclerosis, spinal injuries, stroke damage,* mental handicap, *sight,* speech or *hearing impairment* and by paraplegics, tetraplegics and those who have lost a limb.

The sport is run by the **Riding for the Disabled Association** (O), a national registered charity formed in 1969. The President is HRH the Princess Royal GCVO. Today over 22,000 disabled children and adults ride and drive with the 636 member groups of the association throughout Britain. Each member group of the association belongs to one of the 18 geographical regions in Britain and there is a small headquarters based at the National Agricultural Centre in Kenilworth, Warwickshire.

The object of the association is to provide the opportunity of riding for disabled people who might benefit in their general health and well-being. The strength of the association rests in the capable hands of some 12,000 volunteers who are responsible for the operation of the member groups. All volunteers, including instructors and physiotherapists, give their services free, and training is given at local, regional and national level. No prior horse knowledge is necessary but it does take enthusiasm, dedication and a reasonable level of physical fitness. Member groups normally hold riding sessions once a week. About a quarter of the disabled riders are adult and clearly have differing requirements from the youngsters, but some groups do cater for both categories. The association is funded from voluntary contributions and considerable effort is put into fund-raising.

Progress for the disabled rider depends on the nature and level of the disability, and the regularity with which they ride. It is possible for riders to take a series of proficiency tests which are a guide to progress. Those who progress well – upwards of 100 – are encouraged to participate in pony clubs and riding clubs and even national RDA dressage competitions and riding holidays abroad.

Driving is offered as an alternative to more severely handicapped people. Special vehicles have been designed, some of which will take an occupied wheelchair.

The association publishes *RDA News*, an excellent, glossy, well-illustrated quarterly magazine, and training films and leaflets, and runs courses for instructors.

For more information contact the **Riding for the Disabled Association** (O).

Rubella

If a pregnant mother contracts rubella (German measles) her child may be born disabled. A Rubella baby may be born with some degree of deafness, blindness, brain or heart damage, as well as other serious defects. Deaf/blind children are extremely difficult to bring up and parents need massive support.

The **National Deaf/Blind and Rubella Association** (O) (SENSE) provides a wide range of supportive services for the children and their parents. Their Family Advisory Service offers counselling, guidance, support and advice to parents and caring professionals concerned with deaf/blind children. There is a team of peripatetic teachers who are trained to deal with dual sensory impairment, and they work with specialist paediatricians, *physiotherapists* and speech therapists. The team can help parents to work with their child after an assessment has been made. The service works mainly with pre-school children, but some services are available to children already at school. There is a Family Centre in London for a weekend of assessment and advice.

Teenagers and young adults can have residential training at the Manor House in Market Deeping, Lincolnshire. Here they are prepared for adult life and they are involved with the activities of the local community. They are able to play sports and holidays are arranged in Britain and abroad.

S

Schizophrenia

Schizophrenia is an illness that can manifest itself in many different ways. It is not uncommon – one person in every hundred will suffer from it at some time during their lifetime. It is not known what causes schizophrenia (which starts most often in men and women in their twenties), but it is known that the risk of the illness may be inherited. One in ten children of a schizophrenic parent will develop it themselves in later life.

Schizophrenia is a mental illness which may be due to a chemical imbalance in the brain. Disturbances of thinking are very common, with the person saying things which do not make sense. He may hear voices – in his head, in a cupboard, outside the house – and he may 'see' things which are not there. He has lost the ability to think and, although his thoughts are jumbled, he is not aware of it. He may talk endlessly or become morose. Social relationships are unpredictable and he may apparently hate those he formerly loved. His speech may be hard to follow. Often the schizophrenic will neglect his own personal appearance and virtually lose touch with the world around him. His emotions may be so mixed up he could laugh at something tragic.

Few people with schizophrenia show signs of violence – in fact they tend to be shy and retiring. However, life with a patient can be very difficult for his family and advice and counselling will be needed.

Most people with schizophrenia need to spend some time in hospital, followed by outpatient treatment and time in day centres. Many people get better with treatment, but even if recovery is complete they may have further attacks, perhaps years later. Drug treatment can help but a careful watch for side-effects is necessary. Drug treatment may go on for a long time, even after the patient feels better.

The largest support group is the **National Schizophrenia**

Fellowship (O) which has over 5,000 members and over 100 local groups. Schizophrenia is extremely stressful for the caring relatives, so the information, advice and mutual support which they can get from other members of a local group is invaluable. The fellowship headquarters also gives advice as well as providing training courses for group leaders. They campaign for better services and fund research projects. There is a quarterly newsletter, *NSF News*, and a wide range of leaflets, reports, tapes and video tapes. A very useful book is *Surviving Schizophrenia: a Family Manual* by E Fuller Torrey (Harper & Row, 28 Tavistock Street, London WC2).

Scoliosis

Scoliosis is not a disease. It just means that in an otherwise healthy child the spine is curved or twisted. There is no physical weakness of the back, it is not infectious or contagious, and is not the consequence of any action or inaction on the part of the child or the parent.

It is important to detect scoliosis as early as possible so that remedial action can be taken. The condition will not go away as the child gets older and the earlier it is treated the better for the patient, so children should be examined bare-backed from time to time. This is easily done by getting the child to bend over from the waist, while keeping the knees back and arms straight with the palms together. From the rear a clear rib bulge will be seen if the child has scoliosis. A common sign of the problem is one shoulder blade being more prominent than the other, with the child tending to lean a little to one side. The hips may also be uneven.

Scoliosis usually appears during the fast growth of the early teens, although it can affect younger children. There are many types of scoliosis, varying from slight to severe curvature. About four children in every thousand need treatment.

The **Scoliosis Association (UK)** (O) is a registered charity formed by Ailie Harrison in 1981. This is a nationwide organisation with over 1,300 members, and its main aim is to provide information and make available to parents the experience and reassurance of others. When caring professionals also began to turn to SAUK for information, it became apparent that, outside the specialist treatment centres, very little is known. SAUK has an on-going 'Watch for scoliosis' poster campaign, with the object not only of informing but also of removing fear – 'bring scoliosis out of the closet'. Eventually, posters will appear in every school in the 11–16 age range, so that PE departments can look out for the signs that a child's back is not growing straight.

Many older people whose curvature was untreated in the past suffer chronic pain and breathing problems. Scoliosis in adolescence can sometimes bring psychological problems, for which counselling from SAUK can help. The loneliness can be eased by contact with others, and there is a great deal of information on aids and special clothing in the quarterly newsletter and the *Scoliosis Handbook*.

Scooters

Electric scooters appeared on the disabled scene at the be-
gining of the 1980s, and there are now a score or more
different models, so making a choice requires careful
thought. For many disabled people, the scooter is an attractive alternative to an electric wheelchair because it is a sort of
fun vehicle devoid of association with handicap. The rider of
a scooter should have minimal walking ability, if this only
means being able to stand and transfer into the scooter seat.
Good manual dexterity and use of arms is necessary to steer
and operate the controls. If, for the disabled person, this is
the first outdoor powered pavement vehicle, then it would
be wise to have extended trials of several makes before
making a choice – and, for that matter, deciding whether to
buy one at all. If the rider is not competent, there can be
danger in steep slopes, pot-holes, slippery surfaces or crossing main roads.

Electric scooters are now very popular and there is quite a
brisk second-hand market, so your first decision is whether
to buy new or second-hand. Before buying second-hand, get
catalogues and choose the models that might suit you so you
know the new price and the capability of the machine. New
prices vary between £900 and £1,800, and second-hand prices
will be around half of these. Second-hand scooters are advertised in the monthly bulletins of **RADAR** (O) and the **Multiple Sclerosis Society** (O).

There are three main types of scooter – indoor, indoor/
outdoor, and outdoor. Indoor scooters are light and compact
(25 × 45in (60 × 110cm)) and have small smooth wheels.
They are powered by a single 12-volt motor driving the front
wheel, demount without tools, and will stow easily in a car
boot. Whilst they will cope with slopes of up to 1:12 they are
really designed for flat indoor floors, and are ideal for use by
partly ambulant disabled people in large residential homes,
where indoor distances can be lengthy. Steering is by
handlebars or steering wheel and speed control by gripping
a lever like a bicycle brake. Seat heights can be varied and
they rotate so it is possible to sit at a table or bench. Typical
indoor scooters are made by **Raymar** (M), **Batricar** (M),

Vessa (M) and **BEC** (M). Indoor/outdoor scooters are larger and heavier and would need a fair amount of space indoors. Two of the firms making these are **Everest and Jennings** (M) or the **Electric Mobility Company** (M).

Outdoor scooters are large machines which would normally be kept in a shed or garage. They have larger wheels with big chunky tyres, and power is on the rear wheels, sometimes with two motors. These scooters are very stable and safe on most outdoor terrains. Typical examples are the Ventura (**Vessa** (M)) and the Elva Twin (**Electric Leisure Vehicles Ltd** (M)).

There are a number of features which vary from make to make. There are 'soft' speed controls which prevent a jerky start and progressive brakes which prevent too sharp a stop. Some scooters have handbrakes and a few have lights. Most have a removable 'ignition key' and one or more shopping baskets.

When you have bought your scooter you should get a friend to come with you to a quiet car park on a Sunday morning, and there you should practise until you can drive with confidence. The machine is expensive and attractive so it should be insured. Write to **James Yarrow, Young and Co. Ltd** (M).

There is a very useful chapter on electric scooters in *Wheelchairs and their Use* by Janet Weyers (published by **RADAR** (O)). Never buy a scooter without giving it a thorough trial over the area where you will use it, and always have someone to help you when you are making your decision in front of the salesman.

Scouting

Scouting is highly organised to cope with handicap and it has much to offer disabled people, both young and old. From Cubs to Venture Scouts, in every town there are able-bodied Scouts visiting disabled people, sometimes just to chat, or other times to walk the dog or cut the grass. Able-bodied Scouts also work with handicapped youngsters of their own age. Often the able-bodied half of PHAB clubs come from Scouts and Guides, and both are often to be found helping in Sports Associations for the Disabled.

Scouting makes splendid provision at all ages for its own disabled members. The main aim of the association – the physical, mental and spiritual development of young people so they may take a constructive place in society – is applicable to all, regardless of ability or disability. As far as possible, Scouts with disabilities are to be found in normal troops and there they are treated no differently from anyone else. It is a fundamental principle of scouting that the individual is stretched to the limit. The absolute limit for the boy in a wheelchair may be less than that of another lad, but it requires the same level of determination to achieve it.

At Scout Headquarters there is a Commissioner for the Handicapped who is directly responsible to the Chief Scout. At county and district levels there are Assistant Commissioners for the Handicapped who liaise closely with the voluntary disabled organisations. Management of disability is an integral part of Scout leader training.

The Resource Centre at Gilwell Park produces an excellent range of 26 detailed fact sheets on practical aspects of disability. These are so good I am surprised other organisations do not make greater use of them. The Scout Leader whose troop is joined by a wheelchair rider might use *Down's Syndrome, Scouting with the Handicapped, Scouts with Mobility Problems, Incontinence, Toiletting* and *Camping with the Handicapped*.

The third way in which scouting provides for the needs of disabled youngsters is in those situations where numbers are gathered together. In hospitals, special schools and rehabilitation centres there are over 120 Scout groups all over the country where all the members, sometimes including the Leaders, are disabled.

Scouting has brought about true 'take-it-for-granted' integration. One new boy in a wheelchair may mean structural alterations to the toilet and a ramp at the entrance to the Scout hut. Often these are turned into working exercises for the troop – real 'service to others'.

Security in the Home

A useful device for the disabled or elderly person living alone is the 'Night Companion', which can be used in any light socket. You remove the light bulb, plug it into the Night Companion which is then plugged back into the socket. Any noise – a spoken word, hand clap, rattling keys – will switch on the light. It will not come on in daylight. Once it is activated the light will stay on for three minutes and then switch off automatically. It is therefore very useful for elderly people who wander about the house at night or as a deterrent to intruders. Normal lighting can be resumed by switching off for 10 seconds or more at the usual switch.

Night Companion would enhance safety and security in an unoccupied house as well as giving economy in the use of electricity in halls, landings and passageways. It would be a great comfort at night for a bed-ridden person.

Write to **Manor (Custodians) Ltd** (M).

SEQUAL

Sequal, formerly the Possum Users' Association, was founded 20 years ago. The name was changed in 1983 because confusion arose with Possum Controls Ltd and the Possum Trust. The advancement of technology made the name inappropriate, with so many companies providing environmental control and communications equipment.

The organisation is governed by a committee of disabled members and it employs four people full-time and two part-time. There is an excellent quarterly glossy magazine and a video demonstrating their work is available.

Sequal provides a highly-skilled, full-time welfare staff who will visit any disabled person requiring help and information regarding suitable equipment, mainly micro-chip-based. The equipment ranges from a simple pointer board, to matrices with 16, 32, or 100 squares selected by a scanning light, page turners, electronic typewriters, voice synthesizers and full computer systems. All equipment can be operated by remote control, using whatever residual muscle is left to the individual. There are even devices which enable equipment to be controlled using only the flicker of an eyelid. Sequal maintains and insures all the equipment and they provide 'learning' toys for younger members.

For details contact the Administrator, **Sequal** (O).

Severe Disablement Allowance

This is a benefit similar to *Invalidity Benefit* but it is for people who do not have enough National Insurance contributions. It is for people unable to work because of a disability, is tax-free and there is no means test. There is additional benefit for a spouse or dependent children.

To qualify you must live in the UK. Among the 'passport' qualifications which give automatic eligibility are *Attendance Allowance*, *Mobility Allowance*, blind registration or 80 per cent disability for industrial injuries or war disablement. Assessment is not needed if your incapacity for work started before the age of 20. Otherwise you have to be assessed as 80 per cent disabled by a DHSS doctor. In general you cannot claim this allowance over retirement age or under 16, and you must have been incapable of work for at least 28 weeks. However you should apply after 15 weeks. The leaflet, which includes the application form, is NI 252.

Sexual Problems of Disabled People

For many months, as I lay in an intensive care ward, there was a young man in the next bed who had broken his back falling off a roof. He had a young wife and a three-year-old daughter and he was due to be released from hospital soon. One day, in response to a question, I heard his consultant say 'Sex? – I should forget that old man'.

This summarises the attitude of many of the general able-bodied public towards disabled people and sex. The unspoken thought is 'You're lucky to be alive – so why do you want more?' In fact, sex, which is all about love and being needed, is more important for the disabled person and their spouse than it is for an able-bodied couple.

However, for physically disabled people there will be both psychological and practical problems needing advice and counselling, and for this help can be obtained from **SPOD** (O) (the Association to Aid the Sexual and Personal Relationships of People with a Disability). SPOD was founded in 1979 by a group of professional carers who were concerned that the sexual needs of disabled people were ignored, overlooked and denied. They have carried out a considerable amount of research and several conferences have been run. It is possible to join SPOD as a private member, but it is not essentially a membership organisation and their Advisory and Counselling Service is available to any disabled person. There is an information service for professional and volunteer advice-givers, as well as study days and training courses. Where personal counselling is desirable SPOD can often arrange this in the client's home area. There is a series of advisory leaflets and an extensive range of books, which, together with any other help and information, can be obtained from SPOD.

The Shaftesbury Society

This is one of the oldest charities in Britain, being formed in 1844 as the Ragged School Union. The **Shaftesbury Society** (O) maintains three residential schools for physically handicapped children, nine hostels for men and women with severe physical disabilities, and five hostels for people who are mentally handicapped. There are also two Further Education Centres where physically handicapped young people can learn a trade or study for a profession. Each year the society provides holidays by the sea for elderly handicapped people at their Holiday Centre.

The Shaftesbury Society Housing Association provides modern purpose-built flats in many areas for elderly, frail elderly, and disabled people.

Shopping

Only in the last five years have the agencies of supply – manufacturers and retailers – begun to realise that there is, in the 5,000,000 or so disabled people in Britain, a large untapped market. There are signs that industry is trying to produce goods for the disablement and elderly market, but little is done to inform the potential buyer, or to make the purchasing process easy.

For most of us the biggest problem associated with shopping is finding the money, but for the elderly or severely disabled person there are, in addition, the difficulties of choice, of knowing what is available and of *access* to shops. Getting someone else to shop for you is rarely satisfactory so for the majority of us shopping has to be done either by visiting shops or by mail. However, since either method is expensive in time, energy and money, it pays to find out what is available, what is most suitable for us as disabled people, and what is the best value for money. In some cases it is essential to try the item before buying – or to buy only subject to suitability after trial at home. For an individual physically disabled person the highest-priced in a range of similar items is not necessarily the best – the first rule is 'Does it work for me?' Only then can you look at cost, efficiency and durability.

We live in an age of rapidly expanding technology and

most of us occasionally buy items of household hardware – video recorders, microwave ovens, home computers or satellite television receiver dish aerials – without understanding enough to ask sensible questions of the shopkeeper. The answer to this is to get hold of the appropriate copy of the consumer magazine *Which?* This will explain in simple terms the mysteries of kilobytes, rotating antennae and digital programming; it gives prices and makers' addresses; and tells you the 'best but expensive' and 'best buy', all the way down to the 'could be dangerous'. You are guided towards making your own decision over the best choice for your particular circumstances. *Which?* comes out monthly and it may be found in your public library, your neighbour's house or you can write to the **National Consumer Council** (O).

Apart from consumable products, shopping for the disabled person is for two broad classes of items. There are the products made specially for disabled people – what used to be called 'aids' – and products intended for anybody, but which are found to be very suitable for handicapped people.

There are over 10,000 different items of specialised equipment for disabled people, and these can vary from a drinking mug to an electric bed, or a custom-built vehicle or sailing boat. Whatever the item is, before contemplating buying it, always try and get it 'free' from a statutory source, such as *Social Services*, the local council, or the District Health Authority. In some towns Social Servies will buy, at discounted terms, an article on behalf of a disabled person. Information is the key to success, and a wise disabled person will build up a background of knowledge about equipment over the years related to his own needs. New equipment appears every week and one way to keep up to date with this is to read the monthly magazine *Caring*. Do not assume a particular device does not exist. It is better to say 'Is there something that will enable me to do this?'

Two of the main agencies which will supply leaflets or books on equipment are the **Disabled Living Foundation** (O) and Equipment for the Disabled from **Mary Marlborough Lodge** (O). These give prices, makers and full descriptions, and both services are regularly up-dated. Typical titles include *Beds*, *Hoists and Lifting Equipment*, *Leisure Activities* or

Footwear. The routine is – crystallise the problem, get an information list, and then write to selected manufacturers for catalogues.

If your local **DIAL** (O) is not too far away a visit will enable you to see all the catalogues and price lists, and the staff will advise you. Your local *Community Health Council* will tell you where your nearest *Disabled Living Centre* is. You have to make an appointment to visit a DLC, but it will have a standing equipment exhibition where you can try any item you wish. If the article you need is large and expensive try to wait until you can visit the next NAIDEX. There are two of these each year – a national one in London around October and a provincial one in the spring. With a few exceptions, you cannot buy anything, but you can see and try all the variations of a particular item and make comparisons.

There are a few mail-order firms specialising in products for disabled people. A very innovative mail-order firm which is always introducing new exciting products is **Medipost Ltd** (M). Many of the Medipost products are exclusive to them and most are zero-rated for VAT. They have a wide range of items in Mullipel, long recognised as the best artificial fleece on the market. There is a full wheelchair set, heel and elbow protectors, Mullimitts and a Mullimuff. Any Medipost product may be money-back returned if it is not suitable. Other mail-order catalogues of aids to daily living may be had from **Homecraft Supplies Ltd** (M) or **Medimail** (M).

Many disabled people have the need of regular supplies of products related to personal problems and very good for these is **Home Nursing Supplies** (M). There is a large and thriving second-hand market in expensive things like electric *wheelchairs*, *scooters*, *beds*, *stairlifts* and vehicles. Most DIALs keep lists and the three main national small-ad columns are to be found in the bulletins of **RADAR** (O) and the **Multiple Sclerosis Society** (O), and the newsletter of the **Spinal Injuries Association** (O).

There are many products on the open market which are very suitable for handicapped people. A typical example is the Phillips hand-held electric tin opener which is very good for people with arthritic hands. The **DLF** (O) lists are good for these items.

Disabled people who have difficulty in visiting shops can buy products of this nature from ordinary mail-order catalogues. The Argos catalogues can be used in this way by getting a friend to make the purchase for you. Argos catalogues are renewed frequently so they give a good indication of current prices, and products are described in detail.

As well as the large well-known mail-order catalogues there are a number of small catalogues published at regular intervals. There are many things in these which would be useful to disabled people, such as electric plugs with handles, cable-less intercoms, ionisers, posture cushions, home security devices, television personal sound amplifiers or remote-control systems for household appliances. Many of these products are unobtainable elsewhere. Write to **Innovations (Mail Order) Ltd** (M) or **Kaleidoscope Ltd** (M).

Shopping for disabled people in ordinary shops is possible but needs careful planning, and it may pay to save up your shopping for fewer occasions. It helps to take cash, as cheques and credit cards are difficult to manage in a wheelchair, and you will need a large bag on the back of the wheelchair. Small shops will always send somebody out to serve you if you cannot get an electric wheelchair in. Most supermarkets have small trolleys which clamp on to the front of a wheelchair and often a member of staff will come around with you to take things off high shelves. Boots have sold a wide selection of disablement products for several years – from the Pat Saunders Drinking Straw to wheelchairs and they are also very good for incontinence products.

It should be possible for a disabled person to go into a shop and buy the aid they want. By and large this is not the case, but slowly stores for disabled people are opening up and down the country. These are large shops which carry complete ranges of equipment for people with any form of disablement. Here you can see all the beds, hoists, wheelchairs, armchairs or small aids, and you can really 'shop around' in the sense that you can see it, try it, pay for it and take it away. Disablement stores now open include:

Charles Allardyce Ltd
145 Overgate
Dundee DD1 1QG
(0382 22523)

Archibald Young & Son Ltd
37 Constitution Street
Edinburgh EH6 7BG
(031 554 0591)

W Monroe Ltd
1078 Argyle Street
Glasgow G3 8LZ

Peter Brown Ltd
45 Carlyle Avenue
Hillingdon Industrial Estate
Glasgow G52 4XX

JC Peacock & Son Ltd
Friar House
Clevering Place
Newcastle upon Tyne
(0632 329917)

Alton Aids
Home Health Centre
Park Road
Gateshead NE8 3HL

T Clark & Partners Ltd
80/136 Edmond Road
Sheffield S2 4EE

Collins Aids
2 Strowston Road
Norwich
(0603 414294)

Donald Rose Ltd
34/36 Margaret Street
London W1
(01 629 6994)

Living with Handicaps
6 Ashbourne Parade
Finchley Road
London NW11
(01 209 0195)

Community Health Supplies
16 Dinsdale Gardens
New Barnet
Hertfordshire EN5 1HE
(01 440 4931)

Southern Mobility Centre
Unit 64
Hammonds Drive
Eastbourne
(0323 645067)

J & S Services
Unit N11
Riverside Industrial Estate
Littlehampton
Sussex
(0903 723141)

Keith Jay Ltd
Bognor Regis
West Sussex
(0243 865088)

Disabled Living
Unit 11, Salisbury
   Business Park
Southampton Road
Salisbury, Wilts
(0722 26464)

Disabled Living
333 Lymington Road
Highcliff
Dorset
(0425 278036)

Mobility Care Centre
64a Magdalen Street
Exeter
(0392 210520)

Nought–Ninety
172/174 Kellaway Avenue
Horfield
Bristol
(0272 46703)

Independence
52 Exeter Road
Exmouth
Devon EX8 1PY

Bradbury Surgical Ltd
McKinney Industrial Estate
Mallusk
Co Antrim
(023 13 43831)

Disablecare
57 Donegal Avenue
Belfast BT12 6LS
(0232 230744)

Sight Impairment

In Britain, one person in two uses spectacles or contact lenses to help eyesight that is less than perfect. The most common defects are long sight in which the eyeball is shorter than it should be, and short sight in which the eyeball is too long. Both are commonly the result of ageing. Long sight gives difficulty with focusing on near objects, as in reading, whilst short sight means distant objects cannot be seen clearly. In both cases the subconscious effort to focus may cause headaches. Astigmatism occurs where the curvature of the eyeball varies so that in certain directions you get a blurred or distorted image. These are the three commonest conditions for which spectacles are the answer. In return for a stamped self-addressed envelope very useful free information is available from the **Optical Information Council** (O).

To focus on an object the lens of the eye changes shape. As we grow older the elasticity diminishes and we find ourselves holding the newspaper a long way away. This condition is called presbyopia. An eye test may also reveal a number of more rare defects. 'Lazy eye', a condition which may exist at birth, gives a poorly-focused image. A squint is a condition where the two eyes fail to focus on the same object. It is important that either of these conditions in children should be treated as early in life as possible.

When the lens of the eye becomes cloudy we call this a cataract, and it can cause almost total loss of sight. A very useful book is *In Touch with Cataracts* by Margaret Ford (costing £1.00 from **Age Concern** (O)). Operations are 95 per cent successful but spectacles are always needed after.

A very gradual loss of vision may be the result of glaucoma which can be quite painful, but can be treated successfully. A disorder of the blood vessels in the retina can be the result of diabetes and a severe case can cause blindness, but normally treatment will forestall this. Colour blindness should really be called 'colour deficiency' and it is found in only one person in a million, usually men. These people see in colour but cannot distinguish between red and green. It can be caused by alcohol or tobacco abuse but usually it is inherited.

It is important to have a regular eye examination for which there is a fee, unless you fall into one of the exempted classes. Towards old age, even healthy people who wear glasses have an eye test once a year. Eye examinations may be given only by ophthalmic opticians or ophthalmic medical practitioners. An ophthalmologist is qualified to treat or operate on an eye.

A dispensing optician may fit and supply spectacles but he cannot give an eye examination. Most spectacles may be sold or fitted by anyone, regardless of whether they are a registered optician or not, and spectacles may be supplied only on production of a prescription which must be less than two years old. After an eye examination you will be given a prescription which, if you wish, you can use when and where you like. All spectacles must be made up to match your prescription precisely. It is worth looking out for the shops that are starting to sell spectacles – for example, in some of the larger branches of Boots and Woolworths you can have a pair of spectacles made up to your prescription with only an hour to wait. NHS subsidies may be available on certain complex high-powered lenses.

If you are a wheelchair pilot and you wish to know your

nearest accessible optician write to the **Optical Information Council** (O) or to the **Association of Optical Practitioners** (O). For house-bound or hospitalised disabled people it is possible to arrange for the optician to come to you. Tetraplegics who cannot reach their face have special problems – spectacles have to be put on by the care-giver in the morning and they must stay in place all day, so the frames must be a perfect fit and the lenses must serve all purposes. It is wise to use lightweight frames and plastic lenses. The tetraplegic who moves in and out of doors may need photochromic lenses which darken automatically in bright light.

For the person with severe sight impairment there are a number of aids. Possibly the most popular is the wide range of 'reading substitutes', such as large-print books and 'talking' books and newspapers. An A4 stamped addressed envelope sent to the **Library Association** (O), the **Partially Sighted Society** (O), or **Clio Press** (M) will bring you a catalogue of large-print books. Clio, who publish ISI books, have recently added the *Longmans English Dictionary* and the *Longmans Thesaurus* to their series. There is also a large-print version of the telephone code book. Many towns have local evening or weekly newspapers recorded on standard two-track cassettes, and details of these and the available national magazines can be obtained from the **Talking Newspaper Association of the UK** (O).

A relatively new aid for those with very limited sight is a closed-circuit television producing on the screen a variable but possibly very large magnification of the printed word. Details are available from Brian Payne, **Electronic Aids for the Blind** (M) or from **Alphavision** (M). Viewscan is a miniature fibre-optic hand-held camera which scans the page giving a magnified image on a dot-matrix screen. Write to **Wormaid International Sensory Aids Ltd** (M).

Around a quarter of a million people in the UK have such a degree of reduced vision that they are unable to perform everyday tasks, such as reading the newspaper. These people should be registered as partially-sighted and they can benefit from the use of 'Low Vision Aids' (LVAs). These range from simple hand-held magnifying glasses to a pair of spectacles with very thick lenses. Each device normally has one use only – an aid designed for reading will not help you to see a bus number at a distance. For the latter problem you would use a small telescope which can be concealed in the palm of the hand. For those with poor hand function there are magnifiers on stands and the better ones are combined with lights. Aspheric magnifiers are designed to give a flat, true image right to the edge of the glass, and these are sometimes called 'loupes'. For an excellent catalogue of magnifying aids write to **Combined Optical Industries** (M).

In Touch is the only national radio programme for blind and partially-sighted people. It is broadcast each Tuesday at 9 pm on Radio 4 and from 8.30 to 10 pm on the same night there is an off-air phone-in service on 01 580 4444 to give listeners a chance to ask questions. The *In Touch* quarterly bulletin is available free to blind or partially-sighted people, and to get a year's supply you should send four 8½ × 6in. (21 × 15cm) stamped addressed envelopes to *In Touch*, BBC, Broadcasting House, London W1A 1AA. For a free tape version of the bulletin send one blank C90 cassette to Tape Recording Service for the Blind, 48 Fairfax Road, Farnborough, Hants GU14 8JP.

British Telecom offer a wide range of services and equipment to people with partial sight. There is a simple self-adhesive finger guide for push-button telephones; a push-button telephone with very large buttons; telephones storing up to fifty numbers giving one-button access to each; and a range of telephone-related emergency alarms. In fact there is so much equipment it is well worth while calling at your local Telecom office for a copy of their 1988 *Guide to Equipment and Services for the Disabled*. There is also a free tape to help sight-impaired people use the new public telephones.

Sleep

We do not all require the same amount of sleep. In fact, sleep is not absolutely necessary for everybody – Dr Pavoni, who lived in northern Italy, is said to have died at the age of eighty after going without any significant amount of sleep for sixty years. He made a considerable fortune doing other doctors' night calls! Winston Churchill and Margaret Thatcher are among many famous people who apparently manage on only a few hours sleep at night. However, sleep is both a mental and a physical restorative and few of us can do without it.

Insomnia can be very distressing because it may be a part of a vicious circle which is difficult to break; actually worrying about not sleeping keeps you awake. The first step in curing insomnia is the mental acceptance that no harm can come from it. The human body is a good self-regulating mechanism – on the whole a very effective one – and, given the right circumstances, it will ensure that you get enough sleep. We have to learn to cultivate the right mental approach to sleep. Avoid high levels of emotion just before bed-time – if you must have a row with your spouse, have it at lunch-time! By the same token, avoid stimulating intellectual activity late in the evening when you need an hour to wind down. Look forward to bed-time with a relaxed indifference to whether you sleep or not. Many people use a radio with a snooze button or read a book to put them to sleep.

For those who live alone it is important to remove all worries from real or imagined dangers. This may involve anything from a personal alarm to a cordless telephone you can take to bed with you. For a relatively small outlay the house can be made secure, and a small dog with a big voice can also be a comfort.

Avoid coffee or tea last thing at night, although many people find some kind of hot milky drink helps, or perhaps a single brandy or Scotch. So, now you are approaching bed-time, tired and relaxed, what next? To sleep you have to be comfortable, and comfort is often difficult for disabled people to achieve. Many physically disabled people have poor circulation and they react adversely to both heat and cold, so both pyjamas and bed clothes should be warm. The temperature of the bedroom should be controllable. It may need to be very warm for the disabled person who, with or without assistance, takes a long time to undress and get into bed; in addition the room may have to be held at a 'warm' level throughout the night because the disabled person can use only light bed clothes. Many physically disabled people are unable to turn or move in bed with more than a sheet and a blanket over them. An electric blanket which stays on all night is the answer. These are thermostatically-controlled, and, running on low voltages, they are electrically safe. They are available as over-blankets or under-blankets from Boots.

In most houses the central heating goes off altogether at night. In addition to the central heating radiator in the 'disabled' bedroom there should be a small, electric, thermo-statically-controlled panel heater for use at night. Fresh air is important at night and there should be a good means of ventilating the room without draughts. An electric air puri-fier or ioniser helps sleep for asthmatics or people with lung problems.

Many physically disabled people have to sleep alone in a single bed – from problems associated with getting in and out of bed, the need for anti-pressure-sore precautions, bladder management, cramp and circulation. There are a number of ways of transferring from a wheelchair on to a bed and each disabled person should seek expert guidance in finding his own best method. Very severely disabled people may find that they have to use a hoist such as that supplied by **FJ Payne** (M). These lifts require 3 or 4in (7–10cm) clearance under the bed for the lift chassis. The main problem in transferring the severely disabled person for the single-handed helper is the difficulty of holding them in the standing position, and at the same time removing their lower garments before sitting them on the bed. This can be overcome with a new device called 'Stella' made by **Mecan-aids** (M). Some people can help themselves with a monkey pole which may be free-standing or attached to the bed, while some people who are just able to stand and turn with assistance find a turntable (**Renray** (M) or **BEC** (M)) is a help.

Care is needed to relate the support surfaces to the needs of the disability. Physically disabled peole have to avoid pressure sores; people with 'bad backs' and arthritics may

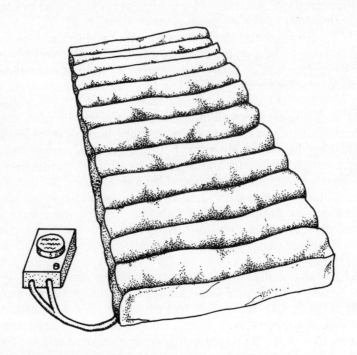

Ripple bed.

need hard mattresses; and others may have problems of lower limb circulation. The **Niagra** (M) electric Adjustamatic bed has a 7in (17.5cm) mattress offering three degrees of hardness, and all the functions are on one hand-held control. You can raise the head for sitting up in bed, raise the feet, vibrate either or both ends, and use the timers. Raising the head is useful for getting in and out of bed and also for angina attacks. Raising and massaging the legs helps lower limb circulation. Many people use the **Spenco** (M) Silicore mattress to avoid pressure sores. Ripple mattresses consist of tubes or sacs which are inflated and deflated alternately, thereby continuously changing the pressure points (**Talley** (M) or **Appollo Medical Supplies Ltd** (M)). RoHo (**Raymar** (M)) and Clinifloat (**Aztec** (M)) are excellent non-mechanical very manageable mattresses for the domestic situation.

Bed clothes should be as light as possible whilst giving

adequate warmth. Plain cotton sheets with an electric over-blanket and a coverlet give warmth, whilst permitting easy movement in bed. Totally paralysed people often sleep without night clothes to avoid skin problems from creases, and there are also electric beds which will turn the sleeper at regular intervals for these people.

There are so many different types of mattresses and beds that it is very necessary to get expert advice. This you may get from your local **DIAL** (O), or from your community OT, or from a Disabled Living Centre. If you can get to London the **DLF** (O) have a good range of beds on permanent display. They will also supply an excellent leaflet called simply *Beds*.

Story

Insomnia Cure

It was 1 am and peace reigned in the hospital male orthopaedic ward when the Ward Sister departed for 'lunch' leaving the attractive young staff nurse in sole charge. Returning an hour later, she heard muffled voices coming from the other end of the darkened ward. One bed had screens around it and as she approached she heard a man's voice say 'Come on, nurse, give me a kiss' followed by a female voice saying 'No, I really shouldn't'. The horrified Sister listened to a few more similar conversational exchanges before opening the screens just as the staff nurse was saying '. . . and anyway I don't really think I should be in bed with you . . .'

Social Fund

See under Social Security.

Social Security

One of the problems with entering the world of disability is the strange new jargon and abbreviations you have to learn if you are not to be disadvantaged in many ways, not least in your dealings with statutory bodies. Of these the two most common are also the two most often confused – *Social Services* and Social Security, run by the Department of Health and the Department of Social Security.

Social Services is run by the local authority, paid for by the rates. Social Services provides services, including meals on wheels, home helps, equipment, care attendants, transport, holidays, residential homes, drug centres and fostering. It does not dole out money to individuals on a regular basis, but may make one-off grants for building alterations or other specific purposes.

Social Security is a system under which we all pay money into a national fund, from which we can draw in the event of one of a wide range of finance-based problems – unemployment, sickness, disability or old age. Most people draw some form of Social Security at some time in their lives. In Britain, the Social Security scheme is funded by National Insurance contributions and taxes; most employed people have to pay National Insurance contributions as deductions from their wage packets. Some Social Security benefits can be paid to people – such as those disabled from birth – even though they have never paid National Insurance contributions.

Our Social Security system was devised by Sir William Beveridge over 40 years ago. By 1985 it had become out of date and failed to satisfy either the consumers or the providers. The original concept was based upon a society in which many people in work contributed to a fund from which a relatively small number of unemployed people were paid. Supplementary Benefit (now called Income Support) was a safety net to care for those in need but without contribution entitlement. Forty years ago unemployment was so low that the system was self-financing, and in fact the Social Security Fund increased as time went on. Now, in the late 1980s unemployment is over 2,000,000; there are 4,000,000 on Supplementary Benefit; the family is no longer the cornerstone of society and there are 1,200,000 one-parent families on Supplementary Benefit; the man is rarely the sole breadwinner in the family; Social Security rates were a disincentive to lower-paid work; and for many, Social Security is a second-generation way of life.

The 1970 Chronically Sick and Disabled Persons Act heralded a decade which saw the introduction of many 'disabled' benefits and allowances, instigated piecemeal over the years as resources became available and needs identified. The result was a social security system of such baffling complexity that many in need failed to apply, the administration costs soared, and staff became demoralised with the work-load. In an average year there were over £1,000 million pounds in uncollected benefits. There was general agreement that there was a need for a massive shake-up of the system. The result was the 1986 Social Security Act which became effective on 11th April 1988.

The 1986 Act introduced five new benefits – Income Support, the Social Fund, Widows' Benefits, Housing Benefits and Family Credit. Not substantially affected by the Act were *Retirement Pension, Invalidity Benefit, Attendance Allowance, Mobility Allowance, Severe Disablement Allowance* or *Invalid Care Allowance*.

Income Support provides help with day-to-day living costs for people out of work, working part-time, and those who are sick, disabled, elderly or caring for children. It is paid in arrears and there is no distinction between householder and non-householder. There is no long-term higher rate. No payment is made for 'additional requirements', housing requirements, water rates or house maintenance. Almost 75 per cent of all disabled people are on Income Support.

Income Support is based upon Personal Allowance,

Dependants' Allowance, and one or more of a number of premiums. It is not payable to people who are working for more than 24 hours a week, to people who are not available for work (with certain exceptions), to full-time students, or to people with over £6,000 in savings. Savings under £3,000 do not affect Income Support, but between £3,000 and £6,000 it will make some difference. As with the former Supplementary Benefit, Income Support is worked out as a 'balance sheet'. On one side is the amount you need and on the other the income you already have.

There are two items on the 'needs' side – allowances and premiums. Allowances are to cover normal expenditure, and there are six levels covering age groups and marriage status. There are seven premiums for special needs. If you have children you may qualify for the Family Premium, the Disabled Child's Premium or the Lone Parent Premium. For people over 60 there is the Pensioner Premium or the Higher Pensioner Premium. For disabled people there is the Disability Premium or the Higher Disability Premium. Normally if you qualify for more than one premium you draw the one paying the most money, but Family Premium, Disabled Child Premium or Higher Disability Premium may be drawn in addition to any other premium.

There has been a major change in the assessment of capital. A person entering a residential home permanently as a former owner/occupier will have the value of his property assessed, irrespective of whether it is sold or not. There is no loan provision. People entering hospital will have Income Support down-rated after six weeks. Income Support is payable in arrears by order book, giro, or it may be collected from unemployment offices. It is claimed on Form B.1 if you are unemployed or Form SB.1 if employed. Both forms are available in post offices. Leaflet SB20 *A Guide to Income Support* is available from any Social Security office.

The Social Fund is a scheme to help people with occasional exceptional expenses which they could not meet from their regular income. It is issued in the form of Budgeting Loans, Crisis Loans or Community Care Grants. Loans are at the discretion of the Social Fund Officer (SFO) and they are interest-free, but repayable over a period of 78 weeks or (exceptionally) 104 weeks. Loans are made for sums between £30 and £1,000. Repayment is between 5 per cent and 15 per cent of income and is deducted directly from Social Security benefit. All loans must be repaid and court action can be taken against any recipient who defaults. Each local Social Security office is allocated a sum of money and this is reviewed monthly – once the allocation is used up further applications will be turned down. To qualify for a Budgeting Loan the recipient must have been drawing Income Support for 26 weeks, and there is a 28-day waiting period on applications. SFOs use discretion in placing loans in priority order. High priority would be given where refusal could cause hardship or risk to the health or safety of the applicant or his family. Claims are made on Form SF.300.

Crisis Loans are also interest-free and these are available to anybody. Loans may be from £5 to £1,000. People drawing Social Security repay the loan by deductions from benefits; other people repay by arrangement, agreed with the SFO. Loans are made from a separate limited local fund which is not interchangeable with the Community Care Grant fund. Capital over £500 is taken into account.

Community Care Grants are to help people to stay in the community (as opposed to entering institutional care), or to help people to settle back into the community. These grants may also be given to relieve stressful family situations or to provide travelling expenses for long journeys for funerals or domestic crises. The priority groups are the elderly, disabled, mentally ill, terminally ill, prisoner rehabilitation and families under stress. Community Care Grants do not have to be repaid if the recipient is getting Income Support. Claim on Form SF 300. For information on the Social Fund get leaflet SB 16 *A Guide to the Social Fund*.

Family Credit is a benefit for people who are working and who have at least one child. It can be paid to married couples or to single parents. To qualify the applicant must be working at least 24 hours a week, support at least one child who is living with them, and have savings under £6,000. The amount you get depends on a threshold income set by the government. Family Credit is worked out on the basis of the number of children in the family and their ages, the money coming in to the family every week, and the total savings of the family. Family Credit is paid for 26 weeks at a time. For information get Leaflet NI 261.

Housing Benefit is a scheme to help people on low incomes pay their rent and rates. It is run by local councils and it can be paid to a person who may or may not be working, who pays rent to a council or a private landlord, or to a person who owns their own home. Housing Benefit can cover some or all of the rent but only up to 80 per cent of the rates. There is no help with mortgage repayments, heating, meals, water charges or service charges. Most people on Income Support are automatically entitled to Housing Benefit. The amount of Housing Benefit depends on the amount of rent and rates, the allowances and premiums, the money coming in from Social Security, and the money coming in from employment (less £5). Housing Benefit is paid either by reducing the rent of a council house or by cheque for private rented accommodation, and owner/occupiers get a reduced rates bill. Apply on Form NHB1 and for detailed information get Leaflet RR2 *A Guide to Housing Benefit*.

If you are turned down for any benefit you will be told whether you can appeal against the decision. Social Fund decisions will be reviewed by a senior SFO within the local office. Housing Benefit decisions will be reviewed by a board of local councillors. Most other claims can be submitted to an independent tribunal. Your nearest **DIAL** (O) will provide an advocate to accompany you to an Appeal Tribunal.

If you are disabled and you have a Social Security problem, seek advice from your nearest **DIAL** (O), Welfare Rights Centre or CAB. For general advice ring Freephone Social Security on 0800 666555. You could also try your public library for *Disability Rights Handbook* – £3.50 from Disability Alliance, 25 Denmark Street, London WC2 8NJ; or *National Welfare Rights Handbook* – £5.50 from CPAG Ltd, 1–5 Bath Street, London EC1V 9PY; or *Your Rights for Retired People* – £1 from Age Concern, 60 Pitcairn Road, Mitcham, Surrey CR4 4LL; or the *Guide to Income Support, Housing Benefit and Family Credit* from the Benefits Research Unit (Services) Ltd, Cherry Tree Buildings, University of Nottingham, Nottingham NG7 2RD.

Special Care Agency

See under Care.

Spina Bifida

See ASBAH.

Spinal Injuries

Spinal injuries are commonly the result of broken backs or broken necks from road accidents or sports injuries, particularly diving accidents. It is interesting to reflect that around the beginning of the twentieth century spinal injuries occurred mainly amongst the gentry, who could easily break crucial bones falling off their horses. The spinal cord can also be damaged in other ways, such as from viral infection (transverse myelitis), cysts and growths.

The spinal cord runs through a chain of bony rings which are called vertebrae, and which together make up the spine. The spinal cord is a set of nerves, each of which acts like a telephone cable sending messages to or from the brain. When the spinal cord is injured, these messages are interrupted, re-routed or cannot get through at all. Sensory nerves send messages of feeling to the brain alerting the body to pain, hot and cold, hard and soft, texture, bladder and bowel needs. Motor nerves transmit instructions to muscles and, in fact, these control almost all bodily functions. Sensory loss can be quite serious – without bladder and bowel signals a person becomes incontinent, while without pain he can scald himself. Loss of motor nerves produces paralysis. Depending on the extent of damage to the spinal cord, a person will be partially or completely paralysed from the lesion (point of damage) downwards.

Paraplegia, which is the result of a broken back, is paralysis from the chest or waist downwards, with little or no movement or feeling in the body below the waist. Tetraplegia, resulting from a broken neck, also affects the arms and hands. Fractures, or compressions of the vertebrae which damage the spinal cord, may lead to loss of sensation, movement, bladder and bowel control, as well as affecting sexual function. A muscle which is unused begins to waste away within a matter of hours; hence the need for the use of passive *physiotherapy* at an early stage. It is possible to mimic nerve messages with electronic equipment and in the future it may be that suitably programmed miniaturised computers will enable paraplegics to walk. Electronic equipment made by **NeuroTech** (M) is claimed to 'regrow' wasted muscles.

The Spinal Injuries Association, now ten years old, is a self-help group, controlled and run by spinal-cord-injured people themselves, which aims to assist those with similar disabilities to get back to an ordinary, everyday life following injury. The SIA philosophy is to help disabled people to help themselves and to this end there are a number of services available, including an Information Service, a confidential Welfare Service and a Care Attendant Agency. Full membership is open to those with spinal cord injury while associated membership is open to those wheelchair riders with other disabilities – spina bifida, poliomyelitis, and so on.

The SIA has a number of holiday facilities including two narrow boats specially built for wheelchair users. Each will take up to six people cruising in comfort. Specially designed mobile homes sleeping up to six are available in Sussex, and on an island off the south-west coast of France.

The Welfare Service gives advice on *Social Security*, housing, *incontinence, sexuality* and parenthood. There are 400 members in the Link Scheme which puts members who want help in touch with members who have the experience to provide it. There is a Relatives Travel Fund to assist with the costs of long journeys to visit patients. There are only nine NHS spinal units in England so relatives often have a journey of over 100 miles.

Up-to-date, accurate and comprehensive information is available by telephone or letter and one of the major activities of the Information Service is the compilation of the excellent quarterly newsletter which is full of ideas, suggestions, experiences, news and views. SIA has published a number of books for wheelchair riders and also for GPs and district nurses. *So You're Paralysed* is a practical introduction to life in a wheelchair which has been translated into several languages. The SIA Care Attendant Agency provides emergency and short-term help for disabled members in England and Wales for periods of up to 14 days. The Care Attendant will live in with the disabled person and provide 24-hour cover. There is a fee structure to meet varying financial circumstances of members.

Sport for Disabled People

The originator of sport for disabled people was the late Ludwig Guttmann, who, at Stoke Mandeville Hospital, first developed rehabilitation when working on young, severely disabled ex-servicemen. He suggested the use of sport as a major feature of long-term rehabilitation, so in those early days a few physically handicapped people were playing sport because it was 'good' for them physically and mentally. Nowadays sport is available to disabled people who want to play for pleasure – no other reason is needed.

Paradoxically, sport is more important to disabled people than to able-bodied people and in sport disability in no way equates with inability. There are many thousands of handicapped participants in sport, and there is an excellent organisation from town to county, region to country, all the way up to the Olympics. In sports such as archery, disabled and able-bodied people compete on even terms. Many disabled people are relatively immobile and they lack the daily exercise necessary to avoid bowel and bladder problems, obesity, problems of circulation, vital capacity and tissue viability.

The only answer is exercise and the most enjoyable way to take exercise is through a chosen sport. Poor lower limb circulation can produce ulcers which can result in the need for amputation; and it can be a contributory factory in *pressure sores*. Simply on preventive grounds alone it is essential for a disabled person to take adequate regular exercise.

Given strength of will you can take your disability where you like, and this is well demonstrated in sport. You can play your game alone (as in angling or weight training), with able-bodied competitors (as in darts, archery, bowls or boule), with other disabled players (as in basketball or fencing), or with both (as in swimming or the marathon). The choice is yours. Sport brings disabled people and ablebods closer together because each is trying not only to beat someone else, but to improve upon his own personal best.

The governing body for disabled sport is the British Sports Association for the Disabled (BSAD), founded at Stoke Mandeville, which is now regarded as the national centre. BSAD is divided into 21 regions, each made up of several counties and in most towns there is a 'SAD' – a Sports Association for the Disabled (for example, HADSAD – Havant and District Sports Association for the Disabled). BSAD makes the rules; in some sports, such as wheelchair basketball, the rules are special for disability, while in others special equipment is prescribed. They also set up new SADs and organise competitions, training and representation at international level. The Junior Multidisabled Games draws well over 400 competitors each year. Complicated handicapping systems have evolved over the years to cater for the meetings between two competitors with different disabilities.

A local disabled sports association has two functions. It provides a gymnasium-based club which meets weekly to play basketball, table tennis, fencing, boule, archery, or any of a dozen other indoor games; and it will arrange for the placement of a single disabled person in a 'normal' club of their choice – perhaps helping a wheelchair rider who wants to join a club for small-bore shooting. The SAD will arrange transport for both individuals as well as teams, it will acquire equipment, and it will organise local competitions. For these purposes it will become a registered charity and raise funds.

Broadly speaking, there are three kinds of equipment used in disabled sport. There is that which belongs to the game being played – as in a table tennis or a snooker table; there are enabling devices – such as sports wheelchairs used for basketball; and there are safety devices, the commonest of which are floor fixings for wheelchairs, used for anglers, fencers, shot putters, javelin throwers and bowls players. Many enabling devices are custom-built for a disabled individual and the local **REMAP** (O) is often the source. Paraplegic canoeists often use fibreglass seats moulded to their shape to give back support. The Caranoe is a broad, cathedral-hull training canoe with considerable lateral stability.

Fibreglass is also used to make breast-plates for one-armed archers; clamps with screw adjustments enable the bow to be fixed to the breast-plate so the string can be pulled with the one good hand. For archers who are unable to grip the string there are special release mechanisms attached to wrist splints. In skiing the disabled learner is at the centre of a 12ft (3.5m) pole held by two experienced skiers. This gives the feeling that they can stop confidently and that their skis will not run away with them. Single leg amputees use elbow crutches with short 17in (42cm) skis on the ends attached with springs; the good leg rides on a single over-sized middle ski. Some disabled skiers use skis with a length of

light chain joining the front ends to prevent unintentional 'splits'. In snooker a special weighted pyramid topped with a ring provides a bridge for the one-armed player. Players of one-armed golf use no special equipment.

Many sports are played by blind people. Cricket, using a sonic ball, is played with two full teams. The umpires are able-bodied – they are probably 'blind' anyway! The blind darts player uses a simple square piece of hardboard with beading down two edges; with his feet he locates himself to take shots.

There are blind show jumpers who use a 'radar' in their hat which, by sound through earphones, gives the range and direction of the fence. Recently the Grimsby REMAP made a sonic football for blind players – strong enough to be kicked without breaking the rather complicated innards. Many blind people compete in athletics track events and both sprint and distance swimming.

Special lightweight wheelchairs, like the Swede and the Quadra, are used in track and distance events. The javelin may be a distance event but it can also be thrown for accuracy using a horizontal target marked out on grass.

However, let it not be thought that competition figures high in disabled sport. Most people play for amusement only. Most SADs provide table games such as chess, dominoes and draughts, which people can play if they tire quickly playing something energetic. A splendid game for disabled people is 'Ukkers' – a naval version of ludo played on a canvas 'board' about 25ft (7.5m) square. The counters are solid timber discs – in Nelson's time they were traditionally cut from old wooden masts – and the wooden dice is shaken in a plastic dustbin.

There are many leaflets and books available and any SAD or local **DIAL** (O) would give you a reading list. A very useful book is Norman Croucher's *Outdoor Pursuits for Disabled People* published by Woodhead-Faulkner. There are many associations for particular disabled sports. There are 42 national disabled sports associations making provision for deaf people, and three devoted to disabled skiing.

There is much benefit to be gained from the social contacts to be found in sport, and the fact that it stimulates disabled people to get out of the house. Once they get to the club, and see people with disabilities far worse than theirs enjoying their game, they are 'hooked'. For disabled people sport is much-needed exercise taken in a pleasant way.

Stairs

For the family with one disabled member who is unable to negotiate stairs there are, at the outset, two choices – move the family to a single-level residence such as a flat or bungalow, or stay and modify the house. Much will depend upon whether the house is on a mortgage or if it is rented. Even if the house can be made to work, is the area suitable for a disabled person – without steep slopes, near shops, the library, a good pub? Many people who have lived near good neighbours for a long time would put up with some disadvantages to stay among friends. It is very important to consider the whole family in making this decision, not allowing sympathy for the disabled member to weigh too much. All will have to sacrifice a little, but in the end everybody should be reasonably happy.

If, after much heart-searching, you decide to stay in your house, then you must consider how it can be adapted. It may be possible in a large house to provide all the disabled person's needs downstairs. Alternatively, where there is land available, a common solution is to build a ground-floor extension which is, in effect, a living unit. Grants for this may be available from Social Services, the local authority or, in some cases, both. It is essential that expert advice is sought. Usually this can be obtained by ringing your local *Social Services* Department and asking for a visit from the domiciliary *occupational therapist*. Advice will also be available from your local **DIAL** (O).

Yet another solution is to provide the means for the disabled person to go upstairs unaided, and there is a wide range of equipment available. For the disabled person needing care during the night it is less work if they are on the same floor as the *caring relative*. The most simple DIY aid consists of a cigar box (or something similar) attached to the end of a wooden walking stick. With this you step from the floor on to the box, then up to the first step and repeat on each step. In effect this makes 12 high steps into 24 shallow steps – quite important, because many ambulant disabled people simply cannot lift a foot high enough for ordinary stairs. Another simple device consists of a rail up the stairs on one side at about waist height. From this a folding arm projects at right angles. If you push it, the arm slides; if you lean on it, it locks. This is called the Paramount Stairs Aid and it is made by **Ellis, Son and Paramore** (M).

Broadly speaking there are three 'powered' methods of moving a disabled person upstairs – homelifts, stairlifts and stair climbers. For both types of lift there may be grant aid under Section 56 of the 1974 Housing Act and also under the 1970 Chronically Sick and Disabled Persons Act; here again you apply through your local domiciliary OT. However, these grants are at the discretion of the local authority and there is a wide variation from place to place in the level of provision. Once the make and model of lift is decided upon, if there is no financial help forthcoming it may be worth looking at the second-hand market. The two best sources are the monthly bulletins from **RADAR** (O) or the **Multiple Sclerosis Society** (O). Some lift makers will remove and re-install their own second-hand equipment.

A homelift is a small box which travels vertically between floors – a miniature version of the sort of lift found in public buildings. These lifts are available with or without shafts and are available in different sizes for one, two, or three standing passengers, for one seated passenger, or for an occupied wheelchair. The lift may be open or enclosed in a shaft. Where a shaft is not used the lift runs on two vertical rails so when it is on the upstairs floor there is clear floor space downstairs. Should somebody leave a chair or a dog in that space, the lift stops automatically when the under side touches any obstruction. When the lift is on the ground floor the bedroom floor is complete. Lifts for 'disabled' domestic use are zero-rated for VAT and are covered by BS 5900.

Prices vary from £4,000 to £12,000 and electric vertical lifts are available from **Wessex Medical Equipment Ltd** (M), **Barron and Shepherd** (M), **Stannah Lifts Ltd** (M), **WJ Furse & Co Ltd** (M), and **Portcullis Home Lift Ltd** (M) whilst **Terry Lifts** (M) make the only manual lift.

Most of the above makers also supply stairlifts for which the common feature is a rail, normally fixed to a load-bearing wall on one side of the stairs. It is quite unobtrusive and projects only 9in (23cm), so the stairs are quite accessible for normal use. Stairlifts are available for single passengers seated or standing, and controlled by the rider or a person at the head or foot of the stairs. They can be fitted without damaging the decoration, normally within a few hours, to straight or curved stairs or where there is a landing. The Liberty Stair Lift (**Stairlift Engineering Ltd** (M)) has a swivel seat, making exit on a top landing easy, and the Chester (**Bison Bede Ltd** (M)) is the most luxurious. The Ease Universal Stairlift (**East Anglian Stair Elevators Ltd** (M)) has a track that is only 6in (15cm) wide and operates on a rechargeable battery.

A stair climber is a wheeled electric one-person vehicle which, with or without an attendant, will ascend or descend stairs. The Escamatic Mobile Stair Rider made by **Baronmead** (M) does need an able-bodied assistant, and is a battery-operated device which can be used indoors or outside. It is a 'crawling' vehicle which requires little physical effort by the attendant. There are two versions. The NM52 Trimline is complete with a comfortable seat for the disabled rider, whilst the NM66 is designed to carry a manual wheelchair with the disabled person in it. Both versions will travel, under power, up stairs, down stairs and on the level. The patented locking system stops the unit on each step. Persons of up to 20 stone (128kg) can be carried from floor to floor without strain on the motor. As the device de-mounts into two relatively small items it could be taken in an estate car.

The Step Rider is an electric wheelchair with two small caster wheels in the front, and the rear powered wheels arranged in two triangular clusters of three. An attendant can easily drive the occupied chair up or down stairs. The electrically-powered three-wheel climbing concept has been

283

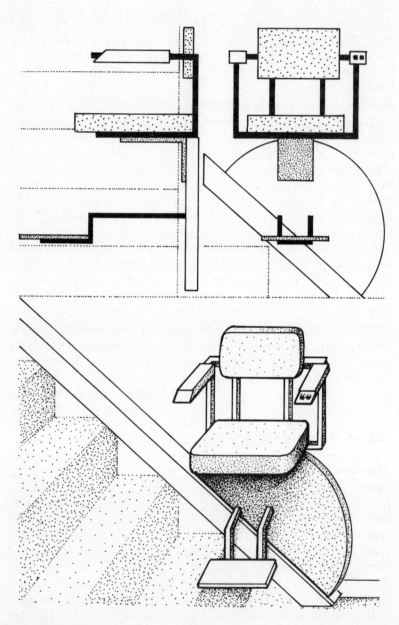

Stairlift.

successful over many years in Italy. The Step Rider grips each step firmly before moving on to the next. A patented braking system controls the rate of descent for added safety, and the chair will cope with steps up to 7¾in (about 19cm) in height and 1,000 steps on one charge. In hospitals, nursing homes, day centres and places of employment and education, the Step Rider will make previously inaccessible areas available at relatively low cost. Only 22in (55cm) wide and 33in (82.5cm) long, this chair can be used in any domestic situation, particularly where there is a straight flight of stairs. On the level, the Mark 1 version is an attendant-operated manual wheelchair; the Mark II Step Rider has an additional power unit which enables it to be driven on the level by the rider unaided. For details write to **Batricar Ltd** (M).

All vertical lifts and stairlifts have different features, and the most expensive is not necessarily the best for a given situation. Safety features are important where the lift is to be used by elderly people or may be misused by children. It is essential to see the range of catalogues, either by sending for them or by visiting your nearest *DIAL* or *Disabled Living Centre*.

Stoke Mandeville

In the county of Buckinghamshire, on the outskirts of Aylesbury, lies the village of Stoke Mandeville, justly world-famous for a hospital specialising in injuries of the spine. Stoke Mandeville is a large district general hospital with many specialities, but it is best known as the home of the National Spinal Injuries Centre. Patients come from all over the UK but the majority come from the counties clustered around London. Stoke Mandeville is one of a number of Spinal Injury Units (SIUs) up and down the country.

Built at the very beginning of the 1939–45 war, the original single-storey hospital was designed for the Emergency

Medical Services to take civilian casualties evacuated from the bombing of London. In fact, almost from its opening in 1940, the hospital was used for service casualties and at the same time patients and staff were evacuated from time to time from the Middlesex Hospital. Fairly quickly, the hospital became used entirely for war casualties.

In the early part of the war many of the injured were airmen with broken backs, broken necks, amputations and severe burns. At Stoke Mandeville in those early days pioneering work on the clinical treatment and subsequent rehabilitation of men and women with spinal injuries was led by the late Dr (later Sir) Ludwig Guttmann. In 1944, as part of the preparations for the Second Front, he opened the National Spinal Injuries Centre, which was to expand eventually to 157 beds. Multiple injuries were common among war casualties and alongside the spinal unit appeared, under the direction of Mr Kilner, the Regional Plastic Surgery and Jaw Injuries Unit.

The National Spinal Injuries Unit has undergone many changes over the years, mainly in response to new techniques, and over the post-war years many of the original hutted wards deteriorated beyond repair. A special swimming pool was opened in 1953 and this has been very effective in the treatment of paraplegia and other paralysing conditions. Sir Ludwig Guttmann originated the use of sport as a major element in the treatment of spinal injuries, and in 1957 a new building was opened for archery, table tennis and snooker. This association with sport continued and quickly out-grew its clinical origins, and today Stoke Mandeville is the world centre for sport for many thousands of disabled people who play for pleasure or competition. Stoke Mandeville now has a large sports stadium and is closely associated with the Paraplegic Games.

The hospital has very close links with the teaching hospitals in London and Oxford; the development of the Post-Graduate Centre has attracted considerable interest from doctors, not only in this country but world-wide, and the programme of studies is continually expanding.

Years ago it was the gentry who suffered most of what were then called 'broken backs' – usually from falling off horses. Nowadays most of the spinal injuries occur to young people, mainly men. Road accidents, especially those involving motorcycles, are the main cause, closely followed by accidents in contact sports such as rugby and soccer. Accidents related to diving into shallow water, riding, motor racing, hang-gliding, parachuting and skiing also often result in spinal injury. Scuba diving accidents resulting in a condition known as the 'bends' are increasing. In this case there is no traumatic spinal injury, but paralysis occurs because the brain is deprived of oxygen.

Stoke Mandeville admits around 20 paraplegics and tetraplegics a month, together with a further 40 former patients who come back for additional treatment or check-ups. In addition the centre handles over 200 out-patients a month. Many patients come in from over 100 miles away to attend the centre, knowing that the services for spinally-injured people are very specialised and after-care can be obtained only from a SIU.

When a spine is broken, apart from the damage to a main vertical supporting element of the body, nerves are also damaged. These nerves normally carry messages from the brain to the muscles, causing limbs to move. If the break in the spine is low, the patient will be a paraplegic – in very broad terms this means he will have lost the control and use of everything below the waist. He will be unable to stand or walk, will have no control of his bowels or bladder, and it is likely that he will have no sensation below the waist. A person with a spinal break high up the spine or the neck will be a tetraplegic, without the use of arms or legs. Some tetraplegics also lose the use of the muscles for breathing, and used to be put in metal chambers called 'iron lungs'. Nowadays they are joined to electric breathing machines, commonly called ventilators or life-support machines. It is normally possible to re-train patients to use their lungs, but a very small proportion do remain on a ventilator for life. Overall, there is a wide variation in the type and severity of the disability, depending on the level of the break in the spinal cord.

There is no cure for a spinal injury but the secondary medical problems – muscle wastage, bowels, bladder, circulation, tissue viability, weight control – can be forestalled. Most spinal injury victims will become wheelchair riders for life; Stoke Mandeville takes them through the period of psychological adjustment and provides the necessary practical training for daily living. The patient has his own programme of activities each day, and this involves learning to dress, management of feeding, toilet and personal appearance, physiotherapy, hydrotherapy and sports activities aimed at conservation and restoration of muscle power.

The National Spinal Injuries Centre, through the expertise of its surgeons and physicians, the dedication of its nurses and therapists, and an unbroken programme of research and education, has earned world fame. It has featured on many television programmes and been visited by many famous people, including members of the Royal Family. However, fame was of little value when, in the late 1970s, it became apparent that the old hutted hospital was beyond repair. One by one wards were closed as rain poured in through the roof.

Many famous names are associated with Stoke Mandeville, but in the mind of the British public, Jimmy Savile will always occupy pride of place. For many years, quietly, and almost without recognition, Jimmy has worked on the wards of the centre, doing portering or any other necessary task. His unfailing sense of humour has often inspired many a patient to try just that little bit harder.

In 1980 Jimmy Savile launched an appeal to raise funds for a new building with all the most up-to-date facilities and equipment for the treatment of those with an injured spinal cord. Work started on the new 120-bed centre in August 1981 and it was officially opened in July 1983. Jimmy's appeal raised over £10,000,000 and the superb new complex included an Out-Patient Department, a patients' dining room and a research institute.

The National Spinal Injuries Centre has a wonderful atmosphere of friendliness, due in no small part to people like Jimmy – where else would you find a fellow who sweeps ward floors and raises millions of pounds? For information write to the National Spinal Injuries Centre, Stoke Mandeville Hospital, Aylesbury, Bucks HP21 8AL.

Stroke

Every year over 100,000 people in the UK suffer a stroke and about one-third of these die. Some recover fairly quickly but around 50,000 are left with a serious disability. A stroke is sudden and traumatic for the individual and devastating for his or her family.

A stroke is a reduction in, or stopping of, the blood flow to the brain. It may be caused by a blood clot blocking an artery, by a blood clot lodging in a narrowed artery, or by the rupture of a blood vessel in the brain. The resulting stroke can vary widely in severity, from a mild 'warning' episode giving pins and needles or weakness in an arm or leg, to paralysis, coma and death. Permanent disability is the result of damage to the brain cells controlling a particular function. There is always some level of recovery as other cells of the brain take over some of the lost functions.

Most stroke victims are over 65. A fairly common result is hemiplegia – paralysis down one side of the body – in which the leg usually recovers more quickly and more completely than the arm. Physiotherapy is essential and should be continued at home after leaving hospital. Without signals from the brain, muscles cease to function. Inactive muscles will waste away and if necessary they must be given passive exercise to retain good condition until the brain recovers. If a right-handed person becomes paralysed down the right side they may also partly or completely lose speech, or an under-standing of the written or spoken word. In the long term speech therapy may help but immediately after a stroke there is a need for simple communication. There is a wide range of electronic portable communication devices available from **QED** (M). Personal mobility will be affected and people under 65 should apply for *Mobility Allowance*. After taking advice from their GP, car drivers will have to inform DVLC at Swansea to exchange their licence for a restricted one –

normally another driving test is not required. For advice about hand controls or automatic transmission contact the **Mobility Information Service** (O).

As the effects of a stroke can vary so widely the impact on employment, social activity, sport and sexual relations will also vary, and advice should be sought in every case. The main agencies are the **Chest, Heart and Stroke Association** (O) (CHSA), the **British Heart Foundation** (O), the **Oxford Prevention of Heart Attack and Stroke Project** (O), **Help for Health** (O) and the **College of Speech Therapy** (O).

The CHSA has an expanding programme of research, health education, conferences and counselling directed towards preventing stroke, and coping with it should it happen. CHSA actively promotes stroke clubs where recovering stroke patients can find practical help as well as social contact with other stroke people. There are over 400 stroke clubs throughout the country and they are very helpful to people with speech difficulties, especially when all the NHS treatment is over. CHSA have a counselling service which gives sympathetic and practical advice to sufferers and their families on the many personal problems arising from their disability.

The **British Heart Foundation** (O) publishes an excellent series of 16 booklets called the 'Heart Research Series'. **Help for Health** (O) will supply a useful book list on request.

T

Talents

I am convinced that we all go to our Maker with many of our talents 'untapped'. Disability forces upon you a changed way of life, but this should be treated as a challenge; maybe now you are in a wheelchair the door of the golf club is closed, but what about the exciting challenge of all the unopened doors in front of you? I was once a patient in a rehabilitation centre in Oxford, and for some weeks I shared a room with a chap who had become a wheelchair rider, having become paralysed from the waist downwards as a result of falling off a roof. He was a plumber by trade, the boss of a small business and he was very depressed because it seemed that his working days were over.

As a part of our training we were taught water colour painting. I was hopeless, but within a week Peter was producing little pictures and selling them to the nurses. When we went our separate ways we agreed to keep in touch, so, writing to him a year later, I asked him what he was doing. He answered 'I never made a drawing in my life before hospital. When I got home someone saw my little paintings and as a consequence the local Lions gave me a set of oil colours and paid for lessons. Now I can turn out several large paintings a week. I make more money selling them than I ever did as a plumber; the tax man doesn't get to find out; and so far my customers have not found out that I keep on producing the same paintings over and over again!'

Talking Newspapers

There are over 500 national and local newspapers and magazines produced in Britain on tape on a regular basis, and the number is rising all the time. Each of these is an independent local registered charity, run by volunteers, helping, with the co-operation of the local newspaper, to keep people who can no longer read print in touch with their community. They do this by recording local news on standard cassette tapes.

The Talking Newspaper Association of the United Kingdom (TNAUK) is the co-ordinating body which has helped many local organisations to set up their talking newspapers. TNAUK set up a national service in 1963 to tape national newspapers and magazines. They have a small paid staff, backed by volunteers who record over 100 national newspapers and magazines. Each taped publication costs the subscriber £7 a year – much less than the cost of the printed versions. There are over 8,000 subscribers.

Whilst the value of this service to blind people is self-evident, it is also of value to many people with physical disabilities. For more information, contact **TNAUK** (O).

Telephone Services

For a mother whose child has been diagnosed as having diabetes, a man who has just been told he has Multiple Sclerosis, or someone who is worried about cancer, for example, instant, reliable information is the only way to allay real or imagined fears. There are a number of very helpful telephone information services available. Before dialling, write all your questions down and be prepared to take notes of what you will be told, as you may be given further contacts.

WEBSTER'S COMPLEMENTARY MEDICINE LINE on 0898 600 440 gives help on choosing the best alternative therapies.

HEALTHCALL is a confidential library of medical information which operates 24 hours a day. You need a directory of the 360+ subjects available as each is on a separate telephone number. This directory will be sent to you free if you telephone Healthcall on 0898 600 600 or write to **Air Call Medical Services Ltd** (O). You look up the subject you want, dial the number beside it, and wait for the tape to start playing. The average duration of a tape is 4 minutes. Calls are charged at British Telecom's 'M' rate, which is 22p per minute cheap rate, or 35p per minute peak rate.

HEALTHLINE is a telephone service on health matters on 01 980 4848. Phone in, ask for the topic you want, and a tape

will be played to you. A list of topics – which includes AIDS, sex, drug abuse and disabilities – is available from **Healthline** (O). Healthline is run by Health Information Trust which is a non-profit-making organisation (office 01 980 6263).

MEDICAL ADVISORY SERVICE is available on 01 994 9874 evenings, from 7–10 pm Monday to Fridays. It provides information on sources of help (private medicine and voluntary organisations) for people with health problems. For additional information write to the **Medical Advisory Service** (O).

NATIONAL AIDS HELPLINE is available 24 hours a day, seven days a week, on 0800 567 123 or 01 992 5522. There is also a Vistel service for deaf people on 0800 521 361. Office contact on **National AIDS Helpline** (O).

WOMEN'S HEALTH INFORMATION CENTRE provides information on female health problems on 01 251 6580 during office hours. Or write to **Women's Health Information Centre** (O) for publications list.

WOMEN'S REPRODUCTIVE RIGHTS INFORMATION CENTRE gives information on 01 251 6332 on reproductive health problems. Write to **Women's Reproductive Rights Information Centre** (O).

Tennis

Tennis players who find themselves confined to a wheel-chair can continue their favourite sport if they wish. Write to Brian Lock, British Wheelchair Tennis Association, The Pavilion, Pryor's Bank, Bishop's Park, Fulham, London SW6.

Tinnitus

In Britain, around 3,000,000 people suffer with tinnitus. For most people it occurs only occasionally or in a mild form, but for some 200,000 it is a disability that is severe enough to affect normal life, with a constant ringing, buzzing or hum-ming noise in the ears.

Tinnitus may be caused by an accumulation of wax in one or both ears, and a family doctor will cure this by syringeing with slightly warm water.

If the tinnitus is due to the erratic flow of blood in an artery or vein then the doctor will be able to hear this with a stethoscope and a surgical cure may be possible. However, most tinnitus 'sounds' are heard only by the sufferer. In this case the condition may be associated with deafness, particu-larly in elderly people, and it is often incurable.

A tinnitus masker is a device worn in the ear, rather like a hearing aid. It makes the tinnitus tolerable by covering it with a sound which is more pleasant. There are also a number of drugs which can be used with or without a masker. Some people find hypnotherapy is of value.

For more information contact **RNID** (O) or the **British Tinnitus Association** (O) which has over 100 local branches up and down the country.

Story

Amazing

Tinnitus – ringing in the ears – has been prevalent since earliest recorded history in Mesopotamia and Egypt. In those days, reported Pliny the Elder, common cures included foam from a horse's mouth, mother's milk and donkey dung.

Toilets

Management of bladder and bowels is of paramount importance for the health of a physically disabled person, and it follows that the actual means of 'going' should be as easy and comfortable as possible. Training is important and for all but the most severely handicapped person the object should be complete independence. Suitable *clothing* is of value particularly for those who need to hold a support rail to stand; write to the Clothing Adviser, **DLF** (O). Most toilets are too low, and weak leg muscles may mean too rapid a descent on to the seat. For those with good arms, fixed or portable support rails help (**Llewellyn** (M), **SML** (M)). Where the toilet is also used by able-bodied members of the family, a removable raised seat (**Nicholls and Clarke** (M)) may be the answer, but the disabled person may need a foot-stool. SML also supply the Easyrise Toilet Chair which is electrically-powered and, having arms and a back rest, gives great confidence to the user. At the touch of a button the seat rises and tilts forward, putting you in a standing position. There are also a variety of padded seats, complete with lids (**Llewellyn** (M), **Nicholls and Clarke** (M)), and inflatable rubber rings to fit over an existing toilet seat (**SML** (M)).

Possibly the greatest infringement of human dignity for the disabled person is the need to have another person to wipe one's bottom after a bowel action. Furthermore, this is an extremely difficult task for a single-handed helper who then has to try to hold the disabled person upright whilst adjusting their clothes. Apart from the restoration of privacy and dignity, cleanliness around your 'tail' will reduce problems arising from possible infection of pressure sores. There is one electric 'wash and blow dry' toilet for which the reliability has been proven over many years. This is the Samoa automatic combined WC and bidet made and supplied by **Clos-o-Mat (GB) Ltd** (M). This is one unit combining the cistern and the toilet, and it is operated by the user pressing either of two large square buttons on the cistern whilst remaining seated. The writer, who has used a Clos-o-Mat for many years, operates it with his elbow. Pressing the button starts a timed cycle of actions. The toilet is flushed, after which an arm comes out from the rear of the pan. This has a warm water spray which continues until the control button is released. At this point the spray arm retracts and a warm air jet operates and stops after a timed interval. The water and air temperatures are thermostatically controlled. The unit can also be used as a conventional toilet. Clos-o-Mat provide a yearly check and emergency servicing contract.

The 'Medic Loo Dryad' is an electric bidet assembly for use with an existing toilet. There is a free-standing unit beside the WC, which takes up 10 × 20in (23 × 51cm) of floor space, and has a similar 'wash and blow dry' cycle. Write to **Medic Bath Ltd** (M). **Nicholls and Clarke** (M) supply toilet roll holders for one-handed operation and bottom wipers are available from **Llewellyn** (M) and **Homecraft** (M). The Maxigrip extends a lever flush handle to give a more comfortable grip whilst the Super Melton is a new raised toilet seat in a choice of three heights (**Nottingham Rehab Ltd** (M)).

Macerators and macerating toilets can be used with smallbore (20–30mm) outlets. This means a toilet can be located anywhere in the house – up to about 60ft (20m) horizontally and 9–12ft (3–4m) vertically from the nearest soil pipe. For the severely disabled or frail elderly person it is now possible to put a toilet in a bedroom. There are two systems. The

Superflush 2002 is an electrically-operated toilet which has no cistern, and all working parts are built into the WC pan. Installation requires no major structural building work (**Edincare Ltd** (M)). The Saniflow (**Transbyn Ltd** (M)) is a unit which fits on to any toilet with a horizontal outlet. Waste matter is shredded and discharged through a 20mm pipe.

Catalogues can be seen at any *DIAL* or *Disabled Living Centre* and Leaflet 7A, *Personal Toilet*, from **DLF** (O) has many useful addresses.

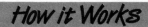

How it Works

1 CONVENTIONAL USE
To use as a conventional W.C., press the operating bar whilst standing.

2 WARM WATER WASHING
WARM AIR DRYING
a. While seated press either operating bar (or foot/hand switch if fitted), keep depressed until water runs cool (W.C. flushing takes place simultaneously).

2 b. Release operating bar and the warm air drier will start. Remain seated until warm air ceases (when W.C. is ready for re-use).

3 NOTE
● The unit must be switched on for 3 minutes before use to ensure correct sequence of functions and water is warm.
● If douche water is not allowed to run cool the air drier may not function or may only operate for a short time.

Story

Sitting Pretty

An English lady, already a wheelchair rider, having suffered a nervous breakdown, decided on a quiet holiday abroad and a friend recommended a hostel in a small German village. It was suggested that she should write for details to the village schoolmaster as he knew a little English. One of the questions in her letter was where the WC was located in the hostel. The German village schoolmaster had never heard the abbreviation WC and he decided that, as the hostel was a religious retreat, the lady must be a devout church-goer, and that she must want to know where the World Chapel was situated. So he wrote:

The WC is situated some seven miles away from your lodgings, in the midst of beautiful scenery, and is open on Tuesdays, Thursdays, Fridays and, of course, all day Sundays. This is unfortunate for you if you are in the habit of going frequently, but you will be glad to know some people take their lunch with them and make a day of it, while others go by car and arrive just in time.

As there are many visitors in summer, I advise you to go early. The accommodation is good and there are about 60 seats, but should you arrive late, you may join in, standing at the side. The bell is rung ten minutes before the WC is open. I advise you especially to pay a call on a Friday when there is an organ performance.

I should be delighted to reserve a seat for you and be the first to take you there. My wife and I have not been for six months and it pains us very much, but it is such a long way to go.

Hoping this information will be of use to you.

Yours &c'

(With acknowledgements to the Multiple Sclerosis Society.)

Toilet Seat Covers

For people who make long journeys by rail or air, and those who use public conveniences frequently, there is a range of disposable toilet seat covers which provide good hygiene. They are designed in such a way that there need be no contact with the toilet either when placing the cover in position or during use. After use the cover is automatically flushed away. Minimum order by post is 5 packs of 20 costing £7.65 (including p & p), from **Bechwell Trading Ltd** (M).

Torticollis

Torticollis, which used to be called 'wry neck', is an irksome condition in which the head is tilted to one side, and turning towards that side may be limited. A child may be born with it and recover without treatment. Torticollis, which appears in early life may be due to a shortening of the mastoid muscle. *Physiotherapy*, which is essentially concerned with stretching of muscles, is usually effective. For more information, write to Mrs Margaret Ball, Torticollis Society, 42b Stakes Road, Purbrook, Portsmouth PO7 5NA.

Tricycles and Bicycles

There are a number of tricycles on the market which, although designed for ablebods, have a particular application to people with certain disabilities.

Where one of a couple of adults is disabled, a machine which enables them to take exercise and fresh air together gives great pleasure. This is particularly so when one partner is blind. There is now a tandem tricycle which is ideal for touring. The machine is supplied with five- or ten-speed gears, wide section tyres, four brakes, including a large diameter hub brake which is useful for coasting down long hills. At the back is a large luggage tray, and the range of optional extras includes puncture-proof tyres, alloy wheels, and a variety of chain sets. Prices vary between £800 and £900. Write to **Broadway Bikes** (M).

For people who can ride a bicycle but lack the muscle power in their legs, there is a range of power-assisted bicycles and tricycles. The design is simple and the electronics kept to a minimum. There is a range of optional extras and a choice of colours. The power comes from a high-capacity battery which can be recharged at night to give a range of about 15 miles – for local shopping a couple of charges a week would suffice. The Urban Cycle folds down so it can be stowed in a car boot. Write to **Scintilla Technology Ltd** (M).

U

Ulcerative Colitis

See under Crohn's Disease.

Unit for Disabled Passengers

The London Regional Transport Unit for Disabled Passengers has two useful cassettes to make travel on the tube easier for blind and visually handicapped people.

The Talking Map of the London Underground takes you in either direction along every Underground line, highlighting interchanges with other lines and with British Rail. It is just like following an ordinary map. The tape is tone-indexed so you can quickly find the line you want.

The Talking Underground Station Guide is a tone-indexed alphabetical list of all 275 stations. It tells which lines each station serves, whether it is an interchange with British Rail, and whether access to the platforms is by stairs, escalator or lift. It is very helpful to guide-dog owners.

For free copies of both, ring the Unit for Disabled Passengers, London Regional Transport, on 01 222 5600. This office will also supply a leaflet about its work and a braille version of the popular handbook *Access to the Underground*.

Urostomy

This is an operation which results in the diversion of urine into a container worn on the stomach. The special needs of people with a urostomy are served by the **Urostomy Association** (O) which helps patients both before and after the operation with counselling and information on appliances, housing work situations, marital problems, and all that is needed to resume as full a life as possible. Trained members of the association will visit new members on request. The UA journal is published twice a year. Research into urinary problems and the development of equipment is promoted.

Vacuum Cleaners

There is a special vacuum cleaner bag for people who are allergic to dust and micro-particles from pets and domestic cleaning. The bag is called Barrier 95 and it is said to be 360 per cent more efficient than conventional disposable paper bags. It is made from micro-porous permeable polyurethane and it retains 95 per cent of the dust it collects. It would be of special value to *asthma* sufferers. Barrier 95 lasts two years with normal use. Contact **Porvair Ltd** (M).

Value Added Tax

Almost all aids and items of equipment designed and made solely for the use of disabled people are exempt from VAT under the terms of the Value Added Tax Act 1983 Schedule 5, Group 14. Help and advice can be obtained from your local VAT office which is in your phone book under 'Customs and Excise'. Everything, from a small item like a special cushion to a modified vehicle, may qualify – if in doubt always ask. It is never possible to get VAT exemption *after* a purchase has been made.

Qualification for zero rating on a purchase depends on proof that the user is disabled by the provision of a declaration signed by the disabled person. There are no printed forms but the following is often used:

'I (full name)

of (address)

declare that I am an eligible person under para 1 of VAT Leaflet 701/7/86, and that I am suffering from:

(description of disability, for example Multiple Sclerosis)

and that I am receiving from:

(name and address of supplier)

the following goods which are being supplied to me for domestic or my personal use:

(description of goods)

and I claim that the supply of these goods is eligible for relief from Value Added Tax under Group 14 of the Zero Rate Schedule to the Value Added Tax Act 1963.
(signature)
(date)'

Thousands of 'disabled' items are zero-rated, but in very broad terms the list includes medical appliances, adjustable beds, commodes and electric toilets, hoists and stairlifts, any equipment designed solely for use by handicapped persons, and vehicles permanently modified for carrying an occupied wheelchair.

Certain services, such as an extension to a dwelling house, may also be zero-rated. Not included are hearing aids, dentures, and spectacles. Any item, such as a walking stick, which could be used by a disabled or an able-bodied person would not be exempt from VAT.

Normally the supplier of the goods or services will provide a VAT exemption form for the disabled customer to sign. However if the supplier normally deals with able-bodied people (for example, a builder or a garage) he may not know the VAT exemption rules. The onus is always upon the customer to produce Leaflet 701/7/86 to prove his entitlement. Where there is any doubt the VAT office will always give a ruling.

The rules are very complicated so it is absolutely essential where any large purchase is contemplated to visit the VAT office to get a letter of agreement. Few people would realise that automatic transmission, power-assisted steering, electric windows or central locking can be VAT-free on a new modified vehicle, but the need for each must be proved separately. If it is near enough it would pay to visit a *DIAL*; they may suggest items you had not considered.

Varicose Veins

Varicose veins cause discomfort, pain, embarrassment and often years of despair for millions of people. Each year, about half a million people, mostly women, see their doctor about varicose veins. In addition, similar problems beset anyone with enforced immobility, such as wheelchair riders and elderly people. The results of poor circulation are found most commonly in the legs, where a large blood supply is needed to 'fuel' active muscles and large bones. When this blood has to return to the heart, it does so against the force of gravity. Veins described as 'varicose' are unsightly, swollen and often distend beyond the level of the adjoining skin.

There are two main 'pumps' in the leg which pump the blood back to the heart for recycling. One is the calf muscle and the other is the foot. Each is associated with one-way valves which prevent back flow, and they operate most efficiently when we walk. A damaged valve, or total inactivity of the leg, allows blood to collect under pressure in the veins near the surface. Cramp pains in the legs at night should be taken as warning signals.

There are a number of causes. Some families seem to suffer from them in several generations, although there is no proven genetic link. Pregnant women are prone but recovery is normal after the birth. Varicose veins can be caused by tight clothing, by obesity and by prolonged standing.

Elastic compression stockings can be prescribed to relieve the effects of varicose veins, and may stop them getting worse. These stockings range from support tights to strong medical hosiery, and in most cases they are of considerable benefit. Under the new Drug Tariff which came into force in April 1988, elastic stockings are easier for the doctor to prescribe and the stockings are more acceptable to the wearer. Severe cases of varicose veins are treated with surgery.

If the skin is broken, even a relatively small wound can take a long time to heal, or fail to heal at all. This is due to the high pressure in the vein. Very careful treatment is needed to prevent the wound developing into a large, chronic leg ulcer – these are notoriously difficult to heal and tend to recur. In some cases, amputation is the only answer. The occurrence of leg ulcers is alarmingly high – 1 per cent of the population as a whole, rising to 3.6 per cent for people over 65. Treatment places a considerable strain on the NHS.

Physically disabled and elderly people can take simple precautions against lower limb problems – simple regular exercise, weight control, avoiding standing, using elastic stockings, taking note of warning signs. Prevention is better than the unsightly and painful alternatives.

Exemption from Vehicle Excise Duty

Disabled people who are drawing certain benefits can claim free tax discs for their cars. The benefits are *Mobility Allowance, Attendance Allowance*, War Pensioners Mobility Supplement or Private Car Allowance. The disc is similar to the normal one but it is marked 'Disabled'. The vehicle must be registered in the name of the disabled person or (as in the case of a child) the appropriate nominee.

Recipients of Mobility Allowance or War Pensioners Mobility Supplement are given entitlement certificates MY182 or MPB1266. Those who have Attendance Allowance, Private Car Allowance or a blue 'Noddy' car will be given entitlement certificate MHS 330.

To get your first exempt licence, take a completed form V10 (from the post office), an entitlement certificate, certificate of insurance, MOT certificate (if necessary), and the Registration Document to the Vehicle Registration Office.

When your licence is due to run out you will get a renewal notice from the DVLC, Swansea, and the instructions for renewal are on this. If a disabled person has had sole use of a car for a period before receiving his Entitlement Certificate, a refund may be claimed at the time of application for the first free disc.

Full details are in leaflet V188, *Exemption from Vehicle Excise Duty for Disabled People*, or from the Vehicle Enquiry Unit, DVLC, Swansea SA99 1BL (0792 72134).

Voluntary Organisations

See National Council for Voluntary Organisations.

W

Webster's Complementary Medicine Line

See Telephone Services.

Wheelchairs

Broadly speaking there are two types of wheelchair – those which are manually operated and those which are powered, usually by electricity. There are also two ways of acquiring a wheelchair – either free from statutory sources or by purchase from commercial sources. Always try to get a 'ministry' chair before thinking about buying one, and do consider the thriving second-hand market.

There are three types of manual wheelchair – those which are operated by the rider, those which have to be pushed by an able-bodied helper (known as 'attendant-controlled'), and high-tech special lightweight wheelchairs used for sports like wheelchair basketball. The most common type of rider-operated manual wheelchair is the type with large wheels at the rear and small caster wheels at the front. A smooth metal ring is attached to the wheel to provide for hand propulsion, with capstan rims available for people with poor grip. To provide for easy entry to the wheelchair, foot-rests are normally designed to lift off or swing around to the sides. Some paraplegics find it easier to propel a chair with large wheels in the front, but these are more difficult to enter.

There are literally scores of types of manual wheelchairs and countless accessories. Wheelchairs come in different sizes, and the overall length and width, and the seat width and height from the ground, all vary, and obviously affect comfort and mobility. Foot-rests, arm-rests and the angle of the back-rest may vary according to choice, and on some chairs they are adjustable. It is very important for both health and comfort to see that your chair fits you. Always treat an aching back, neck, arms or legs as a sign that there may be something wrong with your wheelchair. For hemiplegics there are wheelchairs with both driving rims on one side. There are also chairs that can be propelled with a single lever and steered with the foot. Some wheelchairs have backs which fold down on to the seat.

To obtain a free wheelchair you go to your family doctor. If you are able to walk a little and need a wheelchair only for occasional use, he will prescribe a chair himself and in due course it will be delivered to your house. If your needs are complicated the doctor will refer you to your nearest DSC – Disablement Services Centre. There you will be seen by a consultant and a technical officer and you will be able to try out a number of chairs. It is a good plan to make a list of the things you want to be able to do from your wheelchair – can you transfer from it to the bed, toilet, armchair or car seat? Will it go into the boot of the car? Can your spouse lift it in? Can you eat, read, write or sleep in the chair? You also need a list of accessories – certainly a cushion and maybe lifting foot-rests, desk arms and a shelf. That way you will get a chair suited to your needs. The DSC staff are very helpful but you cannot expect them to be mind-readers.

The DSC range of wheelchairs and accessories is always expanding and their excellent servicing and replacement service is free. Many people go on using an unsuitable or out-of-date wheelchair because they think it cannot be changed, but reasonable requests are always met. The life of a wheelchair varies considerably and it is worth asking for a replacement when you think you need it. The DSC will supply you with a second manual wheelchair where there is a need to keep one at a place of work or education, or where you have two totally incompatible needs. Any disabled person may retain an 'old' wheelchair when they are given a replacement, if they sign a waiver absolving the NHS from the consequences of any accident arising from the use of the old chair. Most wheelchair users make the maximum use of their DSC and buy only that which is unobtainable from statutory sources.

Attendant-operated wheelchairs have 12in (30cm) pneumatic tyres at the back and small casters in the front. These chairs must be tried out by the caring relative at the time of supply.

The DSC supplies rider-controlled electric wheelchairs to disabled people who cannot propel themselves, but for indoor use only, which means within your house and garden. Front wheel drive chairs made by **BEC** (M), with four small wheels, are best for the limited space of a small house. These indoor electric wheelchairs are controlled by left- or right-hand joystick, by chin or suck/blow. If a disabled person is unable to propel himself and his caring relative is not strong enough to push him, or if the immediate environment around his house is full of steep gradients, then the DSC will supply a Model 28B, which is an electric-powered non-folding wheelchair controlled by the pusher rather like a lawn mower.

Few wheelchairs come complete with a cushion so when you get a chair make sure you get a cushion to suit it. No one cushion will suit all purposes. For the person unable to stand the RoHo cushion supplied by **Raymar** (M) is excellent for avoiding pressure sores, but it will not stand rough usage so it should be left in an indoor wheelchair permanently. For a wheelchair which goes in and out of a car frequently a standard NHS 2in or 3in (5cm or 7.5cm) foam cushion is good, whilst a cushion filled with gel, or gel and water, works well in a large outdoor electric wheelchair. **Medipost** (M) supply a very comfortable wheelchair set comprising a seat cushion, back cushion and arm covers all made in Mullipel in a choice of colours and patterns.

Any wheelchair should have all the attachments required for the user to live the way he wishes. **Orange Aids** (M) supply clamp-on units which will take a very large range of equipment for toilet, cookery, office work, reading, hobbies or photography. A simple DIY drink stand can be made by screwing a circular metal ash-tray to the top of a metal rod; two 1in (2.5cm) tool clips attached to the rod about 3in (7.5cm) apart enable the stand to be attached to any wheelchair. Underneath the seat you can fit a full-width canvas shelf for shopping. According to your needs you can fit one or more bags to the back or sides of the chair. **Medipost** (M) supply a parasol which clips on to the back of the chair, and in winter many people cover their legs with waterproof thermal wheelchair rugs.

A wheelchair needs servicing on a regular basis – ideally once a week. Working parts need oil, tyres need air, batteries need distilled water, and the whole thing needs cleaning. Puncture-proof tyres are available from **BG Puncture-Proof Services** (M) or from **Community Health Supplies** (M), and sealed-for-life gel batteries need no maintenance and reduce the risk of spillage. Faulty brakes which allow a chair to roll just when you are going to sit in it are a common cause of accidents, so attend to these regularly. Thought must be given to the caring relative, who has to push the wheelchair, lift it into the car, and maybe lift you in and out of it. So when you are acquiring a wheelchair, picture some of these things being done on a dark night in a wet and windy car park. The value of a wheelchair really becomes apparent when you have to do without it. It is a good idea always to keep a note of the telephone number of your local wheelchair repairer.

The range of commercial wheelchairs, both manual and powered, is vast, and it pays the potential purchaser to see a number of catalogues before making a choice. You can see these and get advice at your nearest *DIAL* or *Disabled Living Centre*, and there are also a few shops carrying a range of wheelchairs. In choosing a manual wheelchair, think about the overall dimensions, getting in and out, ease of folding, weight, size when folded, range of accessories and management by your 'pusher'. The lightest, at 26lb (12kg) is the ultra lightweight by **Newton** (M). This has a handy shelf under the seat and choice of wheels which are all removable without tools.

Powered one-person pavement vehicles fall into two classes – those which look like wheelchairs and those which resemble golf buggies. Most of them are powered by 12 or 24 volt batteries. Prices range from £900 to £3,500, but they can be hire-purchased from **Motability** (O). The most sophisticated outdoor wheelchair is the Meyra wheelchair supplied by **Medinorth Ltd** (M), which has a range of 35 miles, six speed ranges, the ability to 'creep' slowly over a 5in (12.5cm) pavement edge, and full lighting, including indicators and hazard warning. With this chair you can roam the countryside with confidence. This is a vehicle you keep in the garage and it is one of the safest and most reliable long-distance outdoor wheelchairs on the market. It is also available with elevating leg-rests and reclining back. Few electric wheelchairs can be easily loaded into a car single-handed – in fact, lifting a box with two *batteries* in it is a job for two men – so, for days out and holidays, a good electric wheelchair is the Travvla made by **Vessa** (M). This will de-mount, without tools, into as many as ten separate units if required, so each is relatively light for loading into the car. Other large wheelchair makers include **Everest & Jennings** (M), **Carters** (M), **NV Distributors** (M), **Joncare** (M) and **Downs** (M).

There is an ever-increasing number of wheelchairs, both manual and powered, to meet special needs, social or medical. Several firms make chairs which will stand you up, or with elevating seats to enable you to reach a high shelf or sit at a bar. There are chairs which can be driven up or down stairs. The outdoor version is the **Mobility** (M) 2000 which has twelve wheels arranged in four clusters of three. It is a most versatile rider-operated chair which can climb stairs, steps, kerbs, virtually any gradient, and travel over rough or soft ground. Having power on all four wheels gives it tremendous traction. The seat can be lowered to finger-tip height from the ground or raised to work-bench height. The Squirrel, made by **Chair Power** (M) is an electric wheelchair, powered and steered on all four wheels so it can be moved sideways. Most people who 'live' in an electric wheelchair find when they go on holiday that they have to revert to a manual, as most cars will not take two wheelchairs. Now there are portable 'add-on' electric power units which convert a manual chair into a rider-controlled power wheelchair.

To use a golf buggie-type vehicle such as a **Batricar** (M) you have to be able to walk a few paces to get into it, and with most you have to have a good pair of hands and arms to steer using a wheel or tiller. These also have to be kept in a garage. The relatively new **Explorer** (M) vehicles are made in glass-fibre with an integral roof, and are available in electric, petrol or petrol/electric versions. These are rugged 'go-anywhere' vehicles which, in the electric and petrol/electric types, can be controlled with a small joystick. The petrol versions have unlimited range and optional extras include a heater.

The **Car-Chair** (M) is a system in which either or both of the front seats of a car can be replaced with one of a range of manual or electric wheelchairs. The chair, complete with rider, is reversed to the open door of the car and hooked on to a kind of fork-lift. Electrically, the chair is raised, its wheels folded, rotated into the car and lowered into position.

Many specialist manual wheelchairs are available for sport and of these the Quickie, Swede and Kuschall are popular makes available from **Gerald Simonds** (M). There is one sports wheelchair – the Sprint – available free from the DSC. One of the best books for information on wheelchairs is *Motoring and Mobility for Disabled People* by Ann Darnborough and Derek Kinrade and published by **RADAR** (O). This is a thick volume of 700 pages covering all types of wheelchairs and the methods of using them with a motor car. The more expensive wheelchairs can be hire-purchased through **Motability** (O).

Always seek advice before buying a wheelchair. Go to a *DIAL* or *Disabled Living Centre* if you have one near you. Contact your community OT or visit the *Occupational Therapy* Department of your nearest hospital. If you do choose a wheelchair ask the salesman to give you the name and address of someone who has recently bought the model you are about to buy, then you can get an unbiased opinion on it.

Story

The Tribulations of a Wheelchair Pusher

If a wheelchair will not move:
    the brakes are on,
    the tyres are flat,
    the rider has his foot where it shouldn't be,
    his coat is caught in the spokes,
    the front wheel is stuck in a drain,
    the rider's feet are lacerating the ankles of the person in front,
    it's up to its hubcaps in something,
    the carpet was too expensive,
    it won't go any further into the lift.

Story

Time-bomb

Children are refreshingly direct in their approach to a wheelchair. A nine-year-old boy came up to me as I sat in my electric wheelchair in the sun outside our local corner shop. 'Hello,' he began, briskly, 'are you a cripple?'

I admitted that I was.

'Is that chair electric?'

'Yes.'

'Can you make it go?'

Somewhat cautiously, I said I could.

'Does it go fast?'

'Fast enough for me.'

He looked at me enviously and sighed, saying 'It must be great to bomb around in that.'

Story

Living in sin

Out motoring, we stopped outside a village pub. My wife lifted me out of the car into my wheelchair and trundled me into the pub. She left me in front of the bar and disappeared to the ladies toilet. It is odd how many people assume wheelchair riders are deaf. I ordered a pint and the bartender, in a voice that could be heard all over the room, said 'and what will your nurse have?'

A hush fell as, raising my voice slightly, I replied 'I'm sleeping with that nurse tonight so better make it a double brandy.'

The British Association of Wheelchair Distributors

This organisation of the forty largest wheelchair distributors in the UK was formed in 1985 with the object of providing wheelchair riders with straightforward dealing, good assessment of their needs, and a reliable after-sales service. They have a published Code of Practice which includes a conciliation service to deal with any dispute between a wheelchair supplier and a disabled customer. The code also provides a guarantee in respect of all repair work undertaken.

BAWD have negotiated favourable terms with two hire purchase companies and a 'Powerchair Insurance Plan' through MJ Fish & Co., 1–3 Slater Lane, Leyland, Preston PR5 3AL (0772 455111). In association with the Electric Vehicle Association they have set minimum standards for power-chair batteries and these carry the EVA label. Negotiations are in hand for a similar system for battery chargers.

If you own or are about to purchase an electric wheelchair you should use a BAWD supplier. There will be one in your area and you can get a list, complete with phone numbers, from the British Association of Wheelchair Distributors, D Smytheman, Grove Cottage, Packwood Road, Lapworth, Solihull, West Midlands B94 6AS.

Wheelchairs on Pavements

It is legal to use certain powered wheelchairs on pavements, footpaths and to cross roads. Where there are no pedestrian sidewalks, powered wheelchairs may be driven along roads. No driving test, licence or number plates are required, and these rules apply whether the vehicle is controlled by the rider or an attendant. These rules also apply to electric *scooters* and tricycles. All of these vehicles are exempt from compulsory insurance.

If one of these vehicles is used in the dark on a road where there is no pavement it must have a single white light in front, and a single red light plus a reflector at the back. No lights are required in the dark for driving on the pavement or crossing.

The vehicle must be incapable of being driven faster than 4 miles per hour, and its braking system should be able to stop it and hold it stationary on gradients of up to 1 in 5. The unladen weight of the vehicle should not exceed 250lb (about 113kg); this is likely to be increased to 560lb (about 254g).

Wider Horizons

This is a registered charity which for many years has lightened the lives of house-bound disabled or elderly people.

The membership is made up of physically disabled people of all ages, lonely people, people lacking social contacts, and able-bodied folk who are interested in supporting this valuable organisation. As members live in all parts of the UK and some overseas, all the work is carried out by correspondence.

For a modest annual subscription of £3.00 each member receives a bi-monthly magazine, the contents of which are written by the members themselves. The *Wider Horizons Magazine* covers a variety of subjects including nature, travel, hobbies, Christian topics, competitions and anything of general interest. For people with visual handicaps there is a cassette version.

There is a correspondence folder on various subjects and those who prefer to exchange letters individually can be linked up with members with similar interests.

For more information, send a stamped addressed envelope to Mr and Mrs AB Fletcher, 'Westbrook', Back Lane, Malvern, Worcestershire WR14 2HJ.

Womens' National Cancer Control Campaign

The WNCCC was formed in 1965 to help women overcome their fears of cancer and to take simple precautions which could save their lives. They have five mobile clinics and organise screening for women in their places of work and local shopping centres, managing in this way to reach women who could not attend normal clinics.

They provide a wide range of literature and audio-visual aids, as well as speakers for ladies' meetings. This vital tuition enables women to detect early signs of breast or cervical cancer. Contact **Women's National Cancer Control Campaign** (O).

Writing for Disabled People

Writing is an excellent occupation for disabled people, especially wheelchair pilots. Writing is time-consuming and time is something disabled people have plenty of; writing can bring in a little money, and money is something most disabled people are short of; writing can be done at home at a pace and at times which best suit the writer's disability.

Few people know whether they can write until they try. Not many writers are geniuses; the vast majority are merely competent at a craft which can be self-taught. New writers are well advised to write upon subjects with which they are familiar, so start with aspects of your own disability – hospital, adapting your house, your disability, equipment, your partner, caring professionals. If you have a hobby or a favourite sport, write about that. If you have travelled, and particularly if you have some good photographs, write about the places you have seen. Until you have considerable experience do not write about yourself.

Great confidence comes from seeing your work in print and for many people their first experience of this will be a letter to the editor of a national newspaper or magazine; some of the latter pay for letters. *Wider Horizons* (O) is a magazine composed entirely of the work of disabled writers. In the first 12 months be prepared for a great deal of disappointment, but remember that even if your piece is rejected it may have nothing wrong with it – it may just be the case that it did not fit in with that particular publication. Do not throw away rejected material as often it can be refurbished and used again.

By and large, bearing in mind that one person in five has a close daily contact with handicap, the world of disability is poorly served by the media – and this is where you could carve a little niche for your work. No national daily newspaper carries a regular feature devoted to the interests of disabled people, yet weekly columns are to be found on everything from antiques to angling. A few of the provincial papers do carry disabled features and *Caring* (M) will consider material from disabled writers. Women's magazines will take well-written articles, particularly about female disabled achievers. If you can persuade the editor of your local evening paper to give you a weekly column with a disability-related content, this makes a splendid apprenticeship, as your work will be sub-edited and you can learn from your mistakes.

Your first need is to get words on to paper, and this usually means using a typewriter. If your handicap allows you to use a conventional machine then it pays to take a typing course – two hours a week for three terms. At a College of Further Education this course is likely to be free if you are disabled.

For those who find hitting the keys of a standard 'qwerty' keyboard difficult, there are key covers, expanded keyboards and, with computers, a wide range of inputs. There is even a typewriter which will print what you say. Editors usually require material typed double-spaced with a 2in (5cm) margin on the left. Always keep a copy so you can discuss changes over the phone.

Most writers feel they could go on rewriting an article many times and each time it would get better. Few people can get an article right for size, shape and coverage at the first draft. It is a great advantage if you can use a computer with a word processing programme or, better still, a dedicated word processor such as an Olivetti. With this there is no need to draft – you simply play about with the words on the screen until the piece is right. You can correct spelling, insert words or sentences, slide whole paragraphs up and down, and run as many copies as you wish. Some machines have built-in dictionaries, and others will 'seek and change' any word throughout an article. The writer uses the word processor rather like an artist painting in oils. You compose on the screen, altering, correcting, choosing and re-arranging until you are satisfied. You can, over a period, write any number of articles simultaneously, leaving them in the machine and adding to each as and when you wish. You can keep notes, statistics, addresses, phone numbers, or any data you use from time to time.

If you wish to work away from home there are a number of battery-operated electric typewriters, such as those in the Brother and Canon ranges, which have a memory of about five pages of typing. These small machines have many of the word processing features of the bigger machines, including correction before printing. All 'computer-type' typewriters permit the running of multiple copies and for the aspiring writer they are ideal. Fairly new on the market are portable battery-operated computers but printers are needed for typed copies.

Other essential 'tools of the trade' are a good dictionary and *Roget's Thesaurus*. Alternatively, from large office equipment supply shops, these are available in one small machine which has a keyboard and a small LCD window. You key in your spelling of the word and the correct spelling appears in the window. The *Writer's Monthly* is invaluable for budding writers. Write to *Writer's Monthly*, 18–20 High Road, London N22 6DN. For disabled writers aiming at freelance newspaper journalism *All Write Now* by Pat Saunders is priced at 60p (plus 20p p & p) from **RADAR** (O).

Readers of popular newspapers and magazines like that which is familiar. A regular column should appear on the same page of the paper on the same day each week, and should have an eye-catching caption embodying your own personal logo. This 'familiarity' aspect is an important step towards getting your readers turning eagerly to your article to see what you have to say this week.

Careful thought should be given to your style. In popular publications you are writing for a mass reading public, so your style should be chatty, simple, and easy to read. This is quite difficult but it really needs only time and patience. Your disabled readers and their *caring relatives* are a section of society containing all ages and all levels of literacy. Your writing must be liked by the majority and tolerated kindly by the remainder. Humour is very important, both in the text and in cartoon form. Use a working title to identify your piece in the making, and then title it after it is written. Often the title will come from a phrase in the text. Always try to capture your reader's attention from the start, even if you have to say something outrageous.

You do not necessarily have to write about disability, although this may be easier to start with, if only because the competition is poor. You can experiment with different forms of writing – articles, short stories, book criticism, novels, children's stories – always with a clear view of your readership. Do not write a piece first and then try and find an editor to buy it. Decide on the publication you are going to write for, read several copies and thoroughly immerse yourself in their type of material, then think about doing a piece to please their readers. Be content, to start with, to concentrate on getting yourself into print, even if you are paid nothing for it. Every piece you get printed is building up your qualifications as a writer.

A weekly 'disabled' column in a local paper fills a media gap which exists in most towns. In no way does it overlap the publications of the national voluntary associations, but it does draw strength from them. The majority of disabled people belong to no national association, and as a journalist you can reach most of the disabled people in your area through your local newspaper. Disabled readers are prompted to bring local problems to your column. Through reading the column, the general public, including the decision-makers, are made aware of the problems of handicapped people. In every town there are disabled people who could do themselves, and many other people, a lot of good by writing for the local paper on a regular basis.

Young Disabled on Holiday

This charity provides *holidays* for physically handicapped people aged 18–30 years. The aim of the holidays is to provide a wide range of activities specifically catering for the interests of young people. YDH is run by a voluntary committee of disabled and able-bodied young people.

The organisation has run holidays in various locations, including Edinburgh, Lancaster, York, Southampton and Wales; and abroad in Germany, Spain, France, Ireland, Malta and Lanzarote. The holiday accommodation has included tents, boats, universities, chalets and hotels. Each holiday-maker has a helper to suit required needs.

YDH provides holidays for most types and degrees of physical disability. Every applicant is required to complete a medical form, and acceptance for holidays is at the discretion of the Nursing Advisor and holiday organisers. All holidays have a nurse in full-time attendance.

Disabled holiday-makers have to meet the cost of transport to and from the place of residence. Prices are kept to an absolute minimum and include half-board and most transport costs during the holiday.

YDH helpers come from all walks of life and many return every year so there are always some with considerable experience. However, new blood is always welcome. No special skills are required, but it does help to have a strong back and the ability to cope with the unexpected. Helpers are asked to contribute a percentage towards their holiday costs.

For more information write to **Young Disabled on Holiday** (O).

Z

ZZZZZZZZZZZZZZZZZZZZZ

See Sleep!

Appendix 1 – Manufacturers (M)

A & M Hearing Aids
7 Kelvin Way
Crawley
Sussex RH10 2LS
(0923 26976)

Adjustamatic Beds Ltd
46 Holmebury Grove
Forestdale
Croydon
Surrey OR0 9AP

Aerospace Communication
    Systems Ltd
Fringe Meadow Road
North Moors Moat
Redditch
Worcestershire B98 9NS
(0527 67607)

The AID Centre
182 Brighton Road
Coulsdon
Surrey CF3 2NF
(01 645 9014)

All Handling (Movability)
    Ltd
492 Kingston Road
Raynes Park
London SW20 8DX
(01 542 2217)

Alphavision Ltd
61 Beechtree Avenue
Marlow Bottom
Buckinghamshire WS17 3NH

Appollo Medical Supplies
    Ltd
Eagle Works
Eagle Lane
Great Bridge
Tipton
West Midlands DY4 7AZ

Aremco
Grove House
Lenham
Kent ME17 22PX

Arjo Mecanaids Ltd
St Catherine Street
Gloucester GL1 2SL

Austin Taylor Electrical Ltd
Bangor
North Wales LL57 3BX

Aztec Ltd
31 Lynx Crescent
Weston Industrial Estate
Weston-super-Mare
Avon BS23 9DJ

Back Shop
24 New Cavendish Street
London W1
(01 935 9120)

Back Store
324A King Street
Hammersmith
London W6
(01 741 5022)

Baronmead International Ltd
Bank Building
39 Elmer Road
Middleton-on-Sea
West Sussex PO22 6DZ

Barron & Shepherd
134 King Street
Hammersmith
London W6 0QU

Batricar Ltd
Griffin Mill
Thrupp
Stroud
Gloucestershire GL5 2AZ

BEC Mobility Ltd
Fens Pool Avenue
Brierly Hill
West Midlands DY5 1QA

Bechwell Trading Ltd
Newcastle Road
Congleton
Cheshire WA122 4HS

Belco Manufacturing Co. Ltd
Hovefields Avenue
Nore Industrial Estate
Burnt Mills
Basildon
Essex SS113 1EB

Bison Bede Ltd
Units 11A & B
Leadgate Industrial Estate
Consett
Co. Durham DH8 7RN

John Bradburn
　(Microsystems) Ltd
St James Mill Road
Northampton
Northamptonshire NN5 5JW
(0604 55142)

Braid Systems Ltd
130 Buckingham Palace Road
London SW1W 9SA
(01 730 2714)

British Telecom Action for
　Disabled Customers
BT Centre
81 Newgate Street
London EC1A 7AJ
(01 356 5000)

Broadway Bikes
65 Windmill Hill
Enfield
Middlesex
(01 367 6690)

Rod Brotherwood
Station Garage
Yetminster
Sherborne
Dorset

S Burvill & Sons
39 Primrose Road
Hersham
Walton-on-Thames
Surrey
(0932 221124)

Caducee Healthcare
Rye Park Industrial Estate
Rye Road
Hoddeston
Hertfordshire EN11 0EL
(0992 445658)

Candy Domestic Appliances
Candy House
Bridge Street
Guildford
Hampshire GU1 4SB

Canon Business Machines
  Ltd
Waddon House
Stafford Road
Croydon
Surrey

Car Chair Ltd
Carchair House
Station Road Industrial
  Estate
Hailsham
Sussex BN27 2ES

Carters (J & A) Ltd
Alfred Street
Westbury
Wiltshire BA13 3DZ

Cass Electronics Ltd
Delta Way
Thorpe Industrial Estate
Egham
Surrey TW20 8RN
(0784 36266)

CC Products
152 Markham Road
Charminster
Bournemouth
Dorset BH9 1JE
(0202 522260)

Chair Power
Avondale
Freshford
Bath
Avon BA3 6BX

Cleeve House Products
99 Malvern Street
Sapenhill
Burton-on-Trent
Staffordshire DE15 9DZ
(0283 48012)

Cleveland Spastics
  Workshop
Acklam Road
Middlesbrough
Cleveland TS5 4EG

Clio Press Ltd
55 St Thomas Street
Oxford OX1 1JG

Clos-o-Mat (GB) Ltd
2 Brooklands Road
Sale
Cheshire M33 3SS
(061 973 6262)

Coloplast
Peterborough Business Park
Peterborough
Cambridgeshire PE2 0FX

Combined Optical Industries
200 Bath Road
Slough
Berkshire SL1 4DW

Community Health Supplies
  Co.
16 Dinsdale Gardens
New Barnet
Hertfordshire

Complementary Health
  Insurance Plan
99/101 Commercial Street
London E1 6BG

Thos Cook Ltd
101 High Street
Cosham
Portsmouth PO6 3AZ
(0705 381721)

Countrywide Workshops
17c Earls Court Square
London SW5
(01 373 9943)

Dermalux Co Ltd
Unit 21
The Portsmouth Enterprise
  Centre
Quartermaine Road
Portsmouth
Hampshire PO3 5TQ

Dow Corning Wright
Caledonian House
Tatton Street
Knutsford
Cheshire WA16 6AG

Downs Surgical PLC
Church Path
Mitcham
Surrey CR4 3UE
(01 648 6291)

Gerald Duckworth & Co. Ltd
The Old Piano Factory
43 Gloucester Crescent
London NW1
(01 485 3484)

East Anglian Stair Elevators
  Ltd
The Street
Woolpit
Bury St Edmunds
Suffolk IP30 9SA

Edincare Ltd
Unit 2 Tudor Enterprise Park
Tudor Road
Harrow
Middlesex HA3 5JQ

Elap Engineering Ltd
23 Lynwood Road
Huncoat
Accrington
Lancashire BB5 6LR

Electric Leisure Vehicles Ltd
17 St Georges Industrial
  Estate
Frimley Road
Camberley
Surrey GU15 2QW

Electric Mobility Company
FREEPOST
Sea King Road
Lynx Trading Estate
Yeovil
Somerset BA20 2YS

Electronic Aids for the Blind
28 Crofton Avenue
Orpington
Kent BR6 8DU

Ellis Son & Paramore
Spring Street Works
Sheffield
South Yorkshire S3 9PB
(0742 738921)

Enterprise Engineering
157 Ermine Way
Arrington
Royston
Herts SG8 0AU
(0223 207281)

EPC Ltd
Friggle Street
Frome
Somerset
(0373 62542)

Epsom Care Centre
Station House
Longdown Lane South
Epsom Downs
Surrey KT17 4JX
(03727 41655)

Eurocraft
36 Dover Street
Mayfair
London W1X 3RB

Everest & Jennings
FREEPOST
Princewood Road
Corby
Northamptonshire
NN17 2DX

Explorer Cars Ltd
Unit 203
Old Barn Farm Road
Woolsbridge Industrial Park
Three Legged Cross
Dorset BH21 6SP

Fashions for the Disabled
627 High Road
Seven Kings
Ilford
Essex (01 597 8065)

W J Furse & Co Ltd
Traffic Street
Nottingham NG2 1NF

Gladstone Law Electrical Ltd
Ascot House
Windsor
Berkshire (0753 857737)

Guardian Alarms
(Formerly Trunkgate)
24 Cherry Orton Road
Orton Waterville
Peterborough
(0733 231 179)

Hampshire Medical
  Developments Ltd
Appollo House
34 Church Road
Romsey
Hampshire SO51 8EY

Handi Kontrols Ltd
PO Box 75
Warkworth
Morpeth
Northumberland NE65 0HG

Harper & Row Ltd
34 Cleveland Street
London W1
(01 636 8300)

Henleys of Hornsey
Alexandra Works
Clarendon Road
Hornsey
London N8 0DL
(01 889 3151)

Home Nursing Supplies Ltd
Headquarters Road
West Wiltshire Trading
  Estate
Westbury
Wiltshire BA13 4JR
(0373 822313)

Homecraft Supplies Ltd
27 Trinity Road
London SW17 7SF
(01 672 7070/1789)

Homelink Telecom Ltd
Units 24C & D
Perivale Industrial Park
Horsenden Lane South
Perivale
Greenford
Middlesex U86 7RJ
(01 991 1133)

Incare Medical Products
43 Castle Street
Reading
Berkshire RG1 5SN
(0734 597211)

Innovations (Mail Order) Ltd
Campus Road
Listerhills Science Park
Bradford BD7 1HR

Invatravel
9 Derwent Avenue
Southport PR9 7PX

IT World Ltd
Asphalte House
Palace Street
London SW1 5HS
(01 834 6637)

Joncare
Radley Road Industrial
  Estate
Abingdon
Oxon OX14 3RY

Kaleidoscope Ltd
Admail 50
Leicester LE5 5DL

Llewellyn Health Care
  Services
Carlton Street
Liverpool
Merseyside L3 7ED

Loxley Medical
Unit 5D
Lancaster Road
Carnaby Industrial Estate
Bridlington
North Humberside YO15
  3QY

MAR Design Services
7 Elmscroft Gardens
Potters Bar
Hertfordshire EN6 2JP

M & G Electric (Hayes) Ltd
27 Horton Road
Yiewsley
Middlesex
(0895 446854)

Mangar Aids Ltd
Presteigne Industrial Estate
Presteigne
Powys

Manor (Custodians) Ltd
Arndale House
19 High Street
Maltby
Rotherham S66 8LQ

Mecanaids Ltd
St Catherine's Street
Gloucester GL1 2SL

Medelect Ltd
Manor Way
Old Woking
Surrey GU22 9JU

Medic Bath Ltd
PO Box 12
Ashfield Works
Hulme Hill Lane
Manchester M10 8AB

Medimail Ltd
PO Box 12
Bishop's Stortford
Hertfordshire

Medinorth Ltd
York Towers
383 York Road
Leeds LS9 6TA

Medipost Ltd
Unit 1 St John's Estate
Elder Road
Lees
Oldham
Lancashire OL4 3DZ
(061 678 0233)

Mobility 2000 Telford Ltd
Telford Industrial Centre
Stafford Park 4
Telford
Shropshire TF3 3BA

Mobility International
18–21 Church Gate
Thatcham
Newbury
Berkshire RG13 4PH

Mobility Techniques Ltd
The Croft
Great Longstone
Bakewell
Derbyshire DE4 1TF

Molnlycke Ltd
Hospital Products Division
Southfields Road
Dunstable
Bedfordshire LU6 3EJ
(0582 600211)

Neen Pain Management
    Systems
Barn Lodge
Gooseberry Hill
Swanton Morley
Dereham
Norfolk NR20 4NR

NeuroTech Ltd
Dancon House
North Circular Road
London NW10 7SS
(01 965 7273)

Newtech Electronics
Unit 7
Williams Industrial Park
New Milton
Hampshire BH25 6RJ
(0425 620210)

Newton Products
Meadway Works
Garrets Green Lane
Birmingham
West Midlands B33 0SQ

Niagra Therapy (UK) Ltd
Oliver House
243/245 Selhurst Road
London SE25 6LP
(01 771 3631)

Nicholas Laboratories Ltd
225 Bath Road
Slough
Berkshire S11 4AU
(0753 23971)

Nicholls & Clarke Ltd
Niclar House
3–10 Shoreditch High Street
London E1 6PE
(01 247 5432)

Nottingham Rehab Ltd
17 Ludlow Hill Road
West Bridgeford
Nottingham NG2 6HD
(0602 234251)

NV Distributors Ltd
Soothouse Spring
Valley Road Industrial Estate
St Albans
Hertfordshire

Orange Aids Ltd
PO Box 5
Twickenham
Middlesex TW2 6RZ
(01 892 1850)

Ortho-Kinetics Ltd
Gaffney House
190 Commercial Road
Totton
Southampton SO4 3ZZ
(0703 863629)

Parker Bath Developments
    Ltd
Queensway
Stem Lane Industrial Estate
New Milton BH25 5NN

Parker Knoll Furniture Ltd
PO Box 22
Frogmoor
High Wycombe
Buckinghamshire HP13 5DJ
(0494 21144)

F J Payne Ltd
Stanton Harcourt Road
Eynsham
Oxford OX9 1JT

PEL Ltd
PO Box 119
Oldbury
Warley
West Midlands B69 4HN
(021 552 3377)

Pegasus Air Wave Ltd
Unit 21
Portsmouth Enterprise
    Centre
Quartermaine Road
Portsmouth
Hampshire PO3 5QT
(0705 671321)

V W Ponting
Faraday Road
Churchfields Industrial
    Estate
Salisbury
Wiltshire SP2 7NB

Portakabin Ltd
Marketing Manager
Huntington
York YO3 9PT
(Freefone Portakabin)

Portcullis Home Lift Ltd
Unit 71
Soho Mill
Wooburn Green
High Wycombe
Buckinghamshire

Porvair Ltd (Medical
    Products)
Estuary Road
Riverside Industrial Estate
Kings Lynn
Norfolk PE30 2HS

Possum Controls Ltd
Middlegreen Road
Langley
Berkshire SL3 6DF

Powell Seat Co. Ltd
70 Lodge Lane
Derby
Derbyshire DE1 3HB
(0332 47757)

Powex
99 Malvern Street
Stapenhill
Burton-on-Trent
Staffordshire DE15 9DZ
(0283 48012)

Pressalit Ltd
25 Grove Promenade
Ilkley
West Yorkshire LS29 8AF

B G Puncture-Proof Services
Unit 24
Chalon Way Estate
Chalon Way
St Helens
Merseyside WA110 1AU

QED Ltd
1 Prince Alfred Street
Gosport
Hampshire PO12 1QH
(0705 581179)

Raymar
Box 16
Henley-on-Thames
Oxon RG9 1LL
(0491 578446)

Renray Group Ltd
Road Five
Industrial Estate
Winsford
Cheshire CW7 3PB
(0606 593456)

Rhinotherm Ltd
The Novo Centre
9–11 London Lane
London E8 3PR
(01 986 4717)

Ridley Electronics Ltd
206 Wightman Road
Hornsey
London N8 0BU
(01 388 1266)

Safelab Systems Ltd
Bush House
72 Prince Street
Bristol BS1 4HU
(0272 272454)

Scintilla Technology Ltd
Unit 42 City Industrial Park
Southern Road
Southampton SO1 0HA

Seimens Ltd
Seimens House
Windmill Road
Sunbury-on-Thames
Middlesex TW16 7HS

Senflow (UK) Ltd
1a Norton Hill Drive Wyken
Coventry
West Midlands CV2 3AS
(0203 621096)

Sensory Information
  Systems
2b England's Lane
London NW3 4TG

Seton
Tubiton House
Oldham OL1 3HS

Shackletons (Carlinghow)
   Ltd
501 Bradford Road
Batley
West Yorkshire WF17 8LN
(0924 474430)

Shires Bathrooms
Shires Ltd
Guisley
Leeds
West Yorkshire LS20 8AF

Gerald Simonds
9 March Place
Gatehouse Way
Aylesbury
Buckinghamshire HP19 3UG

SML Aids Ltd
Bath Place
High Street
Barnet
Hertfordshire EN5 5EX

Spembly Ltd
Newbury Road
Andover
Hampshire SP10 4DR

Spenco Medical (UK) Ltd
Tanyard Lane
Steyning
West Sussex BN4 3RJ
(0903 815123)

Squibb Surgicare Ltd
Squibb House
141–149 Staines Road
Hounslow
Middlesex TW3 3JA
(01 572 7422)

Stairlift Engineering Ltd
Unit 3b
Chineham Business Park
Chineham
Basingstoke
(0256 843163)

Stannah Lifts Ltd
Watt Close
East Portway
Andover
Hampshire

Talley Medical Equipment
   Ltd
47 Theobald Street
Borehamwood
Hertfordshire WD6 4RT
(01 953 7171)

Threshold Travel
Wrendel House
2 Whitworth Street West
Manchester M1 5WX

Terry Lifts
Parkgate Industrial Estate
Knutsford
Cheshire WA16 8DZ

Toby Churchill Ltd
20 Panton Stret
Cambridge CB2 1HP

C R Toogood & Co. Ltd
Duncombe House
Ockham Road North
East Horsley
Leatherhead
Surrey KT24 6NX
(048 65 4181)

Transbyn Ltd
62 Station Approach
South Ruislip
Middlesex HA4 6SA

Trunkgate
See Guardian Alarms

Tunstall Telecom Ltd
PO Box 1
Whitely Lodge
Whitely Bridge
Yorkshire DN14 0JT
(0977 661234)

Vessa Ltd
Paper Mill Lane
Alton
Hampshire GU34 2PY

Voice Input
7 The Quay
St Ives
Cambridgeshire

Wessex Medical Equipment
 Co. Ltd
Budds Lane Industrial Estate
Romsey
Hampshire SO5 0HA

John Wiley & Sons Ltd
Baffins Lane
Chichester
Sussex PO19 1UD

Woodhead-Faulkner Ltd
Fitzwilliam House
32 Trumpington Street
Cambridge CB2 1QY
(0223 66733)

Wormaid International
 Sensory Aids Ltd
7 Musters Road
West Bridgeford
Nottingham NG2 7PP

James Yarrow, Young & Co.
 Ltd
327 Station Road
Harrow
Middlesex HA1 2XN
(01 863 5577)

Appendix II – Organisations (O)

Access Committee for
England
35 Great Smith Street
London SW1P 3BJ
(01 222 7980)

ACROSS Trust
Crown House
Morden
Surrey SM4 5EW
(01 540 3897)

British **Acupuncture**
Association
34 Alderney Street
London SW1V 4EU
(01 834 1012/3353)

Council for **Acupuncture**
Suite 1
19a Cavendish Square
London W1M 9AD

Age Concern England
Bernard Sunley House
60 Pitcairn Road
Mitcham
Surrey CR4 3LL
(01 640 5431)

National **AIDS** Helpline
c/o Broadcasting Support
Services
252 Western Avenue
London W3 6XJ
(01 992 5522)

Air Call Medical Services Ltd
Ashton House
403 Silbury Boulevard
Central Milton Keynes
Buckinghamshire MK9 2AH
(0808 600 600)

British **Airports** Authority
Head Office
Gatwick Airport
West Sussex RH6 0HZ
(0293 517755)

Alzheimer's Disease Society
3rd Floor Bank Building
Fulham Broadway
London SW6 1EP
(01 381 3177)

Amnesia Association
25 Prebend Gardens
London W4 1TN
(01 747 0039)

British **Amputee** Sports
Association
Harvey Road
Aylesbury
Buckinghamshire HP21 9PP
(0296 27889)

Handicapped **Anglers** Trust
29 Ironlatch Avenue
St Leonards on Sea
East Sussex TN38 9JE
(0424 427931)

National **Ankylosing Spondylitis** Society
6 Grosvenor Crescent
London SW1X 7ER
(01 235 9585)

APHASIC
347 Central Markets
Smithfield
London EC1H 9NH
(01 236 3632)

ARC
Faraday House
8 Charing Cross Road
London WC2H 0HN

Arthritis Care
6 Grosvenor Crescent
London SW1X 7ER
(01 235 0902)

Asthma Society and Friends
of the Asthma Research
Council
300 Upper Street
London N1 2XX
(01 226 2260)

Attendance Allowance Unit
DHSS
North Fylde Central Office
Norcross
Blackpool FY5 3TA
(0253 856123)

National **Autistic** Society
276 Willesden Lane
London NW2 5RB
(01 451 3844)

BACUP
121/123 Charterhouse Street
London EC1M 6AA
(01 608 1785)

National **Back Pain**
Association
Grundy House
31–33 Park Road
Teddington
Middlesex TW11 0AB
(01 977 5474/5)

Royal Society for the
Protection of **Birds**
The Lodge
Sandy
Bedfordshire SG19 2DL
(0767 80551)

BLESMA
Frankland Moore House
185/187 High Road
Chadwell Heath
Essex RM6 6NA
(01 590 1124/5)

Association of **Blind** and
Partially-Sighted Teachers
and Students
58 South Drive
Manchester M21 2FB
(061 881 4147)

Blind Authors Association
John May
'Brierdene'
Croit-e-Quill Road
Lonan
Isle of Man

National Federation for the
Blind
45 South Street
Normanton
West Yorkshire

National Library for the
Blind
Cromwell Road
Bradbury
Stockport SK6 2SG

National Music for the **Blind**
2 High Park Road
Southport
Merseyside PR9 7QL

National Newspaper and
Magazine Tape Service for
the **Blind**
68a High Street
Heathfield
East Sussex TN21 8JB

Research Unit for the **Blind**
Brunel University
Uxbridge
Middlesex UB8 3PH

Royal London Society for the
Blind
105 Salisbury Road
London NW6 6RH
(01 624 8844)

Royal National Institute for
the **Blind**
224 Great Portland Street
London W1N 6AA
(01 388 1266)

South Regional Association
for the **Blind**
55 Eton Avenue
London NW3 3ET

Tape Recording Service for
the **Blind**
48 Fairfax Road
Farnborough
Hampshire GU14 8JP

Braille Chess Association
Stanley Lovell, Hon Sec
36 Partridge Court
Harlow
Essex CM18 6SH
(0279 33960)

BREAK
20 Hooks Hill Road
Sheringham
Norfolk NR26 8NL

Breakthrough Trust
Charles W Gillette Centre
Selly Oak College
Birmingham
West Midlands
(021 472 6447)

Brittle Bone Society
Unit 4 Block 20
Carlunie Road
Dunsinane Industrial Estate
Dundee DD2 3QT
(0382 817771)

Appendix II

Buckets and Spades
Lancaster Road
Hollington
St Leonards-on-Sea
Sussex TN38 9LX
(0424 52119)

CALIBRE (Cassette Library
for the Blind and
Handicapped)
Aylesbury
Buckinghamshire HP20 1HU
(0296 432339)

Calvert Trust Adventure
Centre
Little Crosthwaite
Keswick
Cumbria CA12 4QD
(0596 72254)

Camping for the Disabled
20 Burton Close
Dawley
Telford
Shropshire TF4 2BX
(0952 507653)

Women's National **Cancer**
Control Campaign
1 South Audley Street
London W1Y 5DQ
(01 499 7532)

Jeanne Campbell Breast
Cancer Radiotherapy
Appeal
29 St Luke's Avenue
Ramsgate
Kent CT11 7JZ
(0843 596732)

Cancer Relief
Anchor House
15–19 Brittan Street
London SW3 3TZ

BACUP
(British Association of
Cancer United Patients)
121/123 Charterhouse Street
London EC1M 6AA
(01 608 1785)

Cancerlink
46 Pentonville Road
London N1 9HF
(01 833 2451)

British Federation of **Care-
Home** Proprietors
51 Leopold Road
Felixstowe
Suffolk IP11 7NR

CAREMATCH
286 Camden Road
London N7 0BJ
(01 609 9966)

Carers' National Association
Lilac House
Medway Homes
Balfour Road
Rochester
Kent
(0634 813981)

336

Caring
A E Morgan Publications Ltd
Stanley House
9 West Street
Epsom
Surrey KT18 7RL

Child Poverty Action Group
  (CPAG)
1–5 Bath Street
London EC1V 9PY
(01 253 3406)

The Association for **Children
  with Artificial Arms**
13 Park Terrace
Crimchard
Somerset TA20 1LA
(0460 61578)

National Association for the
  Welfare of **Children in
  Hospitals**
Argyle House
29–31 Euston Road
London NW1 2SD

British **Chiropractic**
  Association
Premier House
10 Greycoat Place
London SW1P 1SB

National Association for
  Colitis and **Crohn's
  Disease**
98a London Road
St Albans
Hertfordshire AL1 1NX

College of Health
2 Marylebone Road
London NW1 4DX
(01 935 3251)

Colostomy Welfare Group
38/39 Ecclestone Square
London SW1V 1PB
(01 323 5175)

ACHCEW (Association of
  **Community Health
  Councils** of England
  and Wales)
Nurses' Home
Langton Close
Wren Street
London WC1X 0HX

Institute for **Complementary
  Medicine**
21 Portland Place
London W1N 3AF
(01 636 9543)

British **Computer** Society
Roger Grout – Disabled
  Specialist Group
22 Abbey Road
West Moors
Wimbourne
Dorset BH22 0AX

Rapid Action for **Conductive
  Education**
14 Mallinson Road
Battersea
London SW11 1BP
(01 394 1731 ext 404)

Conquest
3 Beverley Close
East Ewell
Epsom
Surrey KT17 3HB

National **Consumer** Council
20 Grosvenor Gardens
London SW1W 0DH
(01 7330 3469)

CONTACT
15 Henrietta Street
Covent Garden
London WC2E 8QH
(01 240 0630)

Contact a Family
16 Strutton Ground
London SW1P 2HP
(01 222 2695/3969)
(Contact line 01 222 2211)

Association of **Continence**
Advisers
Mrs J Blannin
Disabled Living Foundation
380–384 Harrow Road
London W9 2HU
(01 289 6111)

Coronary Prevention Group
60 Great Ormond Street
London WC1N 3HR

Country Landowners
Association
16 Belgrave Square
London SW1X 8PQ
(01 235 0511)

Crohn's in Childhood
Research Appeal
56a Uxbridge Road
Shepherds Bush
London W12 8LP
(01 743 4940)

Association of **Crossroads**
Care Attendant Schemes
Ltd
10 Regent Place
Rugby
Warwickshire CV21 2PN

CRUSE
Cruse House
126 Sheen Road
Richmond
Surrey TW9 1UR
(01 940 4818)

HM **Customs** and Excise
King's Beam House
Mark Lane
London EC3R 7HE
(01 626 1515)

Association of **Cystic**
Fibrosis Adults (UK)
288 New Road
Ferndown
Dorset BH22 8EP

Cystic Fibrosis Research
Trust
Alexandra House
5 Blyth Road
Bromley
Kent BR1 3RS
(01 464 7211)

British **Deaf** Association
38 Victoria Place
Carlisle CA1 1HU
(0228 20188)

Friends for the Young **Deaf**
Communication Centre
East Court Mansion
College Lane
East Grinstead
Sussex RH19 3LT

The National **Deaf/Blind**
and Rubella Association
311 Gray's Inn Road
London WC1X 8PT
(01 278 1005)

National **Deaf** Children's
Society
45 Hereford Road
London W2 5AH
(01 229 9272)

Royal National Institute for
the **Deaf**
105 Gower Street
London WC1E 6AH
(01 387 8033)

National **Deaf Blind** Helpers
League
18 Rainbow Court
Paston Ridings
Peterborough PE4 6UP
(0733 73511)

The Royal Association in Aid
of **Deaf People**
27 Old Oak Road
Acton
London W3 7HN
(01 743 6187)

British Centre of **Deafened**
People (LINK)
19 Hartfield Road
Eastbourne
Sussex BN21 2AR

British Society of **Dentistry**
for the Handicapped
Dental Department
3 Kimbolton Road
Bedford
(0234 55122 ext 3451)

Department of Trade and
Industry
(Information Technology
Division)
29 Bressenden Place
London SW1E 5DT

British **Diabetic** Association
10 Queen Anne Street
London W1M 0BD
(01 323 1531)

DIAL UK
DIAL House
117 High Street
Clay Cross
Chesterfield
Derbyshire S45 9DZ
(0246 864498)

DIG
Atlee House
28 Commercial Street
London E1 6LR
(01 790 2424)

Disability Alliance
25 Denmark Street
London WC2H 8NJ
(01 240 0806)

Scottish Council on
Disability
Princes House
5 Shandwick Place
Edinburgh EH2 4RG
(031 229 8632)

Action for **Disabled**
Customers
Room B5049
British Telecom Centre
81 Newgate Street
London EC1A 7AJ
(0345 581456)

Disabled Drivers
Association
Ashwellthorpe Hall
Ashwellthorpe
Norwich
Norfolk NR16 1EX
(050841 449)

Disabled Drivers Federation
Copthorn Community Hall
Shelton Road
Shrewsbury
Salop

Disabled Drivers Motor
Club
1a Dudley Gardens
Ealing
London W13 9LU

Disabled Living Foundation
380–384 Harrow Road
London W9 2HU
(01 289 6111)

British Council of
Organisations of **Disabled**
People
St Mary's Church
Greenlaw Street
Woolwich
London SE18 5AR
(01 316 4184)

Disablement Services
Authority
14 Russell Square
London WC1B 5EP
(01 636 6811)

Disfigurement Guidance
Centre
52 Crossgate
Cupar
Fife KY15 5HS
(03377 281)

Downs Syndrome
Association
1st Floor
12–13 Clapham Common
Southside
London SW4 7AA
(01 720 0008)

British **Dyslexia** Association
98 London Road
Reading
Berkshire RG1 5AU
(0734 668271)

Helen Arkell **Dyslexia**
   Centre
14 Crondace Road
London SW6 4BB

Council and Care for the
   Elderly
131 Middlesex Street
London E1 7JF
(01 621 1624)

Centre on the **Environment**
   for the Handicapped
35 Great Smith Street
London SW1P 3BJ
(01 222 7980)

British **Epilepsy** Association
Anstey House
40 Hanover Square
Leeds LS3 1BE
(0532 439393)

Europe Assistance Ltd
252 High Street
Croydon
Surrey CR0 1NF
(01 680 1234)

Office of **Fair Trading**
Field House
15–25 Bream's Buildings
London EC4A 1PR
(01 242 2858)

The **Family Fund**
PO Box 50
York YO1 1UY

Friedrich's Ataxia Group
Burleigh Lodge
Knowle Lane
Cranleigh
Surrey
(0483 272741)

The Compassionate **Friends**
6 Denmark Street
Bristol BS1 5DQ
(0272 292778)

Garden Club
Marjorie Haines
Church Cottage
Headcorn
Kent TN27 9NP

GLAD
336 Brixton Road
London SW9 7AA
(01 274 0107)

GRACE
PO Box 71
Cobham
Surrey
(0932 62928)

Disabled **Graduates'** Careers
   Information Service
University of Nottingham
University Park
Nottingham NG7 2RD
(0602 506101)

John **Groom**'s Association
    for the Disabled
10 Gloucester Drive
Finsbury Park
London N4 2LP
(01 802 7272)

Guide Dogs for the Blind
Alexander House
113 Uxbridge Road
Ealing
London W5 5TQ
(01 567 7001)

Guide Dogs for the Blind
Alexandra House
9–11 Park Street
Windsor
Berkshire SL4 1JR
(0753 855711)

Handicapped Children's
    Adventure Playground
    Association
Fulham Palace Playground
Bishops Avenue
London SW6
(01 731 2753)

Handicapped Persons
    Research Unit
Newcastle Polytechnic
Coach Lane Campus
Newcastle-upon-Tyne
Tyne and Wear NE7 7TW
(091 235 8211)

Handihols
12 Ormonde Avenue
Rochford
Essex SS4 1QW
(0702 548257)

British Association of the
    Hard of Hearing
7/11 Armstrong Road
London W3 7JL
(01 743 1110)

Headway
200 Mansfield Road
Nottingham NG1 3HX
(0602 622382)

Healthline
PO Box 499
London E2 9PU
(01 980 6263)

Help for Health
Grant Building
Southampton General
    Hospital
Tremona Road
Southampton SO9 4XY
(0703 779091)

British **Heart** Foundation
102 Gloucester Place
London W1H 4DH
(01 935 0185)

Help the Aged
(PR) FREEPOST
London EC1B 1BD

Pauline **Hephaistos** Survey
  Products
39 Bradley Gardens
West Ealing
London W13

Hodgkin's Disease
  Association
PO Box 275
Haddenham
Aylesbury
Buckinghamshire HP17 8JJ
(0844 291500)

Holiday Care Service
2 Old Bank Chambers
Station Road
Horley
Surrey RH6 9HW
(0293 774535)

Horticultural Therapy
Goulds Ground
Vaillis Way
Frome
Somerset BA11 3DW
(0373 64782)

Association to Combat
  Huntington's Chorea
Borough House
34a Station Road
Hinckley
Leicestershire LE10 1AP
(0455 515558)

Ileostomy Association
Amblehurst House
Black Scotch Lane
Mansfield
Nottinghamshire NG18 4PF
(0623 28099)

Ileostomy Association
Central Office
Amblehurst House
Chobham
Woking
Surrey GU24 8PZ
(09905 8277)

In Touch
BBC
Broadcasting House
London W1A 1AA
(01 927 5966)

Invalid Care Allowance Unit
DHSS
Palatine House
Lancaster Road
Preston PR1 1HB

IYDP Holiday Fund
Hon Secretary
39 Cranbrook Road
Thornton Heath
Surrey CR4 8PO

Jubilee Sailing Trust
PO Box 180
The Docks
Southampton
Hampshire SO9 7NF

British **Kidney Patient**
Association
Bordon
Hampshire
(04203 2022)

National Federation of
Kidney Patients'
Associations
Acorn Lodge
Woodsetts
Worksop
Nottinghamshire
(0909 562703)

King's Fund Centre
126 Albert Street
London NW1 7NF
(01 267 6111)

The National Association of
Laryngectomee Clubs
Fourth Floor
39 Ecclestone Square
London SW1V 1PB
(01 834 2857)

Legal Aid Head Office
Newspaper House
8–16 Great New Street
London EC4A 3BN
(01 353 7411)

Library Association
7 Ridgemount Street
Store Street
London WC1E 7AE
(01 636 7543)

National Association for the
Limbless Disabled
31 The Mall
Ealing Broadway
London W5 2PX
(01 579 1758)

LINK
London House
26–40 Kensington High
Street
London W8 4PF
(01 938 2222 ext 2226)

National **Listening Library**
12 Lant Street
London SE1
(01 407 9417)

Mary Marlborough Lodge
Nuffield Orthopaedic Centre
Headington
Oxford OX3 7LD

Breast Care and **Mastectomy**
Association
26 Harrison Street
Kings Cross
London WC1 8JG
(01 837 0908)

MAVIS
Department of Transport
TRRL
Crowthorne
Berkshire RG11 6AU

Medical Advisory Service
Barley Mow Passage
Chiswick
London W4 4PH
(01 994 9874)

MENCAP
123 Golden Lane
London EC17 0RT
(01 253 9433)

British **Migraine** Association
178a High Road
Byfleet
Weybridge
Surrey KT14 7ED

Migraine Trust
45 Great Ormond Street
London WC1N 3HD
(01 278 2676)

MIND (National Association
  for Mental Health)
22 Harley Street
London W1N 2ED
(01 637 0741)

Mobility Allowance Unit
DHSS
North Fylde Central Office
Norcross
Blackpool FY5 3TA
(0253 52311)

Banstead Place **Mobility
  Centre**
Park Road
Bansted
Surrey SM7 3EE

Mobility Information
  Service
Unit 2A
Atcham Estate
Upton Magna
Shrewsbury SY4 4UG

Mobility International
62 Union Street
London SE1 1TD
(01 403 5688)

Mobility Trust
19 Wiseton Road
Wandsworth Common
London SW17 7EE
(01 672 9170)

Moon Branch
RNIB
Holmesdale Road
Reigate
Surrey RH2 0BA

MOTABILITY
Gate House
Westgate
The High
Harlow
Essex CM20 1HR
(0279 635666)

Motor Neurone Disease
  Association
(Roy Price – National
  Director)
61 Derngate
Northampton NN1 1UE
(0604 22269/250505)

Mouth and Foot Painting
  Artists Association
9 Inverness Place
London W2 3JF
(01 229 4491)

Action for Research into
  Multiple Sclerosis
Central Middlesex Hospital
Acton Lane
London NW10
(01 453 0142)

Multiple Sclerosis Society
25 Effie Road
London SW6 1EE
(01 736 6267)

Muscular Dystrophy Group
  of Great Britain
Nattrass House
35 Macauley Road
London SW4 0QP
(01 720 8055)

The Council for **Music** in
  Hospitals
340 Lower Road
Little Bookham
Surrey KT23 4EF

Myalgic Encephalomyelitis
  Association
PO Box 8
Stanford-le-Hope
Essex SS17 8EX
(0375 642466)

Talking **Newspaper**
  Association of the UK
90 High Street
Heathfield
East Sussex TN21 8JD
(04352 6102)

Optical Information Council
Temple Chambers
Temple Avenue
London EC4Y 0DT
(01 353 3556)

Association of **Optical**
  Practitioners
Bridge House
233–234 Blackfriars Road
London SE1 8NW

General Council and
  Register of **Osteopaths**
21 Suffolk Street
London SW1Y 4HG

Oxford Caravans for the
  Disabled
Mrs J A Smith
10 Page Furlong
Dorchester-on-Thames
Oxford
(0865 340760)

Outsiders Club
Box 4ZB
London W1A 4ZB
(01 499 0900)

Pain Relief Foundation
Walton Hospital
Liverpool L9 1AE

Joan Seeley **Pain Relief**
  Memorial Trust
20 Stapley Road
Belvedere
Kent DA17 5JS

Intractible **Pain** Society of
  Great Britain
Derby Royal Infirmary
London Road
Derby DE1 2QY

Parkinson's Disease Society
36 Portland Place
London W1N 3DG
(01 323 1174)

Partially Sighted Society
40 Wandsworth Street
Hove
East Sussex BN5 5BH

PHAB
Tavistock House North
Tavistock Square
London WC1H 9HX
(01 388 1963)

Action on **Phobias**
8/9 The Avenue
Eastbourne
Sussex
(0323 504755)

Phobics Society
4 Cheltenham Road
Chorlton cum Hardy
Manchester M21 1QN
(061 881 1937)

The Chartered Society of
  Physiotherapy
14 Bedford Row
London WC1R 4ED
(01 242 1941)

Play Matters
68 Churchway
London NW1 1LT
(01 387 9592)

British **Polio** Fellowship
Bell Close
West End Road
Ruislip
Middlesex HA4 6LP
(089 56 75515)

National **Portage** Association
4 Clifton Road
Winchester
Hampshire

Possum Trust
14 Greenvale Drive
Timsbury
Bath BA3 1HP

Prader-Willi Syndrome
  Association (UK)
30 Follett Drive
Abbots Langley
Hertfordshire WD5 0LP
(0923 74543)

Association of Disabled
Professionals
Peggy M Marchant – General
Secretary
The Stables
73 Pound Road
Banstead
Surrey SM7 2HU
(0737 352366)

Psoriasis Association
7 Milton Street
Northampton NN2 7JG
(0604 711129)

RACE (Rapid Action for
Conductive Education)
14 Mallinson Road
Battersea
London SW11 1BP
(01 394 1731 ext 404)

RADAR
25 Mortimer Street
London W1N 8AB
(01 637 5400)

Radio Regulatory Division
Department of Trade and
Industry
Waterloo Bridge House
Waterloo Road
London SE1 8UA
(01 834 3000)

National Confederation of
**Registered Rest Home
Associations**
Hon Sec A F Andrews
74 London Road
St Leonards-on-Sea
East Sussex TN37 6AS

Remploy Ltd
Remploy House
415 Edgeware Road
Cricklewood
London NW2 6LR
(01 452 8020)

Renal Society
64 South Hill Park
London NW3 2JJ

Action For Research into
Restricted Growth
61 Lady Walk
Maple Cross
Rickmansworth
Hertfordshire WD3 2YZ
(0923 770759)

Retts Syndrome Association
150 Kingsway
Petts Wood
Orpington
Kent BR5 1PU
(0689 26760)

RICA
14 Buckingham Street
London WC2N 6DS
(01 930 0688)

Riding for the Disabled
  Association
Avenue R
National Agricultural Centre
Kenilworth
Warwickshire CV8 2LY
(0203 56107)

RNIB
224 Great Portland Street
London W1N 6AA
(01 388 1266)

RNID
105 Gower Street
London WC1E 6AH
(01 387 8033)

Schizophrenia Association
  of Great Britain
International Schizophrenia
  Centre
Bryn Hyfryd
The Crescent
Bangor
Gwynedd LL57 2AG
(0248 3540 48)

National **Schizophrenia**
  Fellowship
78 Victoria Road
Surbiton
Surrey KT6 4NS

Scoliosis Association (UK)
380–384 Harrow Road
London W9 2HU
(01 289 5652)

Scouting Association
Gilwell Park
Chingford
London E4 7QW
(01 524 5246)

SEQUAL
Ddol Hir
Glyn Ceiriog
Llangollen
Clwyd LL20 7NP
(0691 72331)

Shaftesbury Society
2a Amity Grove
Raynes Park
London SW20 9LJ
(01 946 6634)

Share-a-Care
National Register for Rare
  Diseases
8 Cornmarket
Faringdon
Oxon

British **Ski** Club for the
  Disabled
Corton House
Corton
Near Warminster
Wiltshire BA12 0SZ
(0985 50321)

Spastics Society
12 Park Crescent
London W1N 4EQ
(01 636 5020)

Special Care Agency
Kiln Bolton House
Upper Basildon
Reading
Berkshire RG8 8TB
(0491 671842)

College of **Speech Therapy**
Harold Poster House
6 Lechmere Road
London NW2 5BU
(01 459 8521)

Association for **Spina Bifida
and Hydrocephalus**
(ASBAH)
22 Upper Woburn Place
London WC1H 0EP
(01 388 1382)

Spinal Injuries Association
76 St James's Lane
London N10 3DF
(01 444 2121)

SPOD
286 Camden Road
London N7 0BJ
(01 607 8851)

British **Sports** Association for
the Disabled
Hayward House
Barnard Crescent
Aylesbury
Buckinghamshire HP21 8PP
(0296 27889)

SSAFA
16–18 Old Queen Street
London SW1H 9HP
(01 222 9221)

**Staffordshire Narrowboats
Ltd**
The Wharf
Newcastle Road
Stone
Staffordshire ST15 8JW
(0785 816871)

National Advisory Service
for Parents of Children
with a **Stoma**
55 Peveril Road
Bowthorpe
Norwich NR5 9AT

Chest Heart and **Stroke**
Association
Tavistock House North
Tavistock Square
London WC1H 9JE
(01 387 3012)

Oxford Prevention of Heart
Attack and **Stroke** Project
University of Oxford
Department of
Community Medicine
Gibson Building
Radcliffe Infirmary
Oxford OX2 6HE
(0865 249891)

Association of **Swimming**
  Therapy
Treetops
Swan Hill
Ellesmere
Salop SY12 0LZ
(069 171 3542)

Talking Newspaper
  Association of the UK
90 High Street
Heathfield
East Sussex TN21 8JD
(04352 6102)

British Library of **Tape
  Recordings** for Hospital
  Patients
12 Lant Street
London SE1 1QR

British **Tinnitus** Association
105 Gower Street
London WC1E 6AH
(01 387 8033)

Urostomy Association
Buckland
Beaumont Park
Danbury
Essex CM3 4DE
(024 541 4294)

National Council for
  Voluntary Organisations
26 Bedford Square
London WC1B 3HU
(01 636 4066)

Wider Horizons
Mr A B Fletcher
Westbrook
Back Lane
Malvern
Worcestershire WR14 2HJ

The National Association of
  Widows
Stafford District Voluntary
  Service Centre
Chell Road
Stafford ST1 2QA
(0785 45465)

Winged Fellowship Trust
Angel House
Pentonville Road
London NE5 2LL
(01 833 2594)

Wireless For the Bedridden
Mr J H Parker – Secretary
81b Corbets Tey Road
Upminster
Essex RM14 2AJ
(040 22 50051)

Women's Health
  Information Centre
52–54 Featherstone Street
London EC1Y 8RT
(01 251 6580)

Appendix II

Women's Reproductive Rights Information Centre
52–54 Featherstone Street
London EC1Y 8RT
(01 251 6332)

Young Disabled on Holiday
6 Yewland Drive
Boothsmere
Knutsford
Cheshire WA16 8AP

For details of other Crowood health and social issues titles and a copy of our latest catalogue, please write to:

The Crowood Press
Ramsbury
Marlborough
Wiltshire SN8 2HE